Mometrix
TEST PREPARATION

I0878904

TerraNova®
NEXT
Grade 6 Reading and Language Test Prep Guide

Written and edited by the Mometrix Test Preparation Team
Printed in the United States of America

TABLE OF CONTENTS

Introduction

Thank you for purchasing this resource! You have made the choice to prepare yourself for a test that could have a huge impact on your future, and this guide is designed to help you be fully ready for test day. Obviously, it's important to have a solid understanding of the test material, but you also need to be prepared for the unique environment and stressors of the test, so that you can perform to the best of your abilities.

For this purpose, the first section that appears in this guide is the **Success Strategies**. We've devoted countless hours to meticulously researching what works and what doesn't, and we've boiled down our findings to the most impactful steps you can take to improve your performance on the test. We start at the beginning with study planning and move through the preparation process, all the way to the testing strategies that will help you get the most out of what you know when you're finally sitting in front of the test.

We recommend that you start preparing for your test as far in advance as possible. However, if you've bought this guide as a last-minute study resource and only have a few days before your test, we recommend that you skip over the first two Success Strategies since they address a long-term study plan.

If you struggle with **test anxiety**, we strongly encourage you to check out our recommendations for how you can overcome it. Test anxiety is a formidable foe, but it can be beaten, and we want to make sure you have the tools you need to defeat it.

Strategy #1 – Plan Big, Study Small

There's a lot riding on your performance. If you want to ace this test, you're going to need to keep your skills sharp and the material fresh in your mind. You need a plan that lets you review everything you need to know while still fitting in your schedule. We'll break this strategy down into three categories.

Information Organization

Start with the information you already have: the official test outline. From this, you can make a complete list of all the concepts you need to cover before the test. Organize these concepts into groups that can be studied together, and create a list of any related vocabulary you need to learn so you can brush up on any difficult terms. You'll want to keep this vocabulary list handy once you actually start studying since you may need to add to it along the way.

Time Management

Once you have your set of study concepts, decide how to spread them out over the time you have left before the test. Break your study plan into small, clear goals so you have a manageable task for each day and know exactly what you're doing. Then just focus on one small step at a time. When you manage your time this way, you don't need to spend hours at a time studying. Studying a small block of content for a short period each day helps you retain information better and avoid stressing over how much you have left to do. You can relax knowing that you have a plan to cover everything in time. In order for this strategy to be effective though, you have to start studying early and stick to your schedule. Avoid the exhaustion and futility that comes from last-minute cramming!

Study Environment

The environment you study in has a big impact on your learning. Studying in a coffee shop, while probably more enjoyable, is not likely to be as fruitful as studying in a quiet room. It's important to keep distractions to a minimum. You're only planning to study for a short block of time, so make the most of it. Don't pause to check your phone or get up to find a snack. It's also important to **avoid multitasking**. Research has consistently shown that multitasking will make your studying dramatically less effective. Your study area should also be comfortable and well-lit so you don't have the distraction of straining your eyes or sitting on an uncomfortable chair.

The time of day you study is also important. You want to be rested and alert. Don't wait until just before bedtime. Study when you'll be most likely to comprehend and remember. Even better, if you know what time of day your test will be, set that time aside for study. That way your brain will be used to working on that subject at that specific time and you'll have a better chance of recalling information.

Finally, it can be helpful to team up with others who are studying for the same test. Your actual studying should be done in as isolated an environment as possible, but the work of organizing the information and setting up the study plan can be divided up. In between study sessions, you can discuss with your teammates the concepts that you're all studying and quiz each other on the details. Just be sure that your teammates are as serious about the test as you are. If you find that your study time is being replaced with social time, you might need to find a new team.

Strategy #2 – Make Your Studying Count

You're devoting a lot of time and effort to preparing for this test, so you want to be absolutely certain it will pay off. This means doing more than just reading the content and hoping you can remember it on test day. It's important to make every minute of study count. There are two main areas you can focus on to make your studying count.

Retention

It doesn't matter how much time you study if you can't remember the material. You need to make sure you are retaining the concepts. To check your retention of the information you're learning, try recalling it at later times with minimal prompting. Try carrying around flashcards and glance at one or two from time to time or ask a friend who's also studying for the test to quiz you.

To enhance your retention, look for ways to put the information into practice so that you can apply it rather than simply recalling it. If you're using the information in practical ways, it will be much easier to remember. Similarly, it helps to solidify a concept in your mind if you're not only reading it to yourself but also explaining it to someone else. Ask a friend to let you teach them about a concept you're a little shaky on (or speak aloud to an imaginary audience if necessary). As you try to summarize, define, give examples, and answer your friend's questions, you'll understand the concepts better and they will stay with you longer. Finally, step back for a big picture view and ask yourself how each piece of information fits with the whole subject. When you link the different concepts together and see them working together as a whole, it's easier to remember the individual components.

Finally, practice showing your work on any multi-step problems, even if you're just studying. Writing out each step you take to solve a problem will help solidify the process in your mind, and you'll be more likely to remember it during the test.

Modality

Modality simply refers to the means or method by which you study. Choosing a study modality that fits your own individual learning style is crucial. No two people learn best in exactly the same way, so it's important to know your strengths and use them to your advantage.

For example, if you learn best by visualization, focus on visualizing a concept in your mind and draw an image or a diagram. Try color-coding your notes, illustrating them, or creating symbols that will trigger your mind to recall a learned concept. If you learn best by hearing or discussing information, find a study partner who learns the same way or read aloud to yourself. Think about how to put the information in your own words. Imagine that you are giving a lecture on the topic and record yourself so you can listen to it later.

For any learning style, flashcards can be helpful. Organize the information so you can take advantage of spare moments to review. Underline key words or phrases. Use different colors for different categories. Mnemonic devices (such as creating a short list in which every item starts with the same letter) can also help with retention. Find what works best for you and use it to store the information in your mind most effectively and easily.

Strategy #3 – Practice the Right Way

Your success on test day depends not only on how many hours you put into preparing, but also on whether you prepared the right way. It's good to check along the way to see if your studying is paying off. One of the most effective ways to do this is by taking practice tests to evaluate your progress. Practice tests are useful because they show exactly where you need to improve. Every time you take a practice test, pay special attention to these three groups of questions:

- The questions you got wrong
- The questions you had to guess on, even if you guessed right
- The questions you found difficult or slow to work through

This will show you exactly what your weak areas are, and where you need to devote more study time. Ask yourself why each of these questions gave you trouble. Was it because you didn't understand the material? Was it because you didn't remember the vocabulary? Do you need more repetitions on this type of question to build speed and confidence? Dig into those questions and figure out how you can strengthen your weak areas as you go back to review the material.

Additionally, many practice tests have a section explaining the answer choices. It can be tempting to read the explanation and think that you now have a good understanding of the concept. However, an explanation likely only covers part of the question's broader context. Even if the explanation makes perfect sense, **go back and investigate** every concept related to the question until you're positive you have a thorough understanding.

As you go along, keep in mind that the practice test is just that: practice. Memorizing these questions and answers will not be very helpful on the actual test because it is unlikely to have any of the same exact questions. If you only know the right answers to the sample questions, you won't be prepared for the real thing. **Study the concepts** until you understand them fully, and then you'll be able to answer any question that shows up on the test.

It's important to wait on the practice tests until you're ready. If you take a test on your first day of study, you may be overwhelmed by the amount of material covered and how much you need to learn. Work up to it gradually.

On test day, you'll need to be prepared for answering questions, managing your time, and using the test-taking strategies you've learned. It's a lot to balance, like a mental marathon that will have a big impact on your future. Like training for a marathon, you'll need to start slowly and work your way up. When test day arrives, you'll be ready.

Start with the strategies you've read in the first two Success Strategies—plan your course and study in the way that works best for you. If you have time, consider using multiple study resources to get different approaches to the same concepts. It can be helpful to see difficult concepts from more than one angle. Then find a good source for practice tests. Many times, the test website will suggest potential study resources or provide sample tests.

Practice Test Strategy

If you're able to find at least three practice tests, we recommend this strategy:

Untimed and Open-Book Practice

Take the first test with no time constraints and with your notes and study guide handy. Take your time and focus on applying the strategies you've learned.

Timed and Open-Book Practice

Take the second practice test open-book as well, but set a timer and practice pacing yourself to finish in time.

Timed and Closed-Book Practice

Take any other practice tests as if it were test day. Set a timer and put away your study materials. Sit at a table or desk in a quiet room, imagine yourself at the testing center, and answer questions as quickly and accurately as possible.

Keep repeating timed and closed-book tests on a regular basis until you run out of practice tests or it's time for the actual test. Your mind will be ready for the schedule and stress of test day, and you'll be able to focus on recalling the material you've learned.

Strategy #4 – Pace Yourself

Once you're fully prepared for the material on the test, your biggest challenge on test day will be managing your time. Just knowing that the clock is ticking can make you panic even if you have plenty of time left. Work on pacing yourself so you can build confidence against the time constraints of the exam. Pacing is a difficult skill to master, especially in a high-pressure environment, so **practice is vital**.

Set time expectations for your pace based on how much time is available. For example, if a section has 60 questions and the time limit is 30 minutes, you know you have to average 30 seconds or less per question in order to answer them all. Although 30 seconds is the hard limit, set 25 seconds per question as your goal, so you reserve extra time to spend on harder questions. When you budget extra time for the harder questions, you no longer have any reason to stress when those questions take longer to answer.

Don't let this time expectation distract you from working through the test at a calm, steady pace, but keep it in mind so you don't spend too much time on any one question. Recognize that taking extra time on one question you don't understand may keep you from answering two that you do understand later in the test. If your time limit for a question is up and you're still not sure of the answer, mark it and move on, and come back to it later if the time and the test format allow. If the testing format doesn't allow you to return to earlier questions, just make an educated guess; then put it out of your mind and move on.

On the easier questions, be careful not to rush. It may seem wise to hurry through them so you have more time for the challenging ones, but it's not worth missing one if you know the concept and just didn't take the time to read the question fully. Work efficiently but make sure you understand the question and have looked at all of the answer choices, since more than one may seem right at first.

Even if you're paying attention to the time, you may find yourself a little behind at some point. You should speed up to get back on track, but do so wisely. Don't panic; just take a few seconds less on each question until you're caught up. Don't guess without thinking, but do look through the answer choices and eliminate any you know are wrong. If you can get down to two choices, it is often worthwhile to guess from those. Once you've chosen an answer, move on and don't dwell on any that you skipped or had to hurry through. If a question was taking too long, chances are it was one of the harder ones, so you weren't as likely to get it right anyway.

On the other hand, if you find yourself getting ahead of schedule, it may be beneficial to slow down a little. The more quickly you work, the more likely you are to make a careless mistake that will affect your score. You've budgeted time for each question, so don't be afraid to spend that time. Practice an efficient but careful pace to get the most out of the time you have.

Test-Taking Strategies

This section contains a list of test-taking strategies that you may find helpful as you work through the test. By taking what you know and applying logical thought, you can maximize your chances of answering any question correctly!

It is very important to realize that every question is different and every person is different: no single strategy will work on every question, and no single strategy will work for every person. That's why we've included all of them here, so you can try them out and determine which ones work best for different types of questions and which ones work best for you.

Question Strategies

✓ Read Carefully

Read the question and the answer choices carefully. Don't miss the question because you misread the terms. You have plenty of time to read each question thoroughly and make sure you understand what is being asked. Yet a happy medium must be attained, so don't waste too much time. You must read carefully and efficiently.

✓ Contextual Clues

Look for contextual clues. If the question includes a word you are not familiar with, look at the immediate context for some indication of what the word might mean. Contextual clues can often give you all the information you need to decipher the meaning of an unfamiliar word. Even if you can't determine the meaning, you may be able to narrow down the possibilities enough to make a solid guess at the answer to the question.

✓ Prefixes

If you're having trouble with a word in the question or answer choices, try dissecting it. Take advantage of every clue that the word might include. Prefixes can be a huge help. Usually, they allow you to determine a basic meaning. *Pre-* means before, *post-* means after, *pro-* is positive, *de-* is negative. From prefixes, you can get an idea of the general meaning of the word and try to put it into context.

✓ Hedge Words

Watch out for critical hedge words, such as *likely, may, can, often, almost, mostly, usually, generally, rarely*, and *sometimes*. Question writers insert these hedge phrases to cover every possibility. Often an answer choice will be wrong simply because it leaves no room for exception. Be on guard for answer choices that have definitive words such as *exactly* and *always.*

✓ Switchback Words

Stay alert for *switchbacks*. These are the words and phrases frequently used to alert you to shifts in thought. The most common switchback words are *but, although*, and *however*. Others include *nevertheless, on the other hand, even though, while, in spite of, despite*, and *regardless of*. Switchback words are important to catch because they can change the direction of the question or an answer choice.

✅ Face Value

When in doubt, use common sense. Accept the situation in the problem at face value. Don't read too much into it. These problems will not require you to make wild assumptions. If you have to go beyond creativity and warp time or space in order to have an answer choice fit the question, then you should move on and consider the other answer choices. These are normal problems rooted in reality. The applicable relationship or explanation may not be readily apparent, but it is there for you to figure out. Use your common sense to interpret anything that isn't clear.

Answer Choice Strategies

✅ Answer Selection

The most thorough way to pick an answer choice is to identify and eliminate wrong answers until only one is left, then confirm it is the correct answer. Sometimes an answer choice may immediately seem right, but be careful. The test writers will usually put more than one reasonable answer choice on each question, so take a second to read all of them and make sure that the other choices are not equally obvious. As long as you have time left, it is better to read every answer choice than to pick the first one that looks right without checking the others.

✅ Answer Choice Families

An answer choice family consists of two (in rare cases, three) answer choices that are very similar in construction and cannot all be true at the same time. If you see two answer choices that are direct opposites or parallels, one of them is usually the correct answer. For instance, if one answer choice says that quantity *x* increases and another either says that quantity *x* decreases (opposite) or says that quantity *y* increases (parallel), then those answer choices would fall into the same family. An answer choice that doesn't match the construction of the answer choice family is more likely to be incorrect. Most questions will not have answer choice families, but when they do appear, you should be prepared to recognize them.

✅ Eliminate Answers

Eliminate answer choices as soon as you realize they are wrong, but make sure you consider all possibilities. If you are eliminating answer choices and realize that the last one you are left with is also wrong, don't panic. Start over and consider each choice again. There may be something you missed the first time that you will realize on the second pass.

✅ Avoid Fact Traps

Don't be distracted by an answer choice that is factually true but doesn't answer the question. You are looking for the choice that answers the question. Stay focused on what the question is asking for so you don't accidentally pick an answer that is true but incorrect. Always go back to the question and make sure the answer choice you've selected actually answers the question and is not merely a true statement.

✅ Extreme Statements

In general, you should avoid answers that put forth extreme actions as standard practice or proclaim controversial ideas as established fact. An answer choice that states the "process should be used in certain situations, if..." is much more likely to be correct than one that states the "process should be discontinued completely." The first is a calm rational statement and doesn't even make a definitive, uncompromising stance, using a hedge word *if* to provide wiggle room, whereas the second choice is far more extreme.

✓ Benchmark

As you read through the answer choices and you come across one that seems to answer the question well, mentally select that answer choice. This is not your final answer, but it's the one that will help you evaluate the other answer choices. The one that you selected is your benchmark or standard for judging each of the other answer choices. Every other answer choice must be compared to your benchmark. That choice is correct until proven otherwise by another answer choice beating it. If you find a better answer, then that one becomes your new benchmark. Once you've decided that no other choice answers the question as well as your benchmark, you have your final answer.

✓ Predict the Answer

Before you even start looking at the answer choices, it is often best to try to predict the answer. When you come up with the answer on your own, it is easier to avoid distractions and traps because you will know exactly what to look for. The right answer choice is unlikely to be word-for-word what you came up with, but it should be a close match. Even if you are confident that you have the right answer, you should still take the time to read each option before moving on.

General Strategies

✓ Tough Questions

If you are stumped on a problem or it appears too hard or too difficult, don't waste time. Move on! Remember though, if you can quickly check for obviously incorrect answer choices, your chances of guessing correctly are greatly improved. Before you completely give up, at least try to knock out a couple of possible answers. Eliminate what you can and then guess at the remaining answer choices before moving on.

✓ Check Your Work

Since you will probably not know every term listed and the answer to every question, it is important that you get credit for the ones that you do know. Don't miss any questions through careless mistakes. If at all possible, try to take a second to look back over your answer selection and make sure you've selected the correct answer choice and haven't made a costly careless mistake (such as marking an answer choice that you didn't mean to mark). This quick double check should more than pay for itself in caught mistakes for the time it costs.

✓ Pace Yourself

It's easy to be overwhelmed when you're looking at a page full of questions; your mind is confused and full of random thoughts, and the clock is ticking down faster than you would like. Calm down and maintain the pace that you have set for yourself. Especially as you get down to the last few minutes of the test, don't let the small numbers on the clock make you panic. As long as you are on track by monitoring your pace, you are guaranteed to have time for each question.

✓ Don't Rush

It is very easy to make errors when you are in a hurry. Maintaining a fast pace in answering questions is pointless if it makes you miss questions that you would have gotten right otherwise. Test writers like to include distracting information and wrong answers that seem right. Taking a little extra time to avoid careless mistakes can make all the difference in your test score. Find a pace that allows you to be confident in the answers that you select.

⊘ Keep Moving

Panicking will not help you pass the test, so do your best to stay calm and keep moving. Taking deep breaths and going through the answer elimination steps you practiced can help to break through a stress barrier and keep your pace.

Final Notes

The combination of a solid foundation of content knowledge and the confidence that comes from practicing your plan for applying that knowledge is the key to maximizing your performance on test day. As your foundation of content knowledge is built up and strengthened, you'll find that the strategies included in this chapter become more and more effective in helping you quickly sift through the distractions and traps of the test to isolate the correct answer.

Now that you're preparing to move forward into the test content chapters of this book, be sure to keep your goal in mind. As you read, think about how you will be able to apply this information on the test. If you've already seen sample questions for the test and you have an idea of the question format and style, try to come up with questions of your own that you can answer based on what you're reading. This will give you valuable practice applying your knowledge in the same ways you can expect to on test day.

Good luck and good studying!

Reading Language Arts

Main Ideas and Supporting Details

Identifying Topics and Main Ideas

One of the most important skills in reading comprehension is the identification of **topics** and **main ideas**. There is a subtle difference between these two features. The topic is the subject of a text (i.e., what the text is all about). The main idea, on the other hand, is the most important point being made by the author. The topic is usually expressed in a few words at the most while the main idea often needs a full sentence to be completely defined. As an example, a short passage might be written on the topic of penguins, and the main idea could be written as *Penguins are different from other birds in many ways*. In most nonfiction writing, the topic and the main idea will be **stated directly** and often appear in a sentence at the very beginning or end of the text. When being tested on an understanding of the author's topic, you may be able to skim the passage for the general idea by reading only the first sentence of each paragraph. A body paragraph's first sentence is often—but not always—the main **topic sentence** which gives you a summary of the content in the paragraph.

However, there are cases in which the reader must figure out an **unstated** topic or main idea. In these instances, you must read every sentence of the text and try to come up with an overarching idea that is supported by each of those sentences.

Note: The main idea should not be confused with the thesis statement. While the main idea gives a brief, general summary of a text, the thesis statement provides a **specific perspective** on an issue that the author supports with evidence.

Review Video: Topics and Main Ideas
Visit mometrix.com/academy and enter code: 407801

Supporting Details

Supporting details are smaller pieces of evidence that provide backing for the main point. In order to show that a main idea is correct or valid, an author must add details that prove their point. All texts contain details, but they are only classified as supporting details when they serve to reinforce some larger point. Supporting details are most commonly found in informative and persuasive texts. In some cases, they will be clearly indicated with terms like *for example* or *for instance*, or they will be enumerated with terms like *first*, *second*, and *last*. However, you need to be prepared for texts that do not contain those indicators. As a reader, you should consider whether the author's supporting details really back up his or her main point. Details can be factual and correct, yet they may not be **relevant** to the author's point. Conversely, details can be relevant, but be ineffective because they are based on opinion or assertions that cannot be proven.

Review Video: Supporting Details
Visit mometrix.com/academy and enter code: 396297

Author's Purpose

AUTHOR'S PURPOSE

Usually, identifying the author's **purpose** is easier than identifying his or her **position.** In most cases, the author has no interest in hiding his or her purpose. A text that is meant to entertain, for instance, should be written to please the reader. Most narratives, or stories, are written to entertain, though they may also inform or persuade. Informative texts are easy to identify, while the most difficult purpose of a text to identify is persuasion because the author has an interest in making this purpose hard to detect. When a reader discovers that the author is trying to persuade, he or she should be skeptical of the argument. For this reason, persuasive texts often try to establish an entertaining tone and hope to amuse the reader into agreement. On the other hand, an informative tone may be implemented to create an appearance of authority and objectivity.

An author's purpose is evident often in the **organization** of the text (e.g., section headings in bold font points to an informative text). However, you may not have such organization available to you in your exam. Instead, if the author makes his or her main idea clear from the beginning, then the likely purpose of the text is to **inform**. If the author begins by making a claim and provides various arguments to support that claim, then the purpose is probably to **persuade**. If the author tells a story or wants to gain the reader's attention more than to push a particular point or deliver information, then his or her purpose is most likely to **entertain**. As a reader, you must judge authors on how well they accomplish their purpose. In other words, you need to consider the type of passage (e.g., technical, persuasive, etc.) that the author has written and if the author has followed the requirements of the passage type.

Review Video: Understanding the Author's Intent
Visit mometrix.com/academy and enter code: 511819

INFORMATIONAL TEXTS

An **informational text** is written to educate and enlighten readers. Informational texts are almost always nonfiction and are rarely structured as a story. The intention of an informational text is to deliver information in the most comprehensible way. So, look for the structure of the text to be very clear. In an informational text, the thesis statement is one or two sentences that normally appears at the end of the first paragraph. The author may use some colorful language, but he or she is likely to put more emphasis on clarity and precision. Informational essays do not typically appeal to the emotions. They often contain facts and figures and rarely include the opinion of the author; however, readers should remain aware of the possibility for bias as those facts are presented. Sometimes a persuasive essay can resemble an informative essay, especially if the author maintains an even tone and presents his or her views as if they were established fact.

Review Video: Informational Text
Visit mometrix.com/academy and enter code: 924964

PERSUASIVE WRITING

In a persuasive essay, the author is attempting to change the reader's mind or **convince** him or her of something that he or she did not believe previously. There are several identifying characteristics of **persuasive writing**. One is **opinion presented as fact**. When authors attempt to persuade readers, they often present their opinions as if they were fact. Readers must be on guard for statements that sound factual but which cannot be subjected to research, observation, or experiment. Another characteristic of persuasive writing is **emotional language**. An author will often try to play on the emotions of readers by appealing to their sympathy or sense of morality.

When an author uses colorful or evocative language with the intent of arousing the reader's passions, then the author may be attempting to persuade. Finally, in many cases, a persuasive text will give an **unfair explanation of opposing positions**, if these positions are mentioned at all.

Entertaining Texts

The success or failure of an author's intent to **entertain** is determined by those who read the author's work. Entertaining texts may be either fiction or nonfiction, and they may describe real or imagined people, places, and events. Entertaining texts are often narratives or poems. A text that is written to entertain is likely to contain **colorful language** that engages the imagination and the emotions. Such writing often features a great deal of figurative language, which typically enlivens the subject matter with images and analogies.

Though an entertaining text is not usually written to persuade or inform, authors may accomplish both of these tasks in their work. An entertaining text may *appeal to the reader's emotions* and cause him or her to think differently about a particular subject. In any case, entertaining texts tend to showcase the personality of the author more than other types of writing.

Descriptive Text

In a sense, almost all writing is descriptive, insofar as an author seeks to describe events, ideas, or people to the reader. Some texts, however, are primarily concerned with **description**. A descriptive text focuses on a particular subject and attempts to depict the subject in a way that will be clear to readers. Descriptive texts contain many adjectives and adverbs (i.e., words that give shades of meaning and create a more detailed mental picture for the reader). A descriptive text fails when it is unclear to the reader. A descriptive text will certainly be informative and may be persuasive and entertaining as well.

Review Video: Descriptive Texts
Visit mometrix.com/academy and enter code: 174903

Expression of Feelings

When an author intends to **express feelings**, he or she may use **expressive and bold language**. An author may write with emotion for any number of reasons. Sometimes, authors will express feelings because they are describing a personal situation of great pain or happiness. In other situations, authors will attempt to persuade the reader and will use emotion to stir up the passions. This kind of expression is easy to identify when the writer uses phrases like *I felt* and *I sense*. However, readers may find that the author will simply describe feelings without introducing them. As a reader, you must know the importance of recognizing when an author is expressing emotion and not to become overwhelmed by sympathy or passion. Readers should maintain some **detachment** so that they can still evaluate the strength of the author's argument or the quality of the writing.

Review Video: Emotional Language in Literature
Visit mometrix.com/academy and enter code: 759390

Expository Passage

An **expository** passage aims to **inform** and enlighten readers. Expository passages are nonfiction and usually center around a simple, easily defined topic. Since the goal of exposition is to teach, such a passage should be as clear as possible. Often, an expository passage contains helpful organizing words, like *first*, *next*, *for example*, and *therefore*. These words keep the reader **oriented** in the text. Although expository passages do not need to feature colorful language and artful writing, they are often more effective with these features. For a reader, the challenge of expository passages is to maintain steady attention. Expository passages are not always about subjects that will naturally interest a reader, so the writer is often more concerned with **clarity** and **comprehensibility** than with engaging the reader. By reading actively, you can ensure a good habit of focus when reading an expository passage.

Review Video: Expository Passages
Visit mometrix.com/academy and enter code: 256515

NARRATIVE PASSAGE

A **narrative** passage is a story that can be fiction or nonfiction. However, there are a few elements that a text must have in order to be classified as a narrative. First, the text must have a **plot** (i.e., a series of events). Narratives often proceed in a clear sequence, but this is not a requirement. If the narrative is good, then these events will be interesting to readers. Second, a narrative has **characters**. These characters could be people, animals, or even inanimate objects—so long as they participate in the plot. Third, a narrative passage often contains **figurative language** which is meant to stimulate the imagination of readers by making comparisons and observations. For instance, a *metaphor*, a common piece of figurative language, is a description of one thing in terms of another. *The moon was a frosty snowball* is an example of a metaphor. In the literal sense this is obviously untrue, but the comparison suggests a certain mood for the reader.

TECHNICAL PASSAGE

A **technical** passage is written to *describe* a complex object or process. Technical writing is common in medical and technological fields, in which complex ideas of mathematics, science, and engineering need to be explained *simply* and *clearly*. To ease comprehension, a technical passage usually proceeds in a very logical order. Technical passages often have clear headings and subheadings, which are used to keep the reader oriented in the text. Additionally, you will find that these passages divide sections up with numbers or letters. Many technical passages look more like an outline than a piece of prose. The amount of **jargon** or difficult vocabulary will vary in a technical passage depending on the intended audience. As much as possible, technical passages try to avoid language that the reader will have to research in order to understand the message, yet readers will find that jargon cannot always be avoided.

Review Video: Technical Passages
Visit mometrix.com/academy and enter code: 478923

Common Organizations of Texts

Organization of the Text

The way a text is organized can help readers understand the author's intent and his or her conclusions. There are various ways to organize a text, and each one has a purpose and use. Usually, authors will organize information logically in a passage so the reader can follow and locate the information within the text. However, since not all passages are written with the same logical structure, you need to be familiar with several different types of passage structure.

Review Video: Sequence of Events in a Story
Visit mometrix.com/academy and enter code: 807512

Chronological

When using **chronological** order, the author presents information in the order that it happened. For example, biographies are typically written in chronological order. The subject's birth and childhood are presented first, followed by their adult life, and lastly the events leading up to the person's death.

Cause and Effect

One of the most common text structures is **cause and effect**. A **cause** is an act or event that makes something happen, and an **effect** is the thing that happens as a result of the cause. A cause-and-effect relationship is not always explicit, but there are some terms in English that signal causes, such as *since*, *because*, and *due to*. Furthermore, terms that signal effects include *consequently, therefore, this leads to*. As an example, consider the sentence *Because the sky was clear, Ron did not bring an umbrella*. The cause is the clear sky, and the effect is that Ron did not bring an umbrella. However, readers may find that sometimes the cause-and-effect relationship will not be clearly noted. For instance, the sentence *He was late and missed the meeting* does not contain any signaling words, but the sentence still contains a cause (he was late) and an effect (he missed the meeting).

Review Video: Cause and Effect
Visit mometrix.com/academy and enter code: 868099

Review Video: Rhetorical Strategy of Cause and Effect Analysis
Visit mometrix.com/academy and enter code: 725944

Multiple Effects

Be aware of the possibility for a single cause to have **multiple effects.** (e.g., *Single cause*: Because you left your homework on the table, your dog engulfed the assignment. *Multiple effects*: As a result, you receive a failing grade, your parents do not allow you to go out with your friends, you miss out on the new movie, and one of your classmates spoils it for you before you have another chance to watch it).

Multiple Causes

Also, there is the possibility for a single effect to have **multiple causes.** (e.g., *Single effect*: Alan has a fever. *Multiple causes*: An unexpected cold front came through the area, and Alan forgot to take his multi-vitamin to avoid getting sick.) Additionally, an effect can in turn be the cause of another effect, in what is known as a cause-and-effect chain. (e.g., As a result of her disdain for procrastination, Lynn prepared for her exam. This led to her passing her test with high marks. Hence, her resume was accepted and her application was approved.)

Cause and Effect in Persuasive Essays

Persuasive essays, in which an author tries to make a convincing argument and change the minds of readers, usually include cause-and-effect relationships. However, these relationships should not always be taken at face value. Frequently, an author will assume a cause or take an effect for granted. To read a persuasive essay effectively, readers need to judge the cause-and-effect relationships that the author is presenting. For instance, imagine an author wrote the following: *The parking deck has been unprofitable because people would prefer to ride their bikes.* The relationship is clear: the cause is that people prefer to ride their bikes, and the effect is that the parking deck has been unprofitable. However, readers should consider whether this argument is conclusive. Perhaps there are other reasons for the failure of the parking deck: a down economy, excessive fees, etc. Too often, authors present causal relationships as if they are fact rather than opinion. Readers should be on the alert for these dubious claims.

Problem-Solution

Some nonfiction texts are organized to **present a problem** followed by a solution. For this type of text, the problem is often explained before the solution is offered. In some cases, as when the problem is well known, the solution may be introduced briefly at the beginning. Other passages may focus on the solution, and the problem will be referenced only occasionally. Some texts will outline multiple solutions to a problem, leaving readers to choose among them. If the author has an interest or an allegiance to one solution, he or she may fail to mention or describe accurately some of the other solutions. Readers should be careful of the author's agenda when reading a problem-solution text. Only by understanding the author's perspective and interests can one develop a proper judgment of the proposed solution.

Compare and Contrast

Many texts follow the **compare-and-contrast** model in which the similarities and differences between two ideas or things are explored. Analysis of the similarities between ideas is called **comparison**. In an ideal comparison, the author places ideas or things in an equivalent structure, i.e., the author presents the ideas in the same way. If an author wants to show the similarities between cricket and baseball, then he or she may do so by summarizing the equipment and rules for each game. Be mindful of the similarities as they appear in the passage and take note of any differences that are mentioned. Often, these small differences will only reinforce the more general similarity.

Review Video: Compare and Contrast
Visit mometrix.com/academy and enter code: 798319

Thinking critically about ideas and conclusions can seem like a daunting task. One way to ease this task is to understand the basic elements of ideas and writing techniques. Looking at the ways different ideas relate to each other can be a good way for readers to begin their analysis. For instance, sometimes authors will write about two ideas that are in opposition to each other. Or, one author will provide his or her ideas on a topic, and another author may respond in opposition. The analysis of these opposing ideas is known as **contrast**. Contrast is often marred by the author's obvious partiality to one of the ideas. A discerning reader will be put off by an author who does not engage in a fair fight. In an analysis of opposing ideas, both ideas should be presented in clear and reasonable terms. If the author does prefer a side, you need to read carefully to determine the areas where the author shows or avoids this preference. In an analysis of opposing ideas, you should proceed through the passage by marking the major differences point by point with an eye that is looking for an explanation of each side's view. For instance, in an analysis of capitalism and communism, there is an importance in outlining each side's view on labor, markets, prices, personal responsibility, etc. Additionally, as you read through the passages, you should note whether the opposing views present each side in a similar manner.

SEQUENCE

Readers must be able to identify a text's **sequence**, or the order in which things happen. Often, when the sequence is very important to the author, the text is indicated with signal words like *first, then, next,* and *last.* However, a sequence can be merely implied and must be noted by the reader. Consider the sentence *He walked through the garden and gave water and fertilizer to the plants.* Clearly, the man did not walk through the garden before he collected water and fertilizer for the plants. So, the implied sequence is that he first collected water, then he collected fertilizer, next he walked through the garden, and last he gave water or fertilizer as necessary to the plants. Texts do not always proceed in an orderly sequence from first to last. Sometimes they begin at the end and start over at the beginning. As a reader, you can enhance your understanding of the passage by taking brief notes to clarify the sequence.

Review Video: Sequence
Visit mometrix.com/academy and enter code: 489027

Making and Evaluating Predictions

MAKING PREDICTIONS

When we read literature, **making predictions** about what will happen in the writing reinforces our purpose for reading and prepares us mentally. A **prediction** is a guess about what will happen next. Readers constantly make predictions based on what they have read and what they already know. We can make predictions before we begin reading and during our reading. Consider the following sentence: *Staring at the computer screen in shock, Kim blindly reached over for the brimming glass of water on the shelf to her side.* The sentence suggests that Kim is distracted, and that she is not looking at the glass that she is going to pick up. So, a reader might predict that Kim is going to knock over the glass. Of course, not every prediction will be accurate: perhaps Kim will pick the glass up cleanly. Nevertheless, the author has certainly created the expectation that the water might be spilled.

As we read on, we can test the accuracy of our predictions, revise them in light of additional reading, and confirm or refute our predictions. Predictions are always subject to revision as the reader acquires more information. A reader can make predictions by observing the title and illustrations; noting the structure, characters, and subject; drawing on existing knowledge relative to the subject; and asking "why" and "who" questions. Connecting reading to what we already know enables us to learn new information and construct meaning. For example, before third-graders read a book about Johnny Appleseed, they may start a KWL chart—a list of what they *Know*, what they *Want* to know or learn, and what they have *Learned* after reading. Activating existing background knowledge and thinking about the text before reading improves comprehension.

Review Video: Predictive Reading
Visit mometrix.com/academy and enter code: 437248

Test-taking tip: To respond to questions requiring future predictions, your answers should be based on evidence of past or present behavior and events.

EVALUATING PREDICTIONS

When making predictions, readers should be able to explain how they developed their prediction. One way readers can defend their thought process is by citing textual evidence. Textual evidence to evaluate reader predictions about literature includes specific synopses of the work, paraphrases of the work or parts of it, and direct quotations from the work. These references to the text must support the prediction by indicating, clearly or unclearly, what will happen later in the story. A text may provide these indications through literary devices such as foreshadowing. Foreshadowing is anything in a text that gives the reader a hint about what is to come by emphasizing the likelihood of an event or development. Foreshadowing can occur through descriptions, exposition, and dialogue. Foreshadowing in dialogue usually occurs when a character gives a warning or expresses a strong feeling that a certain event will occur. Foreshadowing can also occur through irony. However, unlike other forms of foreshadowing, the events that seem the most likely are the opposite of what actually happens. Instances of foreshadowing and irony can be summarized, paraphrased, or quoted to defend a reader's prediction.

Review Video: Textual Evidence for Predictions
Visit mometrix.com/academy and enter code: 261070

Making Inferences and Drawing Conclusions

Inferences are logical conclusions that readers make based on their observations and previous knowledge. An inference is based on both what is found in a passage or a story and what is known from personal experience. For instance, a story may say that a character is frightened and can hear howling in the distance. Based on both what is in the text and personal knowledge, it is a logical conclusion that the character is frightened because he hears the sound of wolves. A good inference is supported by the information in a passage.

IMPLICIT AND EXPLICIT INFORMATION

By inferring, readers construct meanings from text that are personally relevant. By combining their own schemas or concepts and their background information pertinent to the text with what they read, readers interpret it according to both what the author has conveyed and their own unique perspectives. Inferences are different from **explicit information**, which is clearly stated in a passage. Authors do not always explicitly spell out every meaning in what they write; many meanings are implicit. Through inference, readers can comprehend implied meanings in the text, and also derive personal significance from it, making the text meaningful and memorable to them. Inference is a natural process in everyday life. When readers infer, they can draw conclusions about what the author is saying, predict what may reasonably follow, amend these predictions as they continue to read, interpret the import of themes, and analyze the characters' feelings and motivations through their actions.

EXAMPLE OF DRAWING CONCLUSIONS FROM INFERENCES

Read the excerpt and decide why Jana finally relaxed.

> Jana loved her job, but the work was very demanding. She had trouble relaxing. She called a friend, but she still thought about work. She ordered a pizza, but eating it did not help. Then, her kitten jumped on her lap and began to purr. Jana leaned back and began to hum a little tune. She felt better.

You can draw the conclusion that Jana relaxed because her kitten jumped on her lap. The kitten purred, and Jana leaned back and hummed a tune. Then she felt better. The excerpt does not explicitly say that this is the reason why she was able to relax. The text leaves the matter unclear, but the reader can infer or make a "best guess" that this is the reason she is relaxing. This is a logical conclusion based on the information in the passage. It is the best conclusion a reader can make based on the information he or she has read. Inferences are based on the information in a passage, but they are not directly stated in the passage.

Test-taking tip: While being tested on your ability to make correct inferences, you must look for **contextual clues**. An answer can be true, but not the best or most correct answer. The contextual clues will help you find the answer that is the **best answer** out of the given choices. Be careful in your reading to understand the context in which a phrase is stated. When asked for the implied meaning of a statement made in the passage, you should immediately locate the statement and read the **context** in which the statement was made. Also, look for an answer choice that has a similar phrase to the statement in question.

Review Video: Inference
Visit mometrix.com/academy and enter code: 379203

Review Video: How to Support a Conclusion
Visit mometrix.com/academy and enter code: 281653

Critical Reading Skills

Opinions, Facts, and Fallacies

Critical thinking skills are mastered through understanding various types of writing and the different purposes authors can have for writing different passages. Every author writes for a purpose. When you understand their purpose and how they accomplish their goal, you will be able to analyze their writing and determine whether or not you agree with their conclusions.

Readers must always be aware of the difference between fact and opinion. A **fact** can be subjected to analysis and proven to be true. An **opinion**, on the other hand, is the author's personal thoughts or feelings and may not be altered by research or evidence. If the author writes that the distance from New York City to Boston is about two hundred miles, then he or she is stating a fact. If the author writes that New York City is too crowded, then he or she is giving an opinion because there is no objective standard for overpopulation. Opinions are often supported by facts. For instance, an author might use a comparison between the population density of New York City and that of other major American cities as evidence of an overcrowded population. An opinion supported by facts tends to be more convincing. On the other hand, when authors support their opinions with other opinions, readers should employ critical thinking and approach the argument with skepticism.

Review Video: Distinguishing Fact and Opinion
Visit mometrix.com/academy and enter code: 870899

Reliable Sources

When you read an argumentative passage, you need to be sure that facts are presented to the reader from **reliable sources**. An opinion is what the author thinks about a given topic. An opinion is not common knowledge or proven by expert sources, instead the information is the personal beliefs and thoughts of the author. To distinguish between fact and opinion, a reader needs to consider the type of source that is presenting information, the information that backs-up a claim, and the author's motivation to have a certain point-of-view on a given topic. For example, if a panel of scientists has conducted multiple studies on the effectiveness of taking a certain vitamin, then the results are more likely to be factual than those of a company that is selling a vitamin and simply claims that taking the vitamin can produce positive effects. The company is motivated to sell their product, and the scientists are using the scientific method to prove a theory. Remember, if you find sentences that contain phrases such as "I think...", then the statement is an opinion.

BIASES

In their attempts to persuade, writers often make mistakes in their thought processes and writing choices. These processes and choices are important to understand so you can make an informed decision about the author's credibility. Every author has a point of view, but authors demonstrate a **bias** when they ignore reasonable counterarguments or distort opposing viewpoints. A bias is evident whenever the author's claims are presented in a way that is unfair or inaccurate. Bias can be intentional or unintentional, but readers should be skeptical of the author's argument in either case. Remember that a biased author may still be correct. However, the author will be correct in spite of, not because of, his or her bias.

A **stereotype** is a bias applied specifically to a group of people or a place. Stereotyping is considered to be particularly abhorrent because it promotes negative, misleading generalizations about people. Readers should be very cautious of authors who use stereotypes in their writing. These faulty assumptions typically reveal the author's ignorance and lack of curiosity.

Review Video: Bias and Stereotype
Visit mometrix.com/academy and enter code: 644829

Persuasion and Rhetoric

PERSUASIVE TECHNIQUES

To **appeal using reason**, writers present logical arguments, such as using "If... then... because" statements. To **appeal to emotions**, authors may ask readers how they would feel about something or to put themselves in another's place, present their argument as one that will make the audience feel good, or tell readers how they should feel. To **appeal to character**, **morality**, or **ethics**, authors present their points to readers as the right or most moral choices. Authors cite expert opinions to show readers that someone very knowledgeable about the subject or viewpoint agrees with the author's claims. **Testimonials**, usually via anecdotes or quotations regarding the author's subject, help build the audience's trust in an author's message through positive support from ordinary people. **Bandwagon appeals** claim that everybody else agrees with the author's argument and persuade readers to conform and agree, also. Authors **appeal to greed** by presenting their choice as cheaper, free, or more valuable for less cost. They **appeal to laziness** by presenting their views as more convenient, easy, or relaxing. Authors also anticipate potential objections and argue against them before audiences think of them, thereby depicting those objections as weak.

Authors can use **comparisons** like analogies, similes, and metaphors to persuade audiences. For example, a writer might represent excessive expenses as "hemorrhaging" money, which the author's recommended solution will stop. Authors can use negative word connotations to make some choices unappealing to readers, and positive word connotations to make others more appealing. Using **humor** can relax readers and garner their agreement. However, writers must take care: ridiculing opponents can be a successful strategy for appealing to readers who already agree with the author, but can backfire by angering other readers. **Rhetorical questions** need no answer, but create effect that can force agreement, such as asking the question, "Wouldn't you rather be paid more than less?" **Generalizations** persuade readers by being impossible to disagree with. Writers can easily make generalizations that appear to support their viewpoints, like saying, "We all want peace, not war" regarding more specific political arguments. **Transfer** and **association** persuade by example: if advertisements show attractive actors enjoying their products, audiences imagine they will experience the same. **Repetition** can also sometimes effectively persuade audiences.

Review Video: Using Rhetorical Strategies for Persuasion
Visit mometrix.com/academy and enter code: 302658

Classical Author Appeals

In his *On Rhetoric,* ancient Greek philosopher Aristotle defined three basic types of appeal used in writing, which he called *pathos*, *ethos*, and *logos*. ***Pathos*** means suffering or experience and refers to appeals to the emotions (the English word *pathetic* comes from this root). Writing that is meant to entertain audiences, by making them either happy, as with comedy, or sad, as with tragedy, uses *pathos*. Aristotle's *Poetics* states that evoking the emotions of terror and pity is one of the criteria for writing tragedy. ***Ethos*** means character and connotes ideology (the English word *ethics* comes from this root). Writing that appeals to credibility, based on academic, professional, or personal merit, uses *ethos*. ***Logos*** means "I say" and refers to a plea, opinion, expectation, word or speech, account, opinion, or reason (the English word *logic* comes from this root.) Aristotle used it to mean persuasion that appeals to the audience through reasoning and logic to influence their opinions.

Rhetorical Devices

- An **anecdote** is a brief story authors may relate to their argument, which can illustrate their points in a more real and relatable way.
- **Aphorisms** concisely state common beliefs and may rhyme. For example, Benjamin Franklin's "Early to bed and early to rise / Makes a man healthy, wealthy, and wise" is an aphorism.
- **Allusions** refer to literary or historical figures to impart symbolism to a thing or person and to create reader resonance. In John Steinbeck's *Of Mice and Men,* protagonist George's last name is Milton. This alludes to John Milton, who wrote *Paradise Lost*, and symbolizes George's eventual loss of his dream.
- **Satire** exaggerates, ridicules, or pokes fun at human flaws or ideas, as in the works of Jonathan Swift and Mark Twain.
- A **parody** is a form of satire that imitates another work to ridicule its topic or style.
- A **paradox** is a statement that is true despite appearing contradictory.
- **Hyperbole** is overstatement using exaggerated language.
- An **oxymoron** combines seeming contradictions, such as "deafening silence."
- **Analogies** compare two things that share common elements.
- **Similes** (stated comparisons using the words *like* or *as*) and **metaphors** (stated comparisons that do not use *like* or *as*) are considered forms of analogy.
- When using logic to reason with audiences, **syllogism** refers either to deductive reasoning or a deceptive, very sophisticated, or subtle argument.
- **Deductive reasoning** moves from general to specific, **inductive reasoning** from specific to general.
- **Diction** is author word choice that establishes tone and effect.
- **Understatement** achieves effects like contrast or irony by downplaying or describing something more subtly than warranted.
- **Chiasmus** uses parallel clauses, the second reversing the order of the first. Examples include T. S. Eliot's "Has the Church failed mankind, or has mankind failed the Church?" and

John F. Kennedy's "Ask not what your country can do for you; ask what you can do for your country."

- **Anaphora** regularly repeats a word or phrase at the beginnings of consecutive clauses or phrases to add emphasis to an idea. A classic example of anaphora was Winston Churchill's emphasis of determination: "[W]e shall fight on the beaches, we shall fight on the landing grounds, we shall fight in the fields and in the streets, we shall fight in the hills; we shall never surrender..."

Reading Comprehension and Connecting with Texts

Comparing Two Stories

When presented with two different stories, there will be **similarities** and **differences** between the two. A reader needs to make a list, or other graphic organizer, of the points presented in each story. Once the reader has written down the main point and supporting points for each story, the two sets of ideas can be compared. The reader can then present each idea and show how it is the same or different in the other story. This is called **comparing and contrasting ideas**.

The reader can compare ideas by stating, for example: "In Story 1, the author believes that humankind will one day land on Mars, whereas in Story 2, the author believes that Mars is too far away for humans to ever step foot on." Note that the two viewpoints are different in each story that the reader is comparing. A reader may state that: "Both stories discussed the likelihood of humankind landing on Mars." This statement shows how the viewpoint presented in both stories is based on the same topic, rather than how each viewpoint is different. The reader will complete a comparison of two stories with a conclusion.

Review Video: How to Compare and Contrast
Visit mometrix.com/academy and enter code: 833765

Outlining a Passage

As an aid to drawing conclusions, **outlining** the information contained in the passage should be a familiar skill to readers. An effective outline will reveal the structure of the passage and will lead to solid conclusions. An effective outline will have a title that refers to the basic subject of the text, though the title does not need to restate the main idea. In most outlines, the main idea will be the first major section. Each major idea in the passage will be established as the head of a category. For instance, the most common outline format calls for the main ideas of the passage to be indicated with Roman numerals. In an effective outline of this kind, each of the main ideas will be represented by a Roman numeral and none of the Roman numerals will designate minor details or secondary ideas. Moreover, all supporting ideas and details should be placed in the appropriate place on the outline. An outline does not need to include every detail listed in the text, but it should feature all of those that are central to the argument or message. Each of these details should be listed under the corresponding main idea.

Review Video: Outlining as an Aid to Drawing Conclusions
Visit mometrix.com/academy and enter code: 584445

Using Graphic Organizers

Ideas from a text can also be organized using **graphic organizers**. A graphic organizer is a way to simplify information and take key points from the text. A graphic organizer such as a timeline may have an event listed for a corresponding date on the timeline, while an outline may have an event listed under a key point that occurs in the text. Each reader needs to create the type of graphic organizer that works the best for him or her in terms of being able to recall information from a story. Examples include a spider-map, which takes a main idea from the story and places it in a bubble with supporting points branching off the main idea. An outline is useful for diagramming the main and supporting points of the entire story, and a Venn diagram compares and contrasts characteristics of two or more ideas.

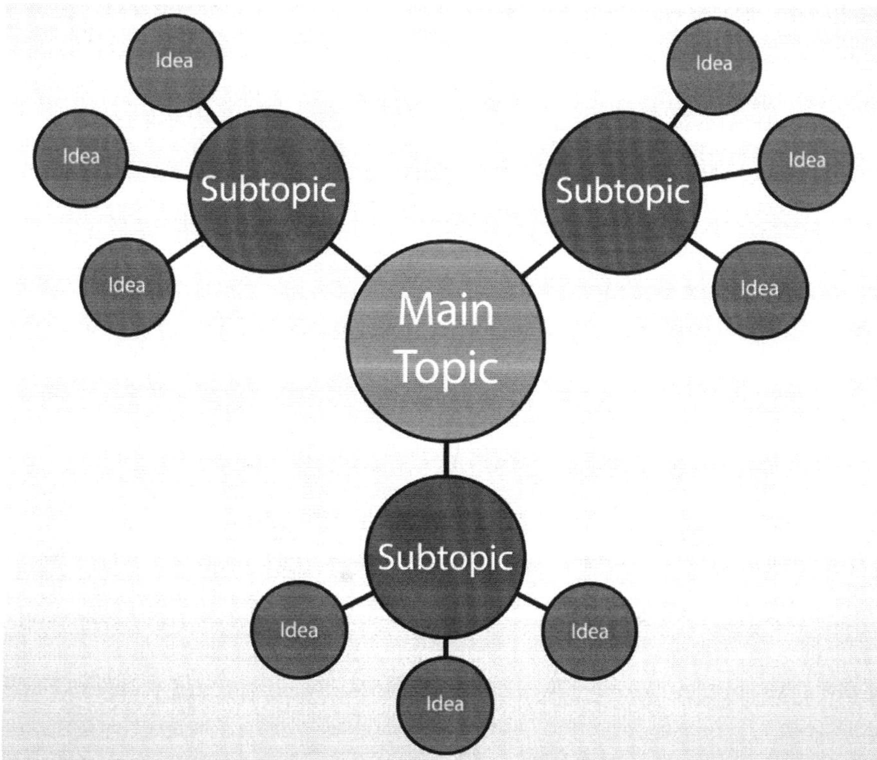

Review Video: Graphic Organizers
Visit mometrix.com/academy and enter code: 665513

Making Logical Conclusions about a Passage

A reader should always be drawing conclusions from the text. Sometimes conclusions are **implied** from written information, and other times the information is **stated directly** within the passage. One should always aim to draw conclusions from information stated within a passage, rather than to draw them from mere implications. At times an author may provide some information and then describe a counterargument. Readers should be alert for direct statements that are subsequently rejected or weakened by the author. Furthermore, you should always read through the entire passage before drawing conclusions. Many readers are trained to expect the author's conclusions at either the beginning or the end of the passage, but many texts do not adhere to this format.

Drawing conclusions from information implied within a passage requires confidence on the part of the reader. **Implications** are things that the author does not state directly, but readers can assume based on what the author does say. Consider the following passage: *I stepped outside and opened my* *umbrella. By the time I got to work, the cuffs of my pants were soaked.* The author never states that it is raining, but this fact is clearly implied. Conclusions based on implication must be well supported by the text. In order to draw a solid conclusion, readers should have **multiple pieces of evidence**. If readers have only one piece, they must be assured that there is no other possible explanation than their conclusion. A good reader will be able to draw many conclusions from information implied by the text, which will be a great help on the exam.

Drawing Conclusions

A common type of inference that a reader has to make is **drawing a conclusion**. The reader makes this conclusion based on the information provided within a text. Certain facts are included to help a reader come to a specific conclusion. For example, a story may open with a man trudging through the snow on a cold winter day, dragging a sled behind him. The reader can logically **infer** from the setting of the story that the man is wearing heavy winter clothes in order to stay warm. Information is implied based on the setting of a story, which is why **setting** is an important element of the text. If the same man in the example was trudging down a beach on a hot summer day, dragging a surf board behind him, the reader would assume that the man is not wearing heavy clothes. The reader makes inferences based on their own experiences and the information presented to them in the story.

Test-taking tip: When asked to identify a conclusion that may be drawn, look for critical "hedge" phrases, such as *likely*, *may*, *can*, and *will often*, among many others. When you are being tested on this knowledge, remember the question that writers insert into these hedge phrases to cover every possibility. Often an answer will be wrong simply because there is no room for exception. Extreme positive or negative answers (such as always or never) are usually not correct. When answering these questions, the reader **should not** use any outside knowledge that is not gathered directly or reasonably inferred from the passage. Correct answers can be derived straight from the passage.

Example

Read the following sentence from *Little Women* by Louisa May Alcott and draw a conclusion based upon the information presented:

> *You know the reason Mother proposed not having any presents this Christmas was because it is going to be a hard winter for everyone; and she thinks we ought not to spend money for pleasure, when our men are suffering so in the army.*

Based on the information in the sentence, the reader can conclude, or **infer**, that the men are away at war while the women are still at home. The pronoun *our* gives a clue to the reader that the character is speaking about men she knows. In addition, the reader can assume that the character is speaking to a brother or sister, since the term "Mother" is used by the character while speaking to another person. The reader can also come to the conclusion that the characters celebrate Christmas, since it is mentioned in the **context** of the sentence. In the sentence, the mother is presented as an unselfish character who is opinionated and thinks about the wellbeing of other people.

Summarizing

A helpful tool is the ability to **summarize** the information that you have read in a paragraph or passage format. This process is similar to creating an effective outline. First, a summary should accurately define the main idea of the passage, though the summary does not need to explain this main idea in exhaustive detail. The summary should continue by laying out the most important supporting details or arguments from the passage. All of the significant supporting details should be included, and none of the details included should be irrelevant or insignificant. Also, the summary should accurately report all of these details. Too often, the desire for brevity in a summary leads to the sacrifice of clarity or accuracy. Summaries are often difficult to read because they omit all of the graceful language, digressions, and asides that distinguish great writing. However, an effective summary should communicate the same overall message as the original text.

Review Video: Summarizing Text
Visit mometrix.com/academy and enter code: 172903

Paraphrasing

Paraphrasing is another method that the reader can use to aid in comprehension. When paraphrasing, one puts what they have read into their own words by rephrasing what the author has written, or one "translates" all of what the author shared into their own words by including as many details as they can.

Evaluating a Passage

It is important to understand the logical conclusion of the ideas presented in an informational text. **Identifying a logical conclusion** can help you determine whether you agree with the writer or not. Coming to this conclusion is much like making an inference: the approach requires you to combine the information given by the text with what you already know and make a logical conclusion. If the author intended for the reader to draw a certain conclusion, then you can expect the author's argumentation and detail to be leading in that direction.

One way to approach the task of drawing conclusions is to make brief **notes** of all the points made by the author. When the notes are arranged on paper, they may clarify the logical conclusion. Another way to approach conclusions is to consider whether the reasoning of the author raises any pertinent questions. Sometimes you will be able to draw several conclusions from a passage. On occasion these will be conclusions that were never imagined by the author. Therefore, be aware that these conclusions must be **supported directly by the text**.

Evaluation of Summaries

A summary of a literary passage is a condensation in the reader's own words of the passage's main points. Several guidelines can be used in evaluating a summary. The summary should be complete yet concise. It should be accurate, balanced, fair, neutral, and objective, excluding the reader's own opinions or reactions. It should reflect in similar proportion how much each point summarized was covered in the original passage. Summary writers should include tags of attribution, like "Macaulay argues that" to reference the original author whose ideas are represented in the summary. Summary writers should not overuse quotations; they should only quote central concepts or phrases they cannot precisely convey in words other than those of the original author. Another aspect of evaluating a summary is considering whether it can stand alone as a coherent, unified composition. In addition, evaluation of a summary should include whether its writer has cited the original source of the passage they have summarized so that readers can find it.

Making Connections to Enhance Comprehension

Reading involves thinking. For good comprehension, readers make **text-to-self**, **text-to-text**, and **text-to-world connections**. Making connections helps readers understand text better and predict what might occur next based on what they already know, such as how characters in the story feel or what happened in another text. Text-to-self connections with the reader's life and experiences make literature more personally relevant and meaningful to readers. Readers can make connections before, during, and after reading—including whenever the text reminds them of something similar they have encountered in life or other texts. The genre, setting, characters, plot elements, literary structure and devices, and themes an author uses allow a reader to make connections to other works of literature or to people and events in their own lives. Venn diagrams and other graphic organizers help visualize connections. Readers can also make double-entry notes: key content, ideas, events, words, and quotations on one side, and the connections with these on the other.

Comparing Two Texts

Synthesis of Multiple Texts

Synthesizing, i.e., understanding and integrating, information from multiple texts can at times be among the most challenging skills for some students to succeed with on tests and in school, and yet it is also among the most important. Students who read at the highest cognitive levels can select related material from different text sources and construct coherent arguments that account for these varied information sources. Synthesizing ideas and information from multiple texts actually combines other reading skills that students should have mastered previously in reading one text at a time, and applies them in the context of reading more than one text. For example, students are required to read texts closely, including identifying explicit and implicit meanings; use critical thinking and reading; draw inferences; assess author reasoning; analyze supporting evidence; and formulate opinions they can justify, based on more passages than one. When two paired texts represent opposing sides of the same argument, students can find analyzing them easier; but this is not always the case.

Similarities in Texts

When students are called upon to compare things two texts share in common, the most obvious commonality might be the same subject matter or specific topic. However, two texts need not be about the same thing to compare them. Some other features texts can share include structural characteristics. For example, they may both be written using a sequential format, such as narrating events or giving instructions in chronological order; listing and/or discussing subtopics by order of importance; or describing a place spatially in sequence from each point to the next. They may both use a comparison-contrast structure, identifying similarities and differences between, among, or within topics. They might both organize information by identifying cause-and-effect relationships. Texts can be similar in type, e.g., description, narration, persuasion, or exposition. They can be similar in using technical vocabulary or using formal or informal language. They may share similar tones and/or styles, e.g., humorous, satirical, serious, etc. They can share similar purposes, e.g., to alarm audiences, incite them to action, reassure them, inspire them, provoke strong emotional responses, etc.

Contrasts in Texts

When analyzing paired or multiple texts, students might observe differences in tone; for example, one text might take a serious approach while another uses a humorous one. Even within approaches or treatments, style can differ: one text may be humorous in a witty, sophisticated, clever way while another may exercise broad, "lowbrow" humor; another may employ mordant sarcasm; another may use satire, couching outrageous suggestions in a "deadpan" logical voice to lampoon social attitudes and behaviors as Jonathan Swift did in *A Modest Proposal.* Serious writing can range from darkly pessimistic to alarmist to objective and unemotional. Texts might have similar information, yet organize it using different structures. One text may support points or ideas using logical arguments, while another may seek to persuade its audience by appealing to their emotions. A very obvious difference in text is genre: for example, the same mythological or traditional stories have been told as oral folk tales, written dramas, written novels, etc.; and/or set in different times and places (e.g., Shakespeare's *Romeo and Juliet* vs. Laurents, Bernstein, and Sondheim's *West Side Story*).

Reading Informational Texts

Language Use

Literal and Figurative Language

As in fictional literature, informational text also uses both **literal language**, which means just what it says, and **figurative language**, which imparts more than literal meaning. For example, an informational text author might use a simile or direct comparison, such as writing that a racehorse "ran like the wind." Informational text authors also use metaphors or implied comparisons, such as "the cloud of the Great Depression." Imagery may also appear in informational texts to increase the reader's understanding of ideas and concepts discussed in the text.

Explicit and Implicit Information

When informational text states something explicitly, the reader is told by the author exactly what is meant, which can include the author's interpretation or perspective of events. For example, a professor writes, "I have seen students go into an absolute panic just because they weren't able to complete the exam in the time they were allotted." This explicitly tells the reader that the students were afraid, and by using the words "just because," the writer indicates their fear was exaggerated out of proportion relative to what happened. However, another professor writes, "I have had students come to me, their faces drained of all color, saying 'We weren't able to finish the exam.'" This is an example of implicit meaning: the second writer did not state explicitly that the students were panicked. Instead, he wrote a description of their faces being "drained of all color." From this description, the reader can infer that the students were so frightened that their faces paled.

Review Video: Explicit and Implicit Information
Visit mometrix.com/academy and enter code: 735771

Making Inferences About Informational Text

With informational text, reader comprehension depends not only on recalling important statements and details, but also on reader inferences based on examples and details. Readers add information from the text to what they already know to draw inferences about the text. These inferences help the readers to fill in the information that the text does not explicitly state, enabling them to understand the text better. When reading a nonfictional autobiography or biography, for example, the most appropriate inferences might concern the events in the book, the actions of the subject of the autobiography or biography, and the message the author means to convey. When reading a nonfictional expository (informational) text, the reader would best draw inferences about problems and their solutions, and causes and their effects. When reading a nonfictional persuasive text, the reader will want to infer ideas supporting the author's message and intent.

Structures or Organizational Patterns in Informational Texts

Informational text can be **descriptive**, appealing to the five senses and answering the questions what, who, when, where, and why. Another method of structuring informational text is sequence and order. **Chronological** texts relate events in the sequence that they occurred, from start to finish, while how-to texts organize information into a series of instructions in the sequence in which the steps should be followed. **Comparison-contrast** structures of informational text describe various ideas to their readers by pointing out how things or ideas are similar and how they are different. **Cause and effect** structures of informational text describe events that occurred and identify the causes or reasons that those events occurred. **Problem and solution** structures of informational texts introduce and describe problems and offer one or more solutions for each problem described.

Determining an Informational Author's Purpose

Informational authors' purposes are why they write texts. Readers must determine authors' motivations and goals. Readers gain greater insight into a text by considering the author's motivation. This develops critical reading skills. Readers perceive writing as a person's voice, not simply printed words. Uncovering author motivations and purposes empowers readers to know what to expect from the text, read for relevant details, evaluate authors and their work critically, and respond effectively to the motivations and persuasions of the text. The main idea of a text is what the reader is supposed to understand from reading it; the purpose of the text is why the author has written it and what the author wants readers to do with its information. Authors state some purposes clearly, while other purposes may be unstated but equally significant. When stated purposes contradict other parts of a text, the author may have a hidden agenda. Readers can better evaluate a text's effectiveness, whether they agree or disagree with it, and why they agree or disagree through identifying unstated author purposes.

Identifying Author's Point of View or Purpose

In some informational texts, readers find it easy to identify the author's point of view and purpose, such as when the author explicitly states his or her position and reason for writing. But other texts are more difficult, either because of the content or because the authors give neutral or balanced viewpoints. This is particularly true in scientific texts, in which authors may state the purpose of their research in the report, but never state their point of view except by interpreting evidence or data.

To analyze text and identify point of view or purpose, readers should ask themselves the following four questions:

1. With what main point or idea does this author want to persuade readers to agree?
2. How does this author's word choice affect the way that readers consider this subject?
3. How do this author's choices of examples and facts affect the way that readers consider this subject?
4. What is it that this author wants to accomplish by writing this text?

Review Video: Understanding the Author's Intent
Visit mometrix.com/academy and enter code: 511819

Review Video: Author's Position
Visit mometrix.com/academy and enter code: 827954

Evaluating Arguments Made by Informational Text Writers

When evaluating an informational text, the first step is to identify the argument's conclusion. Then identify the author's premises that support the conclusion. Try to paraphrase premises for clarification and make the conclusion and premises fit. List all premises first, sequentially numbered, then finish with the conclusion. Identify any premises or assumptions not stated by the author but required for the stated premises to support the conclusion. Read word assumptions sympathetically, as the author might. Evaluate whether premises reasonably support the conclusion. For inductive reasoning, the reader should ask if the premises are true, if they support the conclusion, and if so, how strongly. For deductive reasoning, the reader should ask if the argument is valid or invalid. If all premises are true, then the argument is valid unless the conclusion can be false. If it can, then the argument is invalid. An invalid argument can be made valid through alterations such as the addition of needed premises.

Use of Rhetoric in Informational Texts

There are many ways authors can support their claims, arguments, beliefs, ideas, and reasons for writing in informational texts. For example, authors can appeal to readers' sense of **logic** by communicating their reasoning through a carefully sequenced series of logical steps to help "prove" the points made. Authors can appeal to readers' **emotions** by using descriptions and words that evoke feelings of sympathy, sadness, anger, righteous indignation, hope, happiness, or any other emotion to reinforce what they express and share with their audience. Authors may appeal to the **moral** or **ethical values** of readers by using words and descriptions that can convince readers that something is right or wrong. By relating personal anecdotes, authors can supply readers with more accessible, realistic examples of points they make, as well as appealing to their emotions. They can provide supporting evidence by reporting case studies. They can also illustrate their points by making analogies to which readers can better relate.

Organizational Features in Texts

Text Features in Informational Texts

- The **title of a text** gives readers some idea of its content.
- The **table of contents** is a list near the beginning of a text, showing the book's sections and chapters and their coinciding page numbers. This gives readers an overview of the whole text and helps them find specific chapters easily.
- An **appendix**, at the back of the book or document, includes important information that is not present in the main text.
- Also at the back, an **index** lists the book's important topics alphabetically with their page numbers to help readers find them easily.
- **Glossaries**, usually found at the backs of books, list technical terms alphabetically with their definitions to aid vocabulary learning and comprehension. Boldface print is used to emphasize certain words, often identifying words included in the text's glossary where readers can look up their definitions.
- **Headings** separate sections of text and show the topic of each.
- **Subheadings** divide subject headings into smaller, more specific categories to help readers organize information.
- **Footnotes**, at the bottom of the page, give readers more information, such as citations or links.
- **Bullet points** list items separately, making facts and ideas easier to see and understand.
- A **sidebar** is a box of information to one side of the main text giving additional information, often on a more focused or in-depth example of a topic.

Visual Features in Texts

- **Illustrations** and **photographs** are pictures that visually emphasize important points in text.
- The **captions** below the illustrations explain what those images show.
- **Charts** and **tables** are visual forms of information that make something easier to understand quickly.
- **Diagrams** are drawings that show relationships or explain a process.
- **Graphs** visually show the relationships among multiple sets of information plotted along vertical and horizontal axes.
- **Maps** show geographical information visually to help readers understand the relative locations of places covered in the text.
- **Timelines** are visual graphics that show historical events in chronological order to help readers see their sequence.

Visual Information in Informational Texts

Charts, Graphs, and Visuals

Tables

Tables are presented in a standard format so they will be easy to read and understand. A title is at the top, a short phrase indicating the information the table or graph intends to convey. The title of a table could be something like "Median Income for Various Education Levels" or "Price of Milk Compared to Demand." A table is composed of information laid out in vertical columns and horizontal rows. Typically, each column will have a label. If "Median Income for Various Education Levels" was placed in a table format, the two columns could be labeled "Education Level" and "Median Annual Salary." Each location on the table is called a cell, which holds a piece of information. Cells are defined by their column and row (e.g., second column, fifth row).

Median Annual Salary for Various Education Levels

Education Level	Median Annual Salary
Associate degree	$52,260
Bachelor's degree	$74,464
Master's degree	$86,372
Professional degree	$108,160
Doctoral degree	$108,316

Graphs

Like a table, a graph typically has a title at the top. This title may simply state the identities of the two axes: e.g., "Income vs. Education." However, the title may also be something more descriptive, like "A comparison of average income with level of education." In any case, bar and line graphs are laid out along two perpendicular lines, or axes. The vertical axis is called the *y*-axis, and the horizontal axis is called the *x*-axis. It is typical for the *x*-axis to be the independent variable and the *y*-axis to be the dependent variable. The independent variable is the one manipulated by the researcher or creator of the graph. In the above example, the independent variable would be "education level," since the maker of the graph will define these values (associate degree, bachelor's degree, master's degree, etc.). The dependent value is not controlled by the researcher.

When selecting a graph format, it is important to consider the intention and the structure of the presentation. A bar graph is appropriate for displaying the relations between a series of distinct quantities that are on the same scale. For instance, if one wanted to display the amount of money spent on groceries during the months of a year, a bar graph would be appropriate. The vertical axis would represent values of money, and the horizontal axis would identify each month. A line graph also requires data expressed in common units, but it is better for demonstrating the general trend in that data. If the grocery expenses were plotted on a line graph instead of a bar graph, there would be more emphasis on whether the amount of money spent rose or fell over the course of the year. Whereas a bar graph is good for showing the relationships between the different values plotted, the line graph is good for showing whether the values tended to increase, decrease, or remain stable.

PIE CHART

A pie chart, also known as a circle graph, is useful for depicting how a single unit or category is divided. The standard pie chart is a circle with designated wedges. Each wedge is **proportional** in size to a part of the whole. For instance, consider Shawna, a student at City College, who uses a pie chart to represent her budget. If she spends half of her money on rent, then the pie chart will represent that amount with a line through the center of the pie. If she spends a quarter of her money on food, there will be a line extending from the edge of the circle to the center at a right angle to the line depicting rent. This illustration would make it clear that the student spends twice the amount of money on rent as she does on food.

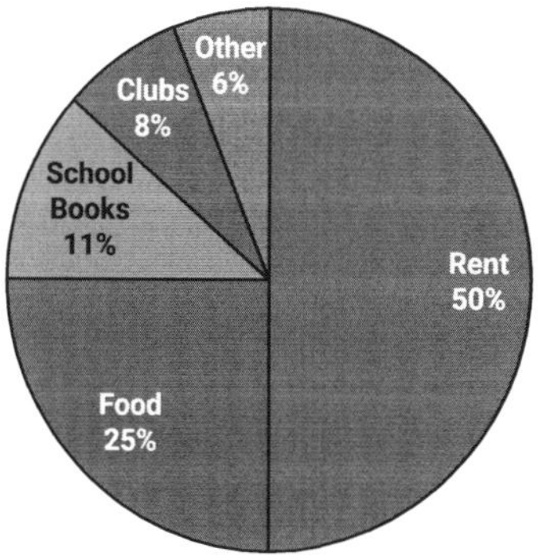

A pie chart is effective at showing how a single entity is divided into parts. They are not effective at demonstrating the relationships between parts of different wholes. For example, an unhelpful use of a pie chart would be to compare the respective amounts of state and federal spending devoted to infrastructure since these values are only meaningful in the context of the entire budget.

BAR GRAPH

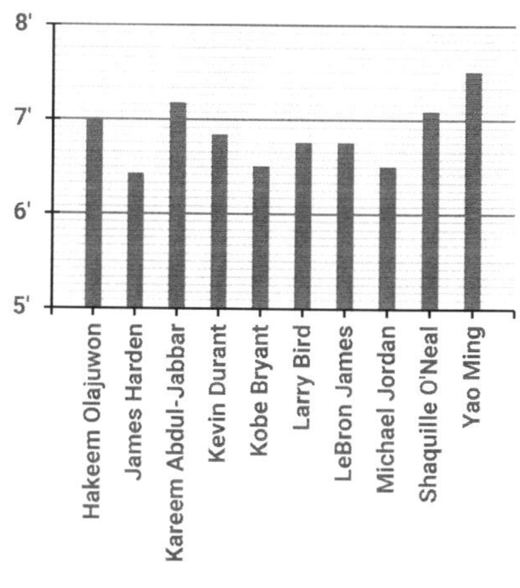

The bar graph is one of the most common visual representations of information. **Bar graphs** are used to illustrate sets of numerical **data**. The graph has a vertical axis (along which numbers are listed) and a horizontal axis (along which categories, words, or some other indicators are placed). One example of a bar graph is a depiction of the respective heights of famous basketball players: the vertical axis would contain numbers ranging from five to eight feet, and the horizontal axis would contain the names of the players. The length of the bar above the player's name would illustrate his height, and the top of the bar would stop perpendicular to the height listed along the left side. In this representation, one would see that Yao Ming is taller than Michael Jordan because Yao's bar would be higher.

Line Graph

A line graph is a type of graph that is typically used for measuring trends over time. The graph is set up along a vertical and a horizontal **axis**. The variables being measured are listed along the left side and the bottom side of the axes. Points are then plotted along the graph as they correspond with their values for each variable. For instance, consider a line graph measuring a person's income for each month of the year. If the person earned $1500 in January, there should be a point directly above January (perpendicular to the horizontal axis) and directly to the right of $1500 (perpendicular to the vertical axis). Once all of the lines are plotted, they are connected with a line from left to right. This line provides a nice visual illustration of the general **trends** of the data, if they exist. For instance, using the earlier example, if the line sloped up, then one would see that the person's income had increased over the course of the year.

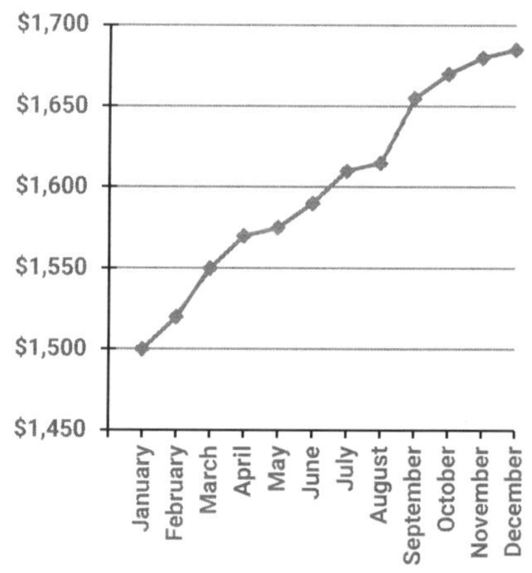

Pictographs

A **pictograph** is a graph, generally in the horizontal orientation, that uses pictures or symbols to represent the data. Each pictograph must have a key that defines the picture or symbol and gives the quantity each picture or symbol represents. Pictures or symbols on a pictograph are not always shown as whole elements. In this case, the fraction of the picture or symbol shown represents the same fraction of the quantity a whole picture or symbol stands for.

Review Video: Pictographs
Visit mometrix.com/academy and enter code: 147860

Genres in Fiction

Common Genres in Prose Fiction

- The **mystery** genre includes stories with plots that follow a protagonist as they work to solve an unexplained situation, such as a murder, disappearance, or robbery. Protagonists of mysteries may be hired professionals or amateurs who solve the mystery despite their lack of experience and resources. Mysteries allow the reader to solve the case along with the protagonist, and often grant the reader an advantageous perspective, creating dramatic irony. The *Sherlock Holmes* novels by Sir Arthur Conan Doyle are examples of mystery novels.
- **Science fiction** is a genre that is based on the manipulation and exaggeration of real scientific discoveries and processes. These works are speculative and frequently depict a world where scientific discoveries and society have progressed beyond the point reached at the time of the work's creation. Works of science fiction often take place in a distant location or time, allowing for the dramatic advancements and conveniences they often depict. *Dune*, written by Frank Herbert, is an example of a science-fiction novel.

- The **fantasy** genre includes stories that feature imaginary creatures and supernatural abilities, but often take place in settings that resemble real places and cultures in history. Fantasy novels usually follow a gifted protagonist from humble beginnings as they embark on a quest, journey, or adventure and encounter mystical beings and personally challenging obstacles. Common themes in the fantasy genre include personal growth, good versus evil, and the value of the journey. J.R.R. Tolkien's *The Lord of the Rings* trilogy belongs to the fantasy genre.
- **Realistic fiction** describes fictional narratives that include events and characters that do not exist, but could appear in reality. Within the narrative, these characters and events may be depicted in real places. For example, Pip, the protagonist of Charles Dickens's *Great Expectations*, was not a real person, but the novel shows him living in London, England for much of his young adulthood. Realistic fiction contains no far-fetched or impossible elements and presents situations that can or do occur in real life. A contemporary example of realistic fiction is *Wonder* by R.J. Palacio.
- **Historical fiction** includes works that take place in the past and model their setting after real historical cultures, societies, and time periods. These works may include real historical figures and events, but they also may not. Works of historical fiction must be fully informed by the period and location they are set in, meaning both the major and minor details of the work must be historically compatible with the work's setting. Examples of historical fiction include Kathryn Stockett's *The Help* and Markus Zusak's *The Book Thief.*
- The phrase **literary nonfiction** describes nonfiction narratives that present true facts and events in a way that entertains readers and displays creativity. Literary nonfiction, also called creative nonfiction, may resemble fiction in its style and flow, but the truth of the events it describes sets it apart from fictional literature. Different types of books may be considered literary nonfiction, such as biographies, if they appear to employ creativity in their writing. An example of literary nonfiction is *The Immortal Life of Henrietta Lacks* by Rebecca Skloot.

REALISM AND SATIRE

REALISM

Realism is a literary form with the goal of representing reality as faithfully as possible. Its genesis in Western literature was a reaction against the sentimentality and extreme emotionalism of the works written during the Romantic literary movement, which championed feelings and emotional expression. Realists focused in great detail on immediacy of time and place, on specific actions of their characters, and the justifiable consequences of those actions. Some techniques of **realism** include writing in vernacular (conversational language), using specific dialects, and placing an emphasis on character rather than plot. Realistic literature also often addresses ethical issues. Historically, realistic works have often concentrated on the middle classes of the authors' societies. Realists eschew treatments that are too dramatic or sensationalistic as exaggerations of the reality that they strive to portray as closely as they are able. Influenced by his own bleak past, Fyodor Dostoevsky wrote several novels, such as *Crime and Punishment* (1866) that shunned romantic ideals and sought to portray a stark reality. Henry James was a prominent writer of realism in novels such as *Daisy Miller* (1879). Samuel Clemens (Mark Twain) skillfully represented the language and culture of lower-class Mississippi in his novel *The Adventures of Huckleberry Finn* (1885).

SATIRE

Satire uses sarcasm, irony, and humor as social criticism to lampoon human folly. Unlike realism, which intends to depict reality as it exists without exaggeration, **satire** often involves creating situations or ideas that deliberately exaggerate reality to appear ridiculous to illuminate flawed behaviors. Ancient Roman satirists included Horace and Juvenal. Alexander Pope's poem "The Rape of the Lock" satirized the values of fashionable members of the 18th-century upper-middle class, which Pope found shallow and trivial. The theft of a lock of hair from a young woman is blown out of proportion: the poem's characters regard it as seriously as they would a rape. Irishman Jonathan Swift satirized British society, politics, and religion in works like "A Modest Proposal" and *Gulliver's Travels*. In "A Modest Proposal," Swift used essay form and mock-serious tone, satirically "proposing" cannibalism of babies and children as a solution to poverty and overpopulation. He satirized petty political disputes in *Gulliver's Travels.*

Types of Stories

OTHER COMMON TYPES OF PROSE

- A **narrative** is any composition that tells a story. Narratives have characters, settings, and a structure. Narratives may be fiction or nonfiction stories and may follow a linear or nonlinear structure. The purpose of a narrative is generally to entertain, but nonfiction narratives can be informative, as well. Narratives also appear in a variety of structures and formats.
- **Biographies** are books written about another person's life. Biographies can be valuable historical resources. Though they provide a narrow view of the relevant time period and culture, their specificity can also provide a unique context for that period or culture. Biographies, especially those whose subject was a well-known and influential figure, can provide a more complete picture of the figure's life or contributions. Biographies can also serve as a source of inspiration or communicate a moral because of their focus on one person over an extended period of time.
- **Myths** that explain how the world works, its creation, and human behavior exist in most ancient cultures and continue to influence modern cultures. Myths are stories that are part of a certain **mythology**, such as Norse mythology. Myths are so influential that they have even inspired numerous pieces of modern literature and media in popular culture. While popular culture most clearly references myths from the Ancient Greek and Roman cultures, literature has been influenced by mythologies from around the entire world. Since myths are so prevalent in ancient literature, it makes sense that universal themes and morals often appear in mythologies from different cultures. The similarities and parallels in different mythologies (e.g., Greek myths about Zeus are very similar to Roman myths about Jupiter) suggest connections between cultures.
- **Folktales** are stories that have withstood time and are usually popular in a particular region or culture. Folktales often depict the clever success of a common person, though the story may, alternatively, end poorly for the protagonist. A collection of folktales relevant to a particular region or culture is referred to as that culture's **folklore**. There are three common types of folktales: fables, fairy tales, and legends.
    - **Fables** are short, didactic stories that typically feature imaginary creatures or talking animals. The famous story "The Tortoise and the Hare" is a fable. Fables are still told and used today because of their universally understandable morals and characters, which also make them suitable for children's literature and media.

- Fairy tales are stories that involve fictional creatures or realistic characters with fantastical traits and abilities. Fairy tales often end happily and depict the victory of good over evil. The plots and characters in fairy tales are often far-fetched and whimsical.
- **Legends** are stories that typically focus on one character and highlight their victory over a particular enemy or obstacle. Legends often feature some facts or are inspired by true events, but are generally considered both unproven and unprovable. Heroes are often the protagonists of legends, and they generally save or protect others as they conquer enemies and obstacles.

- A **short story** is a fictional narrative that is shorter than a novel. However, there is not a definite page or word count that defines the short story category. Short stories tend to focus on one or few elements of a story in order to efficiently tell the story. Though they are often brief, short stories may still contain a moral or impact their readers.

Review Video: Myths, Fables, Legends, and Fairy Tales
Visit mometrix.com/academy and enter code: 347199

Poetry

POETRY TERMINOLOGY

Unlike prose, which traditionally (except in forms like stream of consciousness) consists of complete sentences connected into paragraphs, poetry is written in **verses**. These may form complete sentences, clauses, or phrases. Poetry may be written with or without rhyme. It can be metered, following a particular rhythmic pattern such as iambic, dactylic, spondaic, trochaic, or **anapestic**, or may be without regular meter. The terms **iamb** and **trochee**, among others, identify stressed and unstressed syllables in each verse. Meter is also described by the number of beats or stressed syllables per verse: **dimeter** (2), **trimeter** (3), **tetrameter** (4), **pentameter** (5), and so forth. Using the symbol ᴗ to denote unstressed and / to denote stressed syllables, **iambic** = ᴗ/; **trochaic** = /ᴗ; **spondaic** =//; **dactylic** =/ᴗᴗ; **anapestic** =ᴗᴗ/. **Rhyme schemes** identify which lines rhyme, such as ABAB, ABCA, AABA, and so on. Poetry with neither rhyme nor meter is called **free verse**. Poems may be in free verse, metered but unrhymed, rhymed but without meter, or using both rhyme and meter. In English, the most common meter is iambic pentameter. Unrhymed iambic pentameter is called **blank verse**.

Review Video: Different Types of Rhyme
Visit mometrix.com/academy and enter code: 999342

Review Video: Evocative Words and Rhythm
Visit mometrix.com/academy and enter code: 894610

MAJOR FORMS OF POETRY

From man's earliest days, he expressed himself with poetry. A large percentage of the surviving literature from ancient times is in **epic poetry**, utilized by Homer and other Greco-Roman poets. Epic poems typically recount heroic deeds and adventures, using stylized language and combining dramatic and lyrical conventions. **Epistolary poems**, poems that are written and read as letters, also developed in ancient times. In the fourteenth and fifteenth centuries, the **ballad** became a popular convention. Ballads often follow a rhyme scheme and meter and focus on subjects such as love, death, and religion. Many ballads tell stories, and several modern ballads are put to music. From these early conventions, numerous other poetic forms developed, such as **elegies**, **odes**, and

pastoral poems. Elegies are mourning poems written in three parts: lament, praise of the deceased, and solace for loss. Odes evolved from songs to the typical poem of the Romantic time period, expressing strong feelings and contemplative thoughts. Pastoral poems idealize nature and country living. Poetry can also be used to make short, pithy statements. **Epigrams** (memorable rhymes with one or two lines) and **limericks** (two lines of iambic dimeter followed by two lines of iambic dimeter and another of iambic trimeter) are known for humor and wit.

Haiku

Haiku was originally a Japanese poetry form. In the 13th century, haiku was the opening phrase of renga, a 100-stanza oral poem. By the 16th century, haiku diverged into a separate short poem. When Western writers discovered haiku, the form became popular in English, as well as other languages. A haiku has 17 syllables, traditionally distributed across three lines as 5/7/5, with a pause after the first or second line. Haiku are syllabic and unrhymed. Haiku philosophy and technique are that brevity's compression forces writers to express images concisely, depict a moment in time, and evoke illumination and enlightenment. An example is 17th-century haiku master Matsuo Basho's classic: "An old silent pond... / A frog jumps into the pond, / splash! Silence again." Modern American poet Ezra Pound revealed the influence of haiku in his two-line poem "In a Station of the Metro." In this poem, line 1 has 12 syllables (combining the syllable count of the first two lines of a haiku) and line 2 has 7, but it still preserves haiku's philosophy and imagistic technique: "The apparition of these faces in the crowd; / Petals on a wet, black bough."

Sonnets

The sonnet traditionally has 14 lines of iambic pentameter, tightly organized around a theme. The Petrarchan sonnet, named for 14th-century Italian poet Petrarch, has an eight-line stanza, the octave, and a six-line stanza, the sestet. There is a change or turn, known as the volta, between the eighth and ninth verses, setting up the sestet's answer or summary. The rhyme scheme is ABBA/ABBA/CDECDE or CDCDCD. The English or Shakespearean sonnet has three quatrains and one couplet, with the rhyme scheme ABAB/CDCD/EFEF/GG. This format better suits English, which has fewer rhymes than Italian. The final couplet often contrasts sharply with the preceding quatrains, as in Shakespeare's sonnets—for example, Sonnet 130, "My mistress' eyes are nothing like the sun...And yet, by heaven, I think my love as rare / As any she belied with false compare." Variations on the sonnet form include Edmund Spenser's Spenserian sonnet in the 16th century, John Milton's Miltonic sonnet in the 17th century, and sonnet sequences. Sonnet sequences are seen in works such as John Donne's *La Corona* and Elizabeth Barrett Browning's *Sonnets from the Portuguese.*

Review Video: Structural Elements of Poetry
Visit mometrix.com/academy and enter code: 265216

Plot and Story Structure

PLOT AND STORY STRUCTURE

The **plot** includes the events that happen in a story and the order in which they are told to the reader. There are several types of plot structures, as stories can be told in many ways. The most common plot structure is the chronological plot, which presents the events to the reader in the same order they occur for the characters in the story. Chronological plots usually have five main parts, the **exposition**, **rising action**, the **climax**, **falling action**, and the **resolution**. This type of plot structure guides the reader through the story's events as the characters experience them and is the easiest structure to understand and identify. While this is the most common plot structure, many stories are nonlinear, which means the plot does not sequence events in the same order the characters experience them. Such stories might include elements like flashbacks that cause the story to be nonlinear.

Review Video: How to Make a Story Map
Visit mometrix.com/academy and enter code: 261719

EXPOSITION

The **exposition** is at the beginning of the story and generally takes place before the rising action begins. The purpose of the exposition is to give the reader context for the story, which the author may do by introducing one or more characters, describing the setting or world, or explaining the events leading up to the point where the story begins. The exposition may still include events that contribute to the plot, but the **rising action** and main conflict of the story are not part of the exposition. Some narratives skip the exposition and begin the story with the beginning of the rising action, which causes the reader to learn the context as the story intensifies.

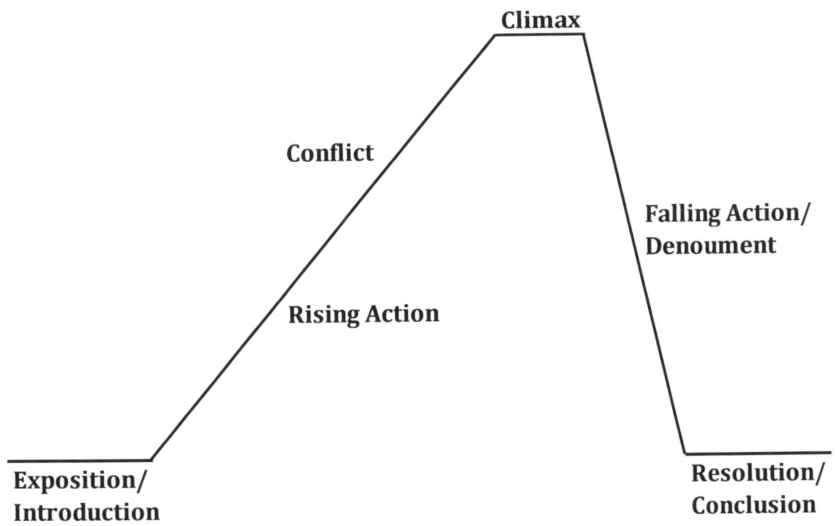

Review Video: Plot Line
Visit mometrix.com/academy and enter code: 944011

Conflict

A **conflict** is a problem to be solved. Literary plots typically include one conflict or more. Characters' attempts to resolve conflicts drive the narrative's forward movement. **Conflict resolution** is often the protagonist's primary occupation. Physical conflicts like exploring, wars, and escapes tend to make plots most suspenseful and exciting. Emotional, mental, or moral conflicts tend to make stories more personally gratifying or rewarding for many audiences. Conflicts can be external or internal. A major type of internal conflict is some inner personal battle, or **man versus self**. Major types of external conflicts include **man versus nature**, **man versus man**, and **man versus society**. Readers can identify conflicts in literary plots by identifying the protagonist and antagonist and asking why they conflict, what events develop the conflict, where the climax occurs, and how they identify with the characters.

Read the following paragraph and discuss the type of conflict present:

> Timothy was shocked out of sleep by the appearance of a bear just outside his tent. After panicking for a moment, he remembered some advice he had read in preparation for this trip: he should make noise so the bear would not be startled. As Timothy started to hum and sing, the bear wandered away.

There are three main types of conflict in literature: **man versus man**, **man versus nature**, and **man versus self**. This paragraph is an example of man versus nature. Timothy is in conflict with the bear. Even though no physical conflict like an attack exists, Timothy is pitted against the bear. Timothy uses his knowledge to "defeat" the bear and keep himself safe. The solution to the conflict is that Timothy makes noise, the bear wanders away, and Timothy is safe.

Review Video: Conflict
Visit mometrix.com/academy and enter code: 559550

Review Video: Determining Relationships in a Story
Visit mometrix.com/academy and enter code: 929925

Rising Action

The **rising action** is the part of the story where conflict **intensifies**. The rising action begins with an event that prompts the main conflict of the story. This may also be called the **inciting incident**. The main conflict generally occurs between the protagonist and an antagonist, but this is not the only type of conflict that may occur in a narrative. After this event, the protagonist works to resolve the main conflict by preparing for an altercation, pursuing a goal, fleeing an antagonist, or doing some other action that will end the conflict. The rising action is composed of several additional events that increase the story's tension. Most often, other developments will occur alongside the growth of the main conflict, such as character development or the development of minor conflicts. The rising action ends with the **climax**, which is the point of highest tension in the story.

Climax

The **climax** is the event in the narrative that marks the height of the story's conflict or tension. The event that takes place at the story's climax will end the rising action and bring about the results of the main conflict. If the conflict was between a good protagonist and an evil antagonist, the climax may be a final battle between the two characters. If the conflict is an adventurer looking for heavily guarded treasure, the climax may be the adventurer's encounter with the final obstacle that protects the treasure. The climax may be made of multiple scenes, but can usually be summarized as one event. Once the conflict and climax are complete, the **falling action** begins.

Falling Action

The **falling action** shows what happens in the story between the climax and the resolution. The falling action often composes a much smaller portion of the story than the rising action does. While the climax includes the end of the main conflict, the falling action may show the results of any minor conflicts in the story. For example, if the protagonist encountered a troll on the way to find some treasure, and the troll demanded the protagonist share the treasure after retrieving it, the falling action would include the protagonist returning to share the treasure with the troll. Similarly, any unexplained major events are usually made clear during the falling action. Once all significant elements of the story are resolved or addressed, the story's resolution will occur. The **resolution** is the end of the story, which shows the final result of the plot's events and shows what life is like for the main characters once they are no longer experiencing the story's conflicts.

Resolution

The way the conflict is **resolved** depends on the type of conflict. The plot of any book starts with the lead up to the conflict, then the conflict itself, and finally the solution, or **resolution**, to the conflict. In **man versus man** conflicts, the conflict is often resolved by two parties coming to some sort of agreement or by one party triumphing over the other party. In **man versus nature** conflicts, the conflict is often resolved by man coming to some realization about some aspect of nature. In **man versus self** conflicts, the conflict is often resolved by the character growing or coming to an understanding about part of himself.

Theme

A **theme** is a central idea demonstrated by a passage. Often, a theme is a lesson or moral contained in the text, but it does not have to be. It also is a unifying idea that is used throughout the text; it can take the form of a common setting, idea, symbol, design, or recurring event. A passage can have two or more themes that convey its overall idea. The theme or themes of a passage are often based on **universal themes**. They can frequently be expressed using well-known sayings about life, society, or human nature, such as "Hard work pays off" or "Good triumphs over evil." Themes are not usually stated **explicitly**. The reader must figure them out by carefully reading the passage. Themes are created through descriptive language or events in the plot. The events of a story help shape the themes of a passage.

Example

Explain why "if you care about something, you need to take care of it" accurately describes the theme of the following excerpt.

> Luca collected baseball cards, but he wasn't very careful with them. He left them around the house. His dog liked to chew. One day, Luca and his friend Bart were looking at his collection. Then they went outside. When Luca got home, he saw his dog chewing on his cards. They were ruined.

This excerpt tells the story of a boy who is careless with his baseball cards and leaves them lying around. His dog ends up chewing them and ruining them. The lesson is that if you care about something, you need to take care of it. This is the theme, or point, of the story. Some stories have more than one theme, but this is not really true of this excerpt. The reader needs to figure out the theme based on what happens in the story. Sometimes, as in the case of fables, the theme is stated directly in the text. However, this is not usually the case.

Review Video: Themes in Literature
Visit mometrix.com/academy and enter code: 732074

Narrator's Point of View

Point of View

Another element that impacts a text is the author's point of view. The **point of view** of a text is the perspective from which a passage is told. An author will always have a point of view about a story before he or she draws up a plot line. The author will know what events they want to take place, how they want the characters to interact, and how they want the story to resolve. An author will also have an opinion on the topic or series of events which is presented in the story that is based on their prior experience and beliefs.

The two main points of view that authors use, especially in a work of fiction, are first person and third person. If the narrator of the story is also the main character, or *protagonist*, the text is written in first-person point of view. In first person, the author writes from the perspective of *I*. Third-person point of view is probably the most common that authors use in their passages. Using third person, authors refer to each character by using *he* or *she*. In third-person omniscient, the narrator is not a character in the story and tells the story of all of the characters at the same time.

Review Video: Point of View
Visit mometrix.com/academy and enter code: 383336

First-Person Narration

First-person narratives let narrators express inner feelings and thoughts, especially when the narrator is the protagonist as Lemuel Gulliver is in Jonathan Swift's *Gulliver's Travels.* The narrator may be a close friend of the protagonist, like Dr. Watson in Sir Arthur Conan Doyle's *Sherlock Holmes.* Or, the narrator can be less involved with the main characters and plot, like Nick Carraway in F. Scott Fitzgerald's *The Great Gatsby.* When a narrator reports others' narratives, she or he is a "**frame narrator**," like the nameless narrator of Joseph Conrad's *Heart of Darkness* or Mr. Lockwood in Emily Brontë's *Wuthering Heights.* **First-person plural** is unusual but can be effective. Isaac Asimov's *I, Robot*, William Faulkner's *A Rose for Emily*, Maxim Gorky's *Twenty-Six Men and a Girl*, and Jeffrey Eugenides' *The Virgin Suicides* all use first-person plural narration. Author Kurt Vonnegut is the first-person narrator in his semi-autobiographical novel *Timequake.* Also unusual, but effective, is a **first-person omniscient** (rather than the more common third-person omniscient) narrator, like Death in Markus Zusak's *The Book Thief* and the ghost in Alice Sebold's *The Lovely Bones.*

Second-Person Narration

While **second-person** address is very commonplace in popular song lyrics, it is the least used form of narrative voice in literary works. Popular serial books of the 1980s like *Fighting Fantasy* or *Choose Your Own Adventure* employed second-person narratives. In some cases, a narrative combines both second-person and first-person voices, using the pronouns *you* and *I*. This can draw readers into the story, and it can also enable the authors to compare directly "your" and "my" feelings, thoughts, and actions. When the narrator is also a character in the story, as in Edgar Allan Poe's short story "The Tell-Tale Heart" or Jay McInerney's novel *Bright Lights, Big City,* the narrative is better defined as first-person despite it also addressing "you."

THIRD-PERSON NARRATION

Narration in the third person is the most prevalent type, as it allows authors the most flexibility. It is so common that readers simply assume without needing to be informed that the narrator is not a character in the story, or involved in its events. **Third-person singular** is used more frequently than **third-person plural**, though some authors have also effectively used plural. However, both singular and plural are most often included in stories according to which characters are being described. The third-person narrator may be either objective or subjective, and either omniscient or limited. **Objective third-person** narration does not include what the characters described are thinking or feeling, while **subjective third-person** narration does. The **third-person omniscient** narrator knows everything about all characters, including their thoughts and emotions, and all related places, times, and events. However, the **third-person limited** narrator may know everything about a particular character, but is limited to that character. In other words, the narrator cannot speak about anything that character does not know.

ALTERNATING-PERSON NARRATION

Although authors more commonly write stories from one point of view, there are also instances wherein they alternate the narrative voice within the same book. For example, they may sometimes use an omniscient third-person narrator and a more intimate first-person narrator at other times. In J. K. Rowling's series of *Harry Potter* novels, she often writes in a third-person limited narrative, but sometimes changes to narration by characters other than the protagonist. George R. R. Martin's series *A Song of Ice and Fire* changes the point of view to coincide with divisions between chapters. The same technique is used by Erin Hunter (a pseudonym for several authors of the *Warriors, Seekers,* and *Survivors* book series). Authors using first-person narrative sometimes switch to third-person to describe significant action scenes, especially those where the narrator was absent or uninvolved, as Barbara Kingsolver does in her novel *The Poisonwood Bible.*

Review Video: The Narrator of a Story
Visit mometrix.com/academy and enter code: 742528

Setting, Mood, and Tone

SETTING AND TIME FRAME

A literary text has both a setting and time frame. A **setting** is the place in which the story as a whole is set. The **time frame** is the period in which the story is set. This may refer to the historical period the story takes place in or if the story takes place over a single day. Both setting and time frame are relevant to a text's meaning because they help the reader place the story in time and space. An author uses setting and time frame to anchor a text, create a mood, and enhance its meaning. This helps a reader understand why a character acts the way he does, or why certain events in the story are important. The setting impacts the **plot** and character **motivations**, while the time frame helps place the story in **chronological context**.

EXAMPLE

Read the following excerpt from The Adventures of Huckleberry Finn by Mark Twain and analyze the relevance of setting to the text's meaning:

> We said there warn't no home like a raft, after all. Other places do seem so cramped up and smothery, but a raft don't. You feel mighty free and easy and comfortable on a raft.

This excerpt from *The Adventures of Huckleberry Finn* by Mark Twain reveals information about the **setting** of the book. By understanding that the main character, Huckleberry Finn, lives on a raft, the reader can place the story on a river, in this case, the Mississippi River in the South before the Civil War. The information about the setting also gives the reader clues about the **character** of Huck Finn: he clearly values independence and freedom, and he likes the outdoors. The information about the setting in the quote helps the reader to better understand the rest of the text.

Syntax and Word Choice

Authors use words and **syntax**, or sentence structure, to make their texts unique, convey their own writing style, and sometimes to make a point or emphasis. They know that word choice and syntax contribute to the reader's understanding of the text as well as to the tone and mood of a text.

Review Video: Syntax
Visit mometrix.com/academy and enter code: 242280

Mood and Tone

Mood is a story's atmosphere, or the feelings the reader gets from reading it. The way authors set the mood in writing is comparable to the way filmmakers use music to set the mood in movies. Instead of music, though, writers judiciously select descriptive words to evoke certain **moods**. The mood of a work may convey joy, anger, bitterness, hope, gloom, fear, apprehension, or any other emotion the author wants the reader to feel. In addition to vocabulary choices, authors also use figurative expressions, particular sentence structures, and choices of diction that project and reinforce the moods they want to create. Whereas mood is the reader's emotions evoked by reading what is written, **tone** is the emotions and attitudes of the writer that she or he expresses in the writing. Authors use the same literary techniques to establish tone as they do to establish mood. An author may use a humorous tone, an angry or sad tone, a sentimental or unsentimental tone, or something else entirely.

Mood and Tone in The Great Gatsby

To understand the difference between mood and tone, look at this excerpt from F. Scott Fitzgerald's *The Great Gatsby*. In this passage, Nick Caraway, the novel's narrator, is describing his affordable house, which sits in a neighborhood full of expensive mansions.

> "I lived at West Egg, the—well the less fashionable of the two, though this is a most superficial tag to express the bizarre and not a little sinister contrast between them. My house was at the very tip of the egg, only fifty yard from the Sound, and squeezed between two huge places that rented for twelve or fifteen thousand a season ... My own house was an eyesore, but it was a small eyesore, and it had been overlooked, so I had a view of the water, a partial view of my neighbor's lawn, and the consoling proximity of millionaires—all for eighty dollars a month."

In this description, the mood created for the reader does not match the tone created through the narrator. The mood in this passage is one of dissatisfaction and inferiority. Nick compares his home to his neighbors', saying he lives in the "less fashionable" neighborhood and that his house is "overlooked," an "eyesore," and "squeezed between two huge" mansions. He also adds that his placement allows him the "consoling proximity of millionaires." A literal reading of these details leads the reader to have negative feelings toward Nick's house and his economic inferiority to his neighbors, creating the mood.

However, Fitzgerald also conveys an opposing attitude, or tone, through Nick's description. Nick calls the distinction between the neighborhoods "superficial," showing a suspicion of the value suggested by the neighborhoods' titles, properties, and residents. Nick also undermines his critique of his own home by calling it "a small eyesore" and claiming it has "been overlooked." However, he follows these statements with a description of his surroundings, claiming that he has "a view of the water" and can see some of his wealthy neighbor's property from his home, and a comparison between the properties' rent. While the mental image created for the reader depicts a small house shoved between looming mansions, the tone suggests that Nick enjoys these qualities about his home, or at least finds it charming. He acknowledges its shortcomings, but includes the benefits of his home's unassuming appearance.

Review Video: Style, Tone, and Mood
Visit mometrix.com/academy and enter code: 416961

Historical and Social Context

Fiction that is heavily influenced by a historical or social context cannot be comprehended as the author intended if the reader does not keep this context in mind. Many important elements of the text will be influenced by any context, including symbols, allusions, settings, and plot events. These contexts, as well as the identity of the work's author, can help to inform the reader about the author's concerns and intended meanings. For example, George Orwell published his novel *1984* in the year 1949, soon after the end of World War II. At that time, following the defeat of the Nazis, the Cold War began between the Western Allied nations and the Eastern Soviet Communists. People were therefore concerned about the conflict between the freedoms afforded by Western democracies versus the oppression represented by Communism. Orwell had also previously fought in the Spanish Civil War against a Spanish regime that he and his fellows viewed as oppressive. From this information, readers can infer that Orwell was concerned about oppression by totalitarian governments. This informs *1984*'s story of Winston Smith's rebellion against the oppressive "Big Brother" government, of the fictional dictatorial state of Oceania, and his capture, torture, and ultimate conversion by that government. Some literary theories also seek to use historical and social contexts to reveal deeper meanings and implications in a text.

Character Development and Dialogue

Character Development

When depicting characters or figures in a written text, authors generally use actions, dialogue, and descriptions as characterization techniques. Characterization can occur in both fiction and nonfiction and is used to show a character or figure's personality, demeanor, and thoughts. This helps create a more engaging experience for the reader by providing a more concrete picture of a character or figure's tendencies and features. Characterizations also gives authors the opportunity to integrate elements such as dialects, activities, attire, and attitudes into their writing.

To understand the meaning of a story, it is vital to understand the characters as the author describes them. We can look for contradictions in what a character thinks, says, and does. We can notice whether the author's observations about a character differ from what other characters in the story say about that character. A character may be dynamic, meaning they change significantly during the story, or static, meaning they remain the same from beginning to end. Characters may be two-dimensional, not fully developed, or may be well developed with characteristics that stand out vividly. Characters may also symbolize universal properties. Additionally, readers can compare and contrast characters to analyze how each one developed.

A well-known example of character development can be found in Charles Dickens's *Great Expectations*. The novel's main character, Pip, is introduced as a young boy, and he is depicted as innocent, kind, and humble. However, as Pip grows up and is confronted with the social hierarchy of Victorian England, he becomes arrogant and rejects his loved ones in pursuit of his own social advancement. Once he achieves his social goals, he realizes the merits of his former lifestyle, and lives with the wisdom he gained in both environments and life stages. Dickens shows Pip's ever-changing character through his interactions with others and his inner thoughts, which evolve as his personal values and personality shift.

Dialogue

Effectively written dialogue serves at least one, but usually several, purposes. It advances the story and moves the plot, develops the characters, sheds light on the work's theme or meaning, and can, often subtly, account for the passage of time not otherwise indicated. It can alter the direction that the plot is taking, typically by introducing some new conflict or changing existing ones. **Dialogue** can establish a work's narrative voice and the characters' voices and set the tone of the story or of particular characters. When fictional characters display enlightenment or realization, dialogue can give readers an understanding of what those characters have discovered and how. Dialogue can illuminate the motivations and wishes of the story's characters. By using consistent thoughts and syntax, dialogue can support character development. Skillfully created, it can also represent real-life speech rhythms in written form. Via conflicts and ensuing action, dialogue also provides drama.

Dialogue in Fiction

In fictional works, effectively written dialogue does more than just break up or interrupt sections of narrative. While **dialogue** may supply exposition for readers, it must nonetheless be believable. Dialogue should be dynamic, not static, and it should not resemble regular prose. Authors should not use dialogue to write clever similes or metaphors, or to inject their own opinions. Nor should they use dialogue at all when narrative would be better. Most importantly, dialogue should not slow the plot movement. Dialogue must seem natural, which means careful construction of phrases rather than actually duplicating natural speech, which does not necessarily translate well to the written word. Finally, all dialogue must be pertinent to the story, rather than just added conversation.

Figurative Language

Literal and Figurative Meaning

When language is used **literally**, the words mean exactly what they say and nothing more. When language is used **figuratively**, the words mean something beyond their literal meaning. For example, "The weeping willow tree has long, trailing branches and leaves" is a literal description. But "The weeping willow tree looks as if it is bending over and crying" is a figurative description—specifically, a **simile** or stated comparison. Another figurative language form is **metaphor**, or an implied comparison. A good example is the metaphor of a city, state, or city-state as a ship, and its governance as sailing that ship. Ancient Greek lyrical poet Alcaeus is credited with first using this metaphor, and ancient Greek tragedian Aeschylus then used it in *Seven Against Thebes,* and then Plato used it in the *Republic.*

Figures of Speech

A **figure of speech** is a verbal expression whose meaning is figurative rather than literal. For example, the phrase "butterflies in the stomach" does not refer to actual butterflies in a person's stomach. It is a metaphor representing the fluttery feelings experienced when a person is nervous or excited—or when one "falls in love," which does not mean physically falling. "Hitting a sales target" does not mean physically hitting a target with arrows as in archery; it is a metaphor for meeting a sales quota. "Climbing the ladder of success" metaphorically likens advancing in one's career to ascending ladder rungs. Similes, such as "light as a feather" (meaning very light, not a feather's actual weight), and hyperbole, like "I'm starving/freezing/roasting," are also figures of speech. Figures of speech are often used and crafted for emphasis, freshness of expression, or clarity.

Review Video: Figures of Speech
Visit mometrix.com/academy and enter code: 111295

FIGURATIVE LANGUAGE

Figurative language extends past the literal meanings of words. It offers readers new insight into the people, things, events, and subjects covered in a work of literature. Figurative language also enables readers to feel they are sharing the authors' experiences. It can stimulate the reader's senses, make comparisons that readers find intriguing or even startling, and enable readers to view the world in different ways. When looking for figurative language, it is important to consider the context of the sentence or situation. Phrases that appear out of place or make little sense when read literally are likely instances of figurative language. Once figurative language has been recognized, context is also important to determining the type of figurative language being used and its function. For example, when a comparison is being made, a metaphor or simile is likely being used. This means the comparison may emphasize or create irony through the things being compared. Seven specific types of figurative language include: alliteration, onomatopoeia, personification, imagery, similes, metaphors, and hyperbole.

Review Video: Figurative Language
Visit mometrix.com/academy and enter code: 584902

ALLITERATION AND ONOMATOPOEIA

Alliteration describes a series of words beginning with the same sounds. **Onomatopoeia** uses words imitating the sounds of things they name or describe. For example, in his poem "Come Down, O Maid," Alfred Tennyson writes of "The moan of doves in immemorial elms, / And murmuring of innumerable bees." The word "moan" sounds like some sounds doves make, "murmuring" represents the sounds of bees buzzing. Onomatopoeia also includes words that are simply meant to represent sounds, such as "meow," "kaboom," and "whoosh."

Review Video: Alliteration in Everyday Expressions
Visit mometrix.com/academy and enter code: 462837

PERSONIFICATION

Another type of figurative language is **personification**. This is describing a non-human thing, like an animal or an object, as if it were human. The general intent of personification is to describe things in a manner that will be comprehensible to readers. When an author states that a tree *groans* in the wind, he or she does not mean that the tree is emitting a low, pained sound from a mouth. Instead, the author means that the tree is making a noise similar to a human groan. Of course, this personification establishes a tone of sadness or suffering. A different tone would be established if the author said that the tree was *swaying* or *dancing*. Alfred Tennyson's poem "The Eagle" uses all of these types of figurative language: "He clasps the crag with crooked hands." Tennyson used alliteration, repeating /k/ and /kr/ sounds. These hard-sounding consonants reinforce the imagery, giving visual and tactile impressions of the eagle.

Review Video: Personification
Visit mometrix.com/academy and enter code: 260066

Similes and Metaphors

Similes are stated comparisons using "like" or "as." Similes can be used to stimulate readers' imaginations and appeal to their senses. Because a simile includes *like* or *as,* the device creates more space between the description and the thing being described than a metaphor does. If an author says that *a house was like a shoebox*, then the tone is different than the author saying that the house *was* a shoebox. Authors will choose between a metaphor and a simile depending on their intended tone.

Similes also help compare fictional characters to well-known objects or experiences, so the reader can better relate to them. William Wordsworth's poem about "Daffodils" begins, "I wandered lonely as a cloud." This simile compares his loneliness to that of a cloud. It is also personification, giving a cloud the human quality loneliness. In his novel *Lord Jim* (1900), Joseph Conrad writes in Chapter 33, "I would have given anything for the power to soothe her frail soul, tormenting itself in its invincible ignorance like a small bird beating about the cruel wires of a cage." Conrad uses the word "like" to compare the girl's soul to a small bird. His description of the bird beating at the cage shows the similar helplessness of the girl's soul to gain freedom.

Review Video: Similes
Visit mometrix.com/academy and enter code: 642949

A **metaphor** is a type of figurative language in which the writer equates something with another thing that is not particularly similar, instead of using *like* or *as.* For instance, *the bird was an arrow arcing through the sky.* In this sentence, the arrow is serving as a metaphor for the bird. The point of a metaphor is to encourage the reader to consider the item being described in a *different way.* Let's continue with this metaphor for a flying bird. You are asked to envision the bird's flight as being similar to the arc of an arrow. So, you imagine the flight to be swift and bending. Metaphors are a way for the author to describe an item *without being direct and obvious.* This literary device is a lyrical and suggestive way of providing information. Note that the reference for a metaphor will not always be mentioned explicitly by the author. Consider the following description of a forest in winter: *Swaying skeletons reached for the sky and groaned as the wind blew through them.* In this example, the author is using *skeletons* as a metaphor for leafless trees. This metaphor creates a spooky tone while inspiring the reader's imagination.

Literary Examples of Metaphor

A **metaphor** is an implied comparison, i.e., it compares something to something else without using "like", "as", or other comparative words. For example, in "The Tyger" (1794), William Blake writes, "Tyger Tyger, burning bright, / In the forests of the night." Blake compares the tiger to a flame not by saying it is like a fire, but by simply describing it as "burning." Henry Wadsworth Longfellow's poem "O Ship of State" (1850) uses an extended metaphor by referring consistently throughout the entire poem to the state, union, or republic as a seagoing vessel, referring to its keel, mast, sail, rope, anchors, and to its braving waves, rocks, gale, tempest, and "false lights on the shore." Within the extended metaphor, Longfellow uses a specific metaphor: "the anchors of thy hope!"

Ted Hughes' Animal Metaphors

Ted Hughes frequently used animal metaphors in his poetry. In "The Thought Fox," a model of concise, structured beauty, Hughes characterizes the poet's creative process with succinct, striking imagery of an idea entering his head like a wild fox. Repeating "loneliness" in the first two stanzas emphasizes the poet's lonely work: "Something else is alive / Beside the clock's loneliness." He treats an idea's arrival as separate from himself. Three stanzas detail in vivid images a fox's approach from the outside winter forest at starless midnight—its nose, "Cold, delicately" touching twigs and leaves; "neat" paw prints in snow; "bold" body; brilliant green eyes; and self-contained, focused progress—"Till, with a sudden sharp hot stink of fox," he metaphorically depicts poetic inspiration as the fox's physical entry into "the dark hole of the head." Hughes ends by summarizing his vision of a poet as an interior, passive idea recipient, with the outside world unchanged: "The window is starless still; the clock ticks, / The page is printed."

> **Review Video: Metaphors in Writing**
> Visit mometrix.com/academy and enter code: 133295

Metonymy

Metonymy is naming one thing with words or phrases of a closely related thing. This is similar to metaphor. However, the comparison has a close connection, unlike metaphor. An example of metonymy is to call the news media *the press*. Of course, *the press* is the machine that prints newspapers. Metonymy is a way of naming something without using the same name constantly.

Synecdoche

Synecdoche points to the whole by naming one of the parts. An example of synecdoche would be calling a construction worker a *hard hat*. Like metonymy, synecdoche is an easy way of naming something without having to overuse a name. The device allows writers to highlight pieces of the thing being described. For example, referring to businessmen as *suits* suggests professionalism and unity.

> **Review Video: Metonymy and Synecdoche**
> Visit mometrix.com/academy and enter code: 900306

Hyperbole

Hyperbole is excessive exaggeration used for humor or emphasis rather than for literal meaning. For example, in *To Kill a Mockingbird*, Harper Lee wrote, "People moved slowly then. There was no hurry, for there was nowhere to go, nothing to buy and no money to buy it with, nothing to see outside the boundaries of Maycomb County." This was not literally true; Lee exaggerates the scarcity of these things for emphasis. In "Old Times on the Mississippi," Mark Twain wrote, "I... could have hung my hat on my eyes, they stuck out so far." This is not literal, but makes his description vivid and funny. In his poem "As I Walked Out One Evening", W. H. Auden wrote, "I'll love you, dear, I'll love you / Till China and Africa meet, / And the river jumps over the mountain / And the salmon sing in the street." He used things not literally possible to emphasize the duration of his love.

Understatement

Understatement is the opposite of hyperbole. This device discounts or downplays something. Think about someone who climbs Mount Everest. Then, they say that the journey was *a little stroll*. As with other types of figurative language, understatement has a range of uses. The device may show self-defeat or modesty as in the Mount Everest example. However, some may think of understatement as false modesty (i.e., an attempt to bring attention to you or a situation). For example, a woman is praised on her diamond engagement ring. The woman says, *Oh, this little thing?* Her understatement might be heard as stuck-up or unfeeling.

Review Video: Hyperbole and Understatement
Visit mometrix.com/academy and enter code: 308470

Literary Devices

Literary Irony

In literature, irony demonstrates the opposite of what is said or done. The three types of irony are **verbal irony**, **situational irony**, and **dramatic irony**. Verbal irony uses words opposite to the meaning. Sarcasm may use verbal irony. One common example is describing something that is confusing as "clear as mud." For example, in his 1986 movie *Hannah and Her Sisters,* author, director, and actor Woody Allen says to his character's date, "I had a great evening; it was like the Nuremburg Trials." Notice these employ similes. In situational irony, what happens contrasts with what was expected. O. Henry's short story *The Gift of the Magi* uses situational irony: a husband and wife each sacrifice their most prized possession to buy each other a Christmas present. The irony is that she sells her long hair to buy him a watch fob, while he sells his heirloom pocket-watch to buy her the jeweled combs for her hair she had long wanted; in the end, neither of them can use their gifts. In dramatic irony, narrative informs audiences of more than its characters know. For example, in *Romeo and Juliet,* the audience is made aware that Juliet is only asleep, while Romeo believes her to be dead, which then leads to Romeo's death.

Review Video: Irony
Visit mometrix.com/academy and enter code: 374204

Idioms

Idioms create comparisons, and often take the form of similes or metaphors. Idioms are always phrases and are understood to have a meaning that is different from its individual words' literal meaning. For example, "break a leg" is a common idiom that is used to wish someone luck or tell them to perform well. Literally, the phrase "break a leg" means to injure a person's leg, but the phrase takes on a different meaning when used as an idiom. Another example is "call it a day," which means to temporarily stop working on a task, or find a stopping point, rather than literally referring to something as "a day." Many idioms are associated with a region or group. For example, an idiom commonly used in the American South is "'til the cows come home." This phrase is often used to indicate that something will take or may last for a very long time, but not that it will literally last until the cows return to where they reside.

Allusion

An allusion is an uncited but recognizable reference to something else. Authors use language to make allusions to places, events, artwork, and other books in order to make their own text richer. For example, an author may allude to a very important text in order to make his own text seem more important. Martin Luther King, Jr. started his "I Have a Dream" speech by saying "Five score years ago…" This is a clear allusion to President Abraham Lincoln's "Gettysburg Address" and served to remind people of the significance of the event. An author may allude to a place to ground his text or make a cultural reference to make readers feel included. There are many reasons that authors make allusions.

Review Video: Allusions
Visit mometrix.com/academy and enter code: 294065

Comic Relief

Comic relief is the use of comedy by an author to break up a dramatic or tragic scene and infuse it with a bit of **lightheartedness**. In William Shakespeare's *Hamlet*, two gravediggers digging the grave for Ophelia share a joke while they work. The death and burial of Ophelia are tragic moments that directly follow each other. Shakespeare uses an instance of comedy to break up the tragedy and give his audience a bit of a break from the tragic drama. Authors sometimes use comic relief so that their work will be less depressing; other times they use it to create irony or contrast between the darkness of the situation and the lightness of the joke. Often, authors will use comedy to parallel what is happening in the tragic scenes.

Review Video: Comic Relief
Visit mometrix.com/academy and enter code: 779604

Foreshadowing

Foreshadowing is a device authors use to give readers **hints** about events that will take place later in a story. Foreshadowing most often takes place through a character's dialogue or actions. Sometimes the character will know what is going to happen and will purposefully allude to future events. For example, consider a protagonist who is about to embark on a journey through the woods. Just before the protagonist begins the trip, another character says, "Be careful, you never know what could be out in those woods!" This alerts the reader that the woods may be dangerous and prompts the reader to expect something to attack the protagonist in the woods. This is an example of foreshadowing through warning. Alternatively, a character may unknowingly foreshadow later events. For example, consider a story where a brother and sister run through their house and knock over a vase and break it. The brother says, "Don't worry, we'll clean it up! Mom will never know!" However, the reader knows that their mother will most likely find out what they have done, so the reader expects the siblings to later get in trouble for running, breaking the vase, and hiding it from their mother.

Symbolism

Symbolism describes an author's use of a **symbol**, an element of the story that **represents** something else. Symbols can impact stories in many ways, including deepening the meaning of a story or its elements, comparing a story to another work, or foreshadowing later events in a story. Symbols can be objects, characters, colors, numbers, or anything else the author establishes as a symbol. Symbols can be clearly established through direct comparison or repetition, but they can also be established subtly or gradually over a large portion of the story. Another form of symbolism is **allusion**, which is when something in a story is used to prompt the reader to think about another work. Many well-known works use **Biblical allusions**, which are allusions to events or details in the Bible that inform a work or an element within it.

Examples of Themes and Plots in Literature

THEMES IN LITERATURE

When we read parables, their themes are the lessons they aim to teach. When we read fables, the moral of each story is its theme. When we read fictional works, the authors' perspectives regarding life and human behavior are their themes. Unlike in parables and fables, themes in literary fiction are usually not meant to preach or teach the readers a lesson. Hence, themes in fiction are not as explicit as they are in parables or fables. Instead, they are implicit, and the reader only infers them. By analyzing the fictional characters through thinking about their actions and behavior, understanding the setting of the story, and reflecting on how its plot develops, the reader comes to infer the main theme of the work. When writers succeed, they communicate with their readers such that common ground is established between author and audience. While a reader's individual experience may differ in its details from the author's written story, both may share universal underlying truths which allow author and audience to connect.

DETERMINING THEME

In well-crafted literature, theme, structure, and plot are interdependent and inextricable: each element informs and reflects the others. The structure of a work is how it is organized. The theme is the central idea or meaning found in it. The plot is what happens in the story. Titles can also inform us of a work's theme. For instance, the title of Edgar Allan Poe's "The Tell-Tale Heart" informs readers of the story's theme of guilt before they even read about the repeated heartbeat the protagonist hears immediately before and constantly after committing and hiding a murder. Repetitive patterns of events or behaviors also give clues to themes. The same is true of symbols. For example, in F. Scott Fitzgerald's *The Great Gatsby,* for Jay Gatsby the green light at the end of the dock symbolizes Daisy Buchanan and his own dreams for the future. More generally, it is also understood as a symbol of the American Dream, and narrator Nick Carraway explicitly compares it to early settlers' sight of America rising from the ocean.

THEMATIC DEVELOPMENT

THEME IN THE GREAT GATSBY

In *The Great Gatsby*, F. Scott Fitzgerald portrayed 1920s America as greedy, cynical, and rife with moral decay. Jay Gatsby's lavish weekly parties symbolize the reckless excesses of the Jazz Age. The growth of bootlegging and organized crime in reaction to Prohibition is symbolized by the character of Meyer Wolfsheim and by Gatsby's own ill-gotten wealth. Fitzgerald symbolized social divisions using geography. The "old money" aristocrats like the Buchanans lived on East Egg, while the "new money" bourgeois like Gatsby lived on West Egg. Fitzgerald also used weather, as many authors have, to reinforce narrative and emotional tones in the novel. Just as in *Romeo and Juliet*, where William Shakespeare set the confrontation of Tybalt and Mercutio and its deadly consequences on the hottest summer day under a burning sun, in *The Great Gatsby*, Fitzgerald did the same with Tom Wilson's deadly confrontation with Gatsby. Both works are ostensible love stories carrying socially critical themes about the destructiveness of pointless and misguided behaviors—family feuds in the former, pursuit of money in the latter.

> **Review Video: Thematic Development**
> Visit mometrix.com/academy and enter code: 576507

THEME IN LES MISÉRABLES

In Victor Hugo's novel *Les Misérables*, the overall metamorphosis of protagonist Jean Valjean from a cynical ex-convict into a noble benefactor demonstrates Hugo's theme of the importance of love and compassion for others. Hugo also reflects this in more specific plot events. For example, Valjean's love for Cosette sustains him through many difficult periods and trying events. Hugo illustrates how love and compassion for others beget the same in them: Bishop Myriel's kindness to Valjean eventually inspires him to become honest. Years later, Valjean, as M. Madeleine, has rescued Fauchelevent from under a fallen carriage, Fauchelevent returns the compassionate act by giving Valjean sanctuary in the convent. M. Myriel's kindness also ultimately enables Valjean to rescue Cosette from the Thénardiers. Receiving Valjean's father-like love enables Cosette to fall in love with and marry Marius, and the love between Cosette and Marius enables the couple to forgive Valjean for his past crimes when they are revealed.

THEME IN "THE TELL-TALE HEART"

In one of his shortest stories, "The Tell-Tale Heart," Poe used economy of language to emphasize the murderer-narrator's obsessive focus on bare details like the victim's cataract-milky eye, the sound of a heartbeat, and insistence he is sane. The narrator begins by denying he is crazy, even citing his extreme agitation as proof of sanity. Contradiction is then extended: the narrator loves the old man, yet kills him. His motives are irrational—not greed or revenge, but to relieve the victim of his "evil eye." Because "eye" and "I" are homonyms, readers may infer that eye/I symbolizes the old man's identity, contradicting the killer's delusion that he can separate them. The narrator distances himself from the old man by perceiving his eye as separate, and dismembering his dead body. This backfires when he imagines the victim's heartbeat, which is really his own, just before he kills him and frequently afterward. Guilty and paranoid, he gives himself away. Poe predated Freud in exploring the paradox of killing those we love and the concept of projecting our own processes onto others.

THEME IN THE WORKS OF WILLIAM FAULKNER AND CHARLES DICKENS

William Faulkner contrasts the traditions of the antebellum South with the rapid changes of post-Civil War industrialization in his short story "A Rose for Emily." Living inside the isolated world of her house, Emily Grierson denies the reality of modern progress. Contradictorily, she is both a testament to time-honored history and a mysterious, eccentric, unfathomable burden. Faulkner portrays her with deathlike imagery even in life, comparing her to a drowned woman and referring to her skeleton. Emily symbolizes the Old South; as her social status is degraded, so is the antebellum social order. Like Miss Havisham in Charles Dickens' *Great Expectations,* Emily preserves her bridal bedroom, denying change and time's passage. Emily tries to control death through denial, shown in her necrophilia with her father's corpse and her killing of Homer Barron to stop him from leaving her, then also denying his death. Faulkner uses the motif of dust throughout to represent not only the decay of Emily, her house, and Old Southern traditions, but also how her secrets are obscured from others.

THEME IN MOBY-DICK

The great White Whale in *Moby-Dick* plays various roles to different characters. In Captain Ahab's obsessive, monomaniacal quest to kill it, the whale represents all evil, and Ahab believes it his duty and destiny to rid the world of it. Ishmael attempts through multiple scientific disciplines to understand the whale objectively, but fails—it is hidden underwater and mysterious to humans—reinforcing Melville's theme that humans can never know everything; here the whale represents the unknowable. Melville reverses white's usual connotation of purity in Ishmael's dread of white, associated with crashing waves, polar animals, albinos—all frightening and unnatural. White is often viewed as an absence of color, yet white light is the sum total of all colors in the spectrum. In the same way, white can signify both absence of meaning, and totality of meaning incomprehensible to humans. As a creature of nature, the whale also symbolizes how 19th-century white men's exploitative expansionistic actions were destroying the natural environment.

THEME IN THE OLD MAN AND THE SEA

Because of the old fisherman Santiago's struggle to capture a giant marlin, some people characterize Ernest Hemingway's *The Old Man and the Sea* as telling of man against nature. However, it can more properly be interpreted as telling of man's role as part of nature. Both man and fish are portrayed as brave, proud, and honorable. In Hemingway's world, all creatures, including humans, must either kill or be killed. Santiago reflects, "man can be destroyed but not defeated," following this principle in his life. As heroes are often created through their own deaths, Hemingway seems to believe that while being destroyed is inevitable, destruction enables living beings to transcend it by fighting bravely with honor and dignity. Hemingway echoes Romantic poet John Keats' contention that only immediately before death can we understand beauty as it is about to be destroyed. He also echoes ancient Greek and Roman myths and the Old Testament with the tragic flaw of overweening pride or overreaching. Like Icarus, Prometheus, and Adam and Eve, the old man "went out too far."

UNIVERSAL THEMES

The Old Testament book of Genesis, the Quran, and the Epic of Gilgamesh all contain flood stories. Versions differ somewhat, yet marketed similarities also exist. Genesis describes a worldwide flood, attributing it to God's decision that mankind, his creation, had become incontrovertibly wicked in spirit and must be destroyed for the world to start anew. The Quran describes the flood as regional, caused by Allah after sending Nuh (notice the similarity in name to Noah) as a messenger to his people to cease their evil. The Quran stipulates that Allah only destroys those who deny or ignore messages from his messengers. In the Gilgamesh poems Utnapishtim, like Noah, is instructed to build a ship to survive the flood. Both men also send out birds afterward as tests, using doves and a raven, though with different outcomes. Many historians and archeologists believe a Middle Eastern tidal wave was a real basis for these stories. However, their universal themes remain the same: the flood was seen as God's way of wiping out humans whose behavior had become ungodly.

THEME OF OVERREACHING

A popular theme throughout literature is the human trait of **reaching too far** or **presuming too much**. In Greek mythology, Daedalus constructed wings of feathers and wax that men might fly like birds. He permitted his son Icarus to try them, but cautioned the boy not to fly too close to the sun. The impetuous youth (in what psychologist David Elkind later named adolescence's myth of invincibility) ignored this, flying too close to the sun. The wax melted, the wings disintegrated, and Icarus fell into the sea and perished. In the Old Testament, God warned Adam and Eve not to eat fruit from the tree of knowledge of good and evil. Because they ignored this command, they were banished from Eden's eternal perfection, condemning them to mortality and suffering. The Romans were themselves examples of overreaching in their conquest and assimilation of most of the then-known world and their ultimate demise. In Christopher Marlowe's *Dr. Faustus* and Johann Wolfgang von Goethe's *Faust,* the protagonist sells his soul to the Devil for unlimited knowledge and success, ultimately leading to his own tragic end.

Story vs. Discourse

In terms of plot, "story" is the characters, places, and events originating in the author's mind, while "discourse" is how the author arranges and sequences events—which may be chronological or not. Story is imaginary; discourse is words on the page. Discourse allows a story to be told in different ways. One element of plot structure is relating events differently from the order in which they occurred. This is easily done with cause-and-effect; for example, in the sentence, "He died following a long illness," we know the illness preceded the death, but the death precedes the illness in words. In Kate Chopin's short story "The Story of an Hour" (1894), she tells some of the events out of chronological order, which has the effect of amplifying the surprise of the ending for the reader. Another element of plot structure is selection. Chopin omits some details, such as Mr. Mallard's trip home; this allows readers to be as surprised at his arrival as Mrs. Mallard is.

Plot and Meaning

Novelist E. M. Forster has made the distinction between story as relating a series of events, such as a king dying and then his queen dying, versus plot as establishing motivations for actions and causes for events, such as a king dying and then his queen dying from grief over his death. Thus, plot fulfills the function of helping readers understand cause-and-effect in events and underlying motivations in characters' actions, which in turn helps them understand life. This affects a work's meaning by supporting its ability to explain why things happen, why people do things, and ultimately the meaning of life. Some authors find that while story events convey meaning, they do not tell readers there is any one meaning in life or way of living, but rather are mental experiments with various meanings, enabling readers to explore. Hence stories may not necessarily be constructed to impose one definitive meaning, but rather to find some shape, direction, and meaning within otherwise random events.

Classic Analysis of Plot Structure

In *Poetics,* Aristotle defined plot as "the arrangement of the incidents." He meant not the story, but how it is structured for presentation. In tragedies, Aristotle found results driven by chains of cause and effect preferable to those driven by the protagonist's personality or character. He identified "unity of action" as necessary for a plot's wholeness, meaning its events must be internally connected, not episodic or relying on *deus ex machina* or other external intervention. A plot must have a beginning, middle, and end. Gustav Freytag adapted Aristotle's ideas into his Pyramid (1863). The beginning, today called the exposition, incentive, or inciting moment, emphasizes causes and de-emphasizes effects. Aristotle called the ensuing cause and effect *desis,* or tying up, today called complications which occur during the rising action. These culminate in a crisis or climax, Aristotle's *peripateia.* This occurs at the plot's middle, where cause and effect are both emphasized. The falling action, which Aristotle called the *lusis* or unraveling, is today called the dénouement. The resolution comes at the catastrophe, outcome, or end, when causes are emphasized and effects de-emphasized.

Review Video: Plot Line
Visit mometrix.com/academy and enter code: 944011

Analysis of Plot Structures Through Recurring Patterns

Authors of fiction select characters, places, and events from their imaginations and arrange them to create a story that will affect their readers. One way to analyze plot structure is to compare and contrast different events in a story. For example, in Kate Chopin's "The Story of an Hour," a very simple but key pattern of repetition is the husband's leaving and then returning. Such patterns fulfill the symmetrical aspect that Aristotle said was required of sound plot structure. In James Baldwin's short story, "Sonny's Blues," the narrator is Sonny's brother. In an encounter with one of Sonny's old friends early in the story, the brother initially disregards his communication. In a subsequent flashback, Baldwin informs us that this was the same way he had treated Sonny. In Nathaniel Hawthorne's "Young Goodman Brown," a pattern is created by the protagonist's recurrent efforts not to go farther into the wood. In Herman Melville's "Bartleby the Scrivener" and in William Faulkner's "Barn Burning," patterns are also created by repetition such as Bartleby's repeated refusals and the history of barn-burning episodes, respectively.

Literary Analysis

Analyzing Literary Texts

The best literary analysis shows special insight into at least one important aspect of a text. When **analyzing literary texts**, it can be difficult to find a starting place. Many texts can be analyzed several different ways, often leaving an overwhelming number of options for writers to consider. However, narrowing the focus to a particular element of literature can be helpful when preparing to analyze a text. Symbolism, themes, and motifs are common starting points for literary analysis. These three methods of analysis can lead to a holistic analysis of a text, since they involve elements that are often distributed throughout the text. However, not all texts feature these elements in a way that facilitates a strong analysis, if they are present at all. It is also common to focus on character or plot development for analysis. These elements are compatible with theme, symbolism, and allusion. Setting and imagery, figurative language, and any external contexts can also contribute to analysis or complement one of these other elements. The application of a critical, or literary, theory to a text can also provide a thorough and strong analysis.

Literary Theories and Criticism and Interpretation

Literary theory includes ideas that guide readers through the process of interpreting literature. Literary theory, as a subject, encompasses several specific, focused theories that lead readers to interpret or analyze literature through the context of the theory using the subjects and elements it involves. Some commonly used and discussed literary theories include **postcolonial theory**, **gender and feminist theory**, **structuralism**, **new historicism**, **reader-response theory**, and **sociological criticism**.

- **Postcolonial theory** involves the historical and geographical context of a work and leads readers to consider how colonization informs the plot, characters, setting, and other elements in the work.
- **Gender and feminist theory** invites readers to interpret a text by looking at its treatment of and suggestions about women and a culture's treatment of women. As with most literary theories, this information can be clearly stated or strongly implied in a work, but it may also be gleaned through looking closely at symbols, characters, and plot elements in a work.
- **Structuralism** uses the structure and organization of a work and the foundations of language to examine how and what a text conveys about the human experience and how those findings connect to common human experiences.

- **New historicism** heavily relies on the cultural and historical context of a work, including when it was written, where the author lives or lived, the culture and history of that location, and other works from the same culture. New historical readings seek to examine these details to expose the ideologies of the location and culture that influenced the work.
- **Reader-response theory** uses the individual reader's response to the text and experience while reading the text to examine the meaning of the reader's relationship with the text and what that relationship suggests about the reader or the factors impacting their experience.
- **Sociological criticism** considers the societies that are relevant to a text. The author's society and any reader's society are important to the text, as sociological criticism seeks to uncover what the text implies or reveals about those societies. This method of criticism can also involve studying the presentation of a society within the text and applying it to the author's society or their other writings.

Language

The Writing Process

Brainstorming

When choosing what to write about, activities like brainstorming can help inspire new ideas or help writers see how their ideas go together. **Brainstorming** means considering a variety of topics or ideas and is mainly used to find a creative approach to a subject or problem. A good first step in brainstorming is simple **free-association** with a topic. One way of doing this is sitting down with paper and pen and writing every thought that comes to mind about the topic in a word or phrase. It does not matter how helpful or good the thought seems at first; the writer should write down everything that comes to mind about the topic. Then, the writer should read the list over a few times. Next, he or she should look for patterns, repetitions, and clusters of ideas. This allows a variety of fresh ideas to come as the writer thinks about the topic.

Free Writing

Free writing is a more organized form of brainstorming. **Free writing** means taking a limited amount of time, like 2 to 3 minutes, to write everything that comes to mind about a topic in complete sentences. When the time is up, the writer should review everything he or she has written down. Many of the sentences may not make sense, but they may contain ideas and details that help the writer organize his or her ideas and prepare to plan the composition. Usually, free writing results in more useful ideas than brainstorming because the writer's thoughts and connections are written in complete sentences. However, both methods can be used together to help the writer prepare to plan and write a composition.

Mapping

One specific way to use graphic organizers is to map an essay. There are many different types of graphic organizers. One easy method to create one is to draw a circle in the middle of the page and write a broad topic in it. Then, draw smaller circles with related topics and ideas, or with topics that fit within the broad topic, written inside and draw line to connect each circle to the main circle. This method can show ideas that fit within the broad topic and will help guide the essay, or it can show which ideas may work better as the main topic of the essay.

Once the main idea and other ideas and details for the essay have been chosen, they can be used to map the essay. Mapping is another word for using a certain type of graphic organizer. These graphic organizers look like a map and organize ideas and details as they will appear in the essay. The essay map can have the main idea at the top or in the center. If the main idea is at the top, the supporting ideas will appear below it in a row, and any additional details will appear under the supporting idea they go with. If the main idea appears in the center, the supporting ideas may appear around it, and the additional details will appear around the supporting ideas they go with.

Planning

Planning is the process of organizing a piece of writing before writing a draft. At the beginning of planning, writers should decide **why they are writing** and **who will read what they write**. The writer must also choose a **genre**, which is the **type** of composition he or she will write. There are fiction genres, such as comedy, folklore, action, and mystery. There are also nonfiction genres, such as essays, reports, poems, and journals. To plan his or her composition, a writer may create an outline or a graphic organizer, such as a Venn diagram, a spider-map, or a flowchart. These methods should help the writer choose their topic, main ideas, and how to organize the composition. If the writer needs to do research for the composition, he or she may also do so as they plan. Planning helps writers organize all of their ideas and decide if they have enough information to begin their first draft. However, writers should remember that the decisions they make during planning may change later, so their plan does not have to be perfect.

Drafting

Writers may then use their plan, outline, or graphic organizer to compose their first draft. They may write more drafts after the first one to improve their writing. Writing multiple drafts can help writers think of different ways to state their ideas and correct mistakes that may be hard to fix without rewriting a section of the composition, or the whole composition. There is no "right" number of drafts, so different writers may write a different number of drafts. Writing drafts also makes it easier to write freely because a writer can improve his or her composition with each draft they write.

Revising, Editing, and Proofreading

Once a writer completes a draft, he or she can move on to revising, editing, and proofreading to improve the draft. **Revising** is making sure that the composition is right for the audience, is not missing important information, is on topic, and is well organized. The writer should also consider the composition's style when revising and ensure that it is appropriately formal or serious. Revising may happen after the first draft so that errors are not repeated in the next draft. Each draft should be revised before the next one is written so that no mistakes are missed. **Editing** comes next. Editing a composition includes steps like improving transitions between paragraphs and making sure each paragraph is on topic. While editing, the writer must pay attention to the words he or she uses and the way the information in each paragraph is organized. Writers may also fix grammar mistakes in the editing phase, since some errors will require a writer to rewrite large parts of their work. **Proofreading** means fixing misspelled words, errors in grammar, and any other small mistakes in the composition.

During the revising, editing, and proofreading steps, it can be helpful for writers to ask a peer to read their work, since he or she may notice mistakes or problems the writer missed before. A writer may also choose to read his or her own work aloud, or listen to someone else read it. Hearing a composition aloud can help writers find mistakes or opportunities for improvement in their work more easily. This happens because when something is read aloud, the person reading the text must pay closer attention to the words on the page. When a writer or a peer reads the composition, they should point out any sentence that confuses them the first time they read it. Most of these sentences can be revised in a way that makes it easier to read and understand.

Adding and Removing Information

While both revising and editing may involve changing the words in a composition, they can also involve adding or taking away words. When a writer has completed a draft and reread it, he or she may notice that something, such as a transition, important details, or an explanatory sentence, is missing. Simply changing the words to make the passage sound better will not solve this problem, so the writer must **add** whatever words and information is needed to make the passage make sense and achieve the writer's purpose.

In other cases, a writer may have words, a sentence, or sometimes an entire paragraph that gives unnecessary information or explains the information in a way that is confusing. When this happens, the extra words and information weaken the composition and must be **removed**. Sometimes, this is difficult for writers to do because it may require them to remove writing they are proud of or a fact they find interesting. Despite this, revising and editing are steps meant to improve and strengthen a composition, so the writer should change, add, or remove parts of his or her writing in a way that makes it better and achieves his or her purpose.

Revising Sentences

Sentence variety is important to consider when writing an essay. A variety of sentence lengths and types can make an essay more engaging, and different types of sentences can sometimes help readers better understand information. For example, a sentence containing a list may make more sense when written with a simple sentence structure, since writing a compound sentence containing a list may give the reader too much information at once. On the other hand, information that is closely related and can be connected with a conjunction should be written in a compound sentence, rather than a simple sentence, since a compound sentence helps the reader see that the information goes together.

Using only simple sentences often makes writing boring and bothersome to read. Writing using only compound sentences makes it difficult for writers to explain information well and difficult for readers to understand, since every sentence will include a coordinating conjunction. To check an essay for sentence variety, it is helpful to look at whether the essay contains different sentence structures and lengths. It is also important to pay attention to the way each sentence starts and avoid beginning with the same words or phrases.

Revising Vocabulary

When writing informational or argumentative texts, it is important to use **precise vocabulary**, or **word choice**, to explain your main idea and supporting details. Generalized vocabulary will not help the audience fully understand the points that you are attempting to make because it will not accurately explain your main idea and supporting details. Precise vocabulary is important to use because it will accurately describe the ideas that are central to your text. When you research a subject, make sure to familiarize yourself with any vocabulary that is involved in its explanation. Use context clues, dictionaries, or, if necessary, a technical dictionary to decode any words that you are not familiar with. Precise vocabulary also impacts the effectiveness of narrative text. Carefully choosing vocabulary to describe sensory details, or imagery, helps writers paint the best possible picture of the events they are describing through their writing.

Recursive Writing Process

Brainstorming, planning, drafting, revising, editing, and proofreading are all steps in the **writing process**. This process is helpful to remember when beginning a new composition, but once a writer has practiced these steps in this order, he or she can use the **recursive writing process**. The recursive writing process is the same as the normal writing process, but the steps in the recursive writing process do not have to happen in the same order. For example, one writer may need to repeat steps after completing other steps. A different writer may discover that he or she can practice the planning and revising steps as he or she writes a draft. The recursive writing process involves moving back and forth between planning, drafting, and revising, followed by more planning, more drafting, and more revising until the writer is happy with his or her work. Each writer can use the recursive writing process in their own way, as long as it helps them improve their work and write the best they can.

Review Video: Recursive Writing Process
Visit mometrix.com/academy and enter code: 951611

Essay Structure and Organization

Central Ideas and Supporting Details

In the first paragraph of a composition, writers include a sentence that explains the **central idea.** This sentence is also known as the **thesis**. The rest of the paragraph shows the reader why the topic of the essay is interesting and includes details that support the central idea. One way to understand the relationship between the central idea and supporting information is to think about a table: the tabletop is the central idea, and each of the table's legs is a supporting detail or group of details. All of the legs work together to support the tabletop and create a table, just like the supporting details work together to support the central idea and create a composition.

Introduction

The introduction is used to capture the reader's attention and announce the essay's central idea. Normally, the introduction contains about 3-5 sentences. An introduction can begin with an interesting quote, a question, a strong opinion, or something else that will **interest** the reader's and prompt them to keep reading. If the composition has a prompt, the introduction should **restate** or **summarize** some part of the prompt so that the reader will have an idea of what information will be in the essay. Finally, your introduction should include the **central idea**, the primary thing the essay will tell the reader.

Review Video: Introduction
Visit mometrix.com/academy and enter code: 961328

Body

In an essay's introduction, the writer states the central idea and prepares the reader for the information in the rest of the composition. In the body of the composition, the writer **explains**, **demonstrates**, and **gives more information about** the **central idea**. This is done using supporting details and examples that are relevant to the central idea of the composition. For example, if the composition's central idea is a vacation the writer took, the body will include descriptions of where the writer went, what they experienced, and what they thought of the trip. If the composition's central idea is the writer's opinion, the body will include examples and facts that show why he or she has formed that opinion. If composition's central idea is a topic and the writer wants to instruct the reader, the body will contain facts, explanations, and examples that help teach the reader about the central idea. A writer will use supporting details to explain the central idea throughout the body.

The body should also contain multiple paragraphs, and the order the writer puts these paragraphs in is important. Each paragraph should include at least one supporting detail, but a paragraph may include more than one if two or more supporting details work together to support the central idea. If the central idea is to describe something that happened, the paragraphs should match the order in which the events occurred. If the central idea is to present an opinion or instruct the reader, the paragraphs should be ordered in the way that would make the most sense to the reader. The order of body paragraphs is important because it can impact how easy a composition is to read.

Review Video: Drafting Body Paragraphs
Visit mometrix.com/academy and enter code: 724590

Choosing Supporting Details and Examples

When writing an informative or argumentative text, writers must choose supporting details carefully. Including details that are irrelevant, inaccurate, or vague does not strengthen the author's writing, while relevant, accurate, provable, and specific details do strengthen the author's writing. These details can make the writer's meaning clearer or give evidence that the author's points are true or logical. Such details may include examples or facts, such as statistics, statements from others who have authority on the subject, and common events or experiences. Choosing appropriate supporting details can also help the author show that they put effort into forming their ideas. This can also make the composition more intriguing and enjoyable to read, since the writer's own interest and insight will be apparent to the reader.

Paragraphs

After the introduction of a passage, the body paragraphs will explain and elaborate upon the central idea. While each paragraph should relate to the central idea of the composition, each paragraph should focus on one point or supporting detail. Normally, a paragraph has a good topic sentence that summarizes the paragraph's main point. A topic sentence is a sentence that gives an introduction to the paragraph and its contents. Topic sentences should contain information that is more specific than what is in the introduction and may include a supporting detail, but they should not contain explanations or examples.

The next sentences in the paragraph should support the topic sentence. These sentences can contain examples, explanations, or other specific information that supports the topic sentence, which supports the central idea of the composition. While a paragraph may be structured in any way, as long as it logically provides information that supports the central idea, it can be best to use a template or pattern to make sure that each paragraph is complete and well organized. For example, a good template to follow is topic sentence, evidence, explanation, conclusion. This means that after the topic sentence, the next sentence should provide evidence, like a quote or example, that supports the paragraph's main point. Next, the paragraph should include a sentence that explains how that evidence supports the paragraph's main point. If there are multiple examples or quotes, more than one sentence may be used to explain them. Finally, there should be a concluding sentence that helps the reader understand the paragraph and prepares them for the next one.

A paragraph must contain enough information to support its main point and the composition's central idea. A paragraph of two or three sentences will most likely not support the main point or central idea because it is not likely to contain enough information, explanation, or evidence. When a paragraph does not support the main point or central idea, it does not help the writer achieve their purpose or goal for writing the essay. A helpful, informative paragraph will often have somewhere from three to five sentences. Also, it is important that the sentences within the paragraph lead the reader through the information. Each paragraph should flow logically and stay on topic throughout.

Starting a New Paragraph

For most forms of writing, you will need to use multiple paragraphs. This means that deciding when to start a new paragraph is very important. Reasons for starting a new paragraph include:

- To separate the introduction and conclusion from the body paragraphs
- To move from one supporting detail or point to another
- To indicate an important shift in time or place
- To show a comparison, contrast, or cause and effect relationship

Transitions

Transitions between sentences and paragraphs guide readers from idea to idea and show relationships between sentences and paragraphs. Writers should use transitions carefully and only when they are truly helpful. They should also be selected to fit the author's purpose. Transitions can show relationships such as time, comparison, an order of events, and cause and effect. Transitions are often used at the beginning of a phrase, sentence, or paragraph, since this helps prepare the reader for the next piece of information.

Review Video: Transitions in Writing
Visit mometrix.com/academy and enter code: 233246

Types of Transitional Words

Time	Afterward, immediately, earlier, meanwhile, recently, lately, now, since, soon, when, then, until, before, etc.
Sequence	too, first, second, further, moreover, also, again, and, next, still, besides, finally
Comparison	similarly, in the same way, likewise, also, again, once more
Contrasting	but, although, despite, however, instead, nevertheless, on the one hand... on the other hand, regardless, yet, in contrast
Cause and Effect	because, consequently, thus, therefore, then, to this end, since, so, as a result, if... then, accordingly
Examples	for example, for instance, such as, to illustrate, indeed, in fact, specifically
Place	near, far, here, there, to the left/right, next to, above, below, beyond, opposite, beside
Repetition, Summary, or Conclusion	as mentioned earlier, as noted, in other words, in short, on the whole, to summarize, therefore, as a result, to conclude, in conclusion
Addition	and, also, furthermore, moreover

Review Video: Transition Words
Visit mometrix.com/academy and enter code: 707563

Conclusion

The conclusion of a composition should summarize the central idea and show that it has been explained well. A good conclusion shows the reader why the author's central idea is meaningful and important and how the supporting details should help the reader understand the central idea. The conclusion should also give the reader something to think about that is related to the central idea. For example, in the conclusion, the author can invite readers to think about how they feel or what they think after reading the composition. Some things to avoid when writing conclusions include:

- Introducing a completely new idea
- Apologizing for one's opinions or writing
- Repeating the central idea word for word rather than summarizing them
- Using the conclusion to summarize every detail in the composition

Review Video: Drafting Conclusions
Visit mometrix.com/academy and enter code: 209408

Grammar

SUBJECTS AND PREDICATES

SUBJECTS

Every sentence needs a subject and a predicate. The **subject** of a sentence names who or what the sentence is about. The subject may be directly stated in a sentence, or the subject may be implied. The **complete subject** includes the simple subject and any **modifiers**, such as adjectives, articles, prepositions, and adverbs, that go with it. To find the complete subject, ask *Who* or *What* before the verb to complete the question. The answer, including any modifiers, is the complete subject. To find the **simple subject**, remove all of the modifiers in the complete subject.

Examples:

simple subject

The small, red car is the one that he wants for Christmas.

complete subject

simple subject

The young artist is coming over for dinner.

complete subject

Review Video: Subjects in English
Visit mometrix.com/academy and enter code: 444771

An imperative sentence is a sentence that gives someone instructions or makes a request to someone. In **imperative** sentences, the verb's subject is understood, but is not actually present in the sentence. For example, this about the sentence *Drive to the store*. This sentence is a command, and the subject is *you*. If the subject were directly stated, the sentence would be *You, drive to the store*. Another fact to consider is that, normally, the subject comes before the verb. However, the subject comes after the verb in sentences that begin with *There are* or *There was*.

Direct:

John knows the way to the park.	Who knows the way to the park?	John
The cookies need ten more minutes.	What needs ten minutes?	The cookies
By five o'clock, Bill will need to leave.	Who needs to leave?	Bill
There are five letters on the table for him.	What is on the table?	Five letters
There were coffee and doughnuts in the house.	What was in the house?	Coffee and doughnuts

Implied:

Go to the post office for me.	Who is going to the post office?	You
Come and sit with me, please?	Who needs to come and sit?	You

Predicates

In a sentence, there is always a predicate and a subject. The subject tells what the sentence is about, and the **predicate** explains or describes the subject.

Think about the sentence *He sings*. In this sentence, we have a subject, *He*, and a predicate, *sings*. This is all that is needed for a sentence to be complete. Most sentences contain more information, but if this is all the information that is given in a sentence, then it is a complete sentence.

Now, let's look at another sentence: *John and Jane sing on Tuesday nights at the dance hall.*

subject: John and Jane | predicate: sing on Tuesday nights at the dance hall.

John and Jane sing on Tuesday nights at the dance hall.

Subject-Verb Agreement

Verbs **agree** with their subjects in number. In other words, singular subjects need singular verbs. Plural subjects need plural verbs. **Singular** is for **one** person, place, or thing. **Plural** is for **more than one** person, place, or thing. Subjects and verbs must also share the same point of view, as in first, second, or third person.

Review Video: Subject-Verb Agreement
Visit mometrix.com/academy and enter code: 479190

Number Agreement Examples:

Single Subject and Verb: Dan (singular subject) calls (singular verb) home.

Dan is one person. So, the singular verb *calls* is needed.

Plural Subject and Verb: Dan and Bob (plural subject) call (plural verb) home.

More than one person needs the plural verb *call.*

Person Agreement Examples:

First Person: I *am* walking.

Second Person: You *are* walking.

Third Person: He *is* walking.

Complications with Subject-Verb Agreement

Words Between Subject and Verb

Words that come between the simple subject and the verb do not affect subject-verb agreement.

Examples:

singular subject — singular verb

The joy of my life returns home tonight.

The phrase *of my life* does not affect the verb *returns*.

singular subject — singular verb

The question that still remains unanswered is "Who are you?"

Don't let the phrase "*that still remains...*" confuse you. The subject *question* goes with the verb *is*.

Compound Subjects

A compound subject is formed when two or more nouns joined by *and*, *or*, or *nor* act together as the subject of the sentence.

Joined by And

When a compound subject is joined by *and*, it is treated as a plural subject and requires a plural verb.

Examples:

plural subject — plural verb

You and Jon are invited to come to my house.

plural subject — plural verb

The pencil and paper belong to me.

Joined by Or/Nor

For a compound subject joined by *or* or *nor*, the verb must agree in number with the part of the subject that is closest to the verb.

Examples:

subject — verb

Today or tomorrow is the day.

subject — verb

Stan or Phil wants to read the book.

subject — verb

Neither the pen nor the book is on the desk.

subject — verb

Either the blanket or pillows arrive this afternoon.

Indefinite Pronouns as Subject

An indefinite pronoun is a pronoun that does not refer to a specific noun. Different indefinite pronouns are used as a singular noun, a plural noun, or change depending on how they are used.

Always Singular

Pronouns such as *each*, *either*, *everybody*, *anybody*, *somebody*, and *nobody* are always singular. This is because these pronouns always stand in for one person, place, or thing.

Examples:

singular subject — singular verb
Each of the runners has a different bib number.

singular verb — singular subject
Is either of you ready for the game?

Note: The words *each* and *either* can also be used as adjectives. For example, *each* person is unique. When one of these adjectives modifies the subject of a sentence, it is always a singular subject.

singular subject — singular verb
Everybody grows a day older every day.

singular subject — singular verb
Anybody is welcome to bring a tent.

Always Plural

Pronouns such as *both*, *several*, and *many* are always plural. This is because these pronouns always stand in for more than one person, place, thing, or idea.

Examples:

plural subject — plural verb
Both of the siblings were too tired to argue.

plural subject — plural verb
Many have tried, but none have succeeded.

Depend on Context

Pronouns such as *some*, *any*, *all*, *none*, *more*, and *most* can be either singular or plural depending on what they are representing in the context of the sentence.

Examples:

singular subject — singular verb
All of my dog's food was still there in his bowl.

plural subject — plural verb
By the end of the night, all of my guests were already excited about coming to my next party.

Other Cases Involving Plural or Irregular Form

Some nouns are **singular in meaning but plural in form**: news, mathematics, physics, and economics.

The *news is* coming on now.

Mathematics is my favorite class.

Some nouns are plural in form and meaning, and have **no singular equivalent**: scissors and pants.

Do these *pants come* with a shirt?

The *scissors are* for my project.

Note: Look to your **dictionary** for help when you aren't sure whether a noun with a plural form has a singular or plural meaning.

Example

Which word should go in the blank?

If Kelly if going to the party, Joan and Susan ____ going to the store.

a. Is
b. Are
c. Am
d. Was

Try using each choice in the sentence. Choice A, *is*, forms this sentence: If Kelly is going to the party, Joan and Susan is going to the store. There are two people, Joan and Susan, who are going to the store. This makes the subject of the clause plural. *Is* is a singular verb, meaning it does not agree with the subject and cannot be the answer.

Choice B, *are*, forms this sentence: If Kelly is going to the party, Joan and Susan are going to the store. The subject of the clause is still plural. But *are* is a plural verb! The subject and verb agree, so *are* is the correct answer.

Choice C, *am*, forms this sentence: If Kelly is going to the party, Joan and Susan am going to the store. *Am* is a singular verb, and it is also only used in first person, when the writer or speaker is referring to themself. The subject of the clause is plural, and the sentence is in third person, so *am* is not the correct answer.

Choice D, *was*, forms this sentence: If Kelly is going to the party, Joan and Susan was going to the store. *Was* is a singular verb, so it does not agree with the plural subject in this clause.

Complements

A complement is a noun, pronoun, or adjective that is used to give more information about the subject or verb in the sentence.

DIRECT OBJECTS

A direct object is a noun or pronoun that takes or receives the **action** of a verb. A complete sentence does not need a direct object, so not all sentences will have them. When you are looking for a direct object, find the verb and ask *who* or *what*.

Examples:

> I took *the blanket.*
>
> Jane read *books*.

INDIRECT OBJECTS

An indirect object is a word or group of words that show how an action had an **influence** on someone or something. If there is an indirect object in a sentence, then you always have a direct object in the sentence. When you are looking for the indirect object, find the verb and ask *to*, *for*, *whom*, or *what*.

Examples:

> We taught the old dog (indirect object) a new trick (direct object).
>
> I gave them (indirect object) a math lesson (direct object).

Review Video: Direct and Indirect Objects
Visit mometrix.com/academy and enter code: 817385

PRONOUN-ANTECEDENT AGREEMENT

The **antecedent** is the noun that has been replaced by a pronoun. A pronoun and its antecedent **agree** when they have the same number (singular or plural) and gender (male, female, or neutral).

Examples:

> **Singular agreement**: John (antecedent) came into town, and he (pronoun) played for us.
>
> **Plural agreement**: John and Rick (antecedent) came into town, and they (pronoun) played for us.

To determine which is the correct pronoun to use in a compound subject or object, try each pronoun **alone** in place of the compound in the sentence. Your knowledge of pronouns will tell you which one is correct.

Example:

> Bob and (I, me) will be going.
>
> Test: (1) *I will be going* or (2) *Me will be going*. The second choice cannot be correct because *me* cannot be used as the subject of a sentence. Instead, *me* is used as an object.
>
> **Answer**: Bob and I will be going.

When a pronoun is used with a noun immediately following (as in "we boys"), try the sentence **without the added noun**.

Example:

(We/Us) boys played football last year.

Test: (1) *We played football last year* or (2) *Us played football last year*. Again, the second choice cannot be correct because *us* cannot be used as a subject of a sentence. Instead, *us* is used as an object.

Answer: We boys played football last year.

Review Video: Pronoun Usage
Visit mometrix.com/academy and enter code: 666500

Review Video: Pronoun-Antecedent Agreement
Visit mometrix.com/academy and enter code: 919704

A pronoun should point clearly to the **antecedent**. Here is how a pronoun reference can be unhelpful if it is puzzling or not directly stated.

Unhelpful: Ron and Jim (antecedent) went to the store, and he (pronoun) bought soda.

Who bought soda? Ron or Jim?

Helpful: Jim (antecedent) went to the store, and he (pronoun) bought soda.

The sentence is clear. Jim bought the soda.

EXAMPLE

Tom printed his ticket to the concert, but he forgot ____ at home.

Which pronoun should go in the blank?

a. It
b. Them
c. Him
d. He

What is the antecedent that the missing pronoun must match? There are only four nouns in the sentence. They are *Tom*, *ticket*, *concert*, and *home*. Which one should the missing pronoun refer to? Tom is the one who forgot something, so the pronoun does not refer to Tom. The concert is not at Tom's home, so he cannot forget the concert at home. It is also not logical to say that Tom forgot his home at home The antecedent must be *ticket*.

Choice A says that the missing pronoun is *it*. The pronoun refers to *ticket*, which is a singular noun. A ticket is also a nonliving thing. The missing pronoun is also the object in the second clause. *It* is singular, refers to nonliving nouns, and can be used as the object. Choice A is correct.

Choice B says that the missing pronoun is *them*. The pronoun refers to the singular noun *ticket*. While *them* can be used to refer to nonliving nouns and can be the object of a sentence, it is a plural pronoun. Choice B is incorrect.

Choice C says that the missing pronoun is *him*. The missing pronoun refers to a nonliving thing, not a human or animal. *Him* is an objective personal pronoun and is singular, but it only refers to living nouns. *Him* cannot represent *ticket*, so choice C is incorrect.

Choice D says that the missing pronoun is *he*. The missing pronoun refers to a nonliving noun and is the object of the second sentence. While *he* is a singular pronoun, it can only be used as the subject of a sentence and only refers to living nouns. Choice D is incorrect.

Phrases

A phrase is a group of words that functions as a single part of speech, usually a noun, adjective, or adverb. A **phrase** is not a complete thought, and does not contain a subject, but it adds detail or explanation to a sentence, or renames something within the sentence.

Clauses

A clause is a group of words that contains both a subject and a predicate (verb). There are two types of clauses: independent and dependent. An **independent clause** contains a complete thought, while a **dependent (or subordinate) clause** does not. A dependent clause includes a subject and a verb, and may also contain additional information, but it cannot stand as a complete thought without being joined to an independent clause. Dependent clauses function within sentences as adjectives, adverbs, or nouns.

Example:

independent clause	dependent clause
I am running	because I want to stay in shape.

The clause *I am running* is an independent clause: it has a subject and a verb, and it gives a complete thought. The clause *because I want to stay in shape* is a dependent clause: it has a subject and a verb, but it does not express a complete thought. This is due to the fact that it begins with *because*, which shows that there is more information needed to complete the thought. This dependent clause adds detail to the independent clause to which it is attached.

Review Video: Independent and Dependent Clauses
Visit mometrix.com/academy and enter code: 556903

SENTENCE STRUCTURE

Sentence structure is based on the type and number of clauses in the sentence. Two common sentence structures are simple sentences and compound sentences:

Simple: A simple sentence has one independent clause with no dependent clauses. A simple sentence may have a **compound subject** or a **compound verb**, or both.

Examples:

single subject: Judy; single verb: watered
Judy watered the lawn.

compound subject: Judy and Alan; single verb: watered
Judy and Alan watered the lawn.

single subject: Judy; compound verb: watered, pulled
Judy watered the lawn and pulled weeds.

compound subject: Judy and Alan; compound verb: watered, pulled
Judy and Alan watered the lawn and pulled weeds.

Compound: A compound sentence has two or more independent clauses with no dependent clauses. Usually, the independent clauses are joined with a comma and a coordinating conjunction or with a semicolon.

Examples:

independent clause: The time has come; independent clause: we are ready
The time has come, and we are ready.

independent clause: I woke up at dawn; independent clause: the sun was just coming up
I woke up at dawn; the sun was just coming up.

Complex: A complex sentence has one independent clause and at least one dependent clause.

Examples:

dependent clause: Although he had the flu; independent clause: Harry went to work
Although he had the flu, Harry went to work.

independent clause: Marcia got married; dependent clause: after she finished college
Marcia got married after she finished college.

Review Video: Sentence Structure
Visit mometrix.com/academy and enter code: 700478

Sentence Fragments

Recall that a group of words must contain at least one **independent clause** in order to be considered a sentence. If it doesn't contain even one independent clause, it is called a **sentence fragment**.

Choosing the best steps for **repairing** a sentence fragment depends on what type of fragment it is. If the fragment is a dependent clause, it can sometimes be fixed by simply removing a subordinating word, such as *when*, *because*, or *if*, from the beginning of the fragment. Alternatively, a dependent clause can be joined to a closely related neighboring sentence. If the fragment is missing some required part, like a subject or a verb, it may be fixed by simply adding the missing part.

Examples:

> **Fragment**: Because he wanted to sail the Mediterranean.
>
> **Removed subordinating word**: He wanted to sail the Mediterranean.
>
> **Combined with another sentence**: Because he wanted to sail the Mediterranean, he booked a Greek island cruise.

Example

Which of the following changes will NOT correct this sentence fragment?

Although she had found the coin first.

a. Remove *Although.*
b. Add a comma and *she let her brother keep it* after *first.*
c. Add *She let her brother keep the coin* before *although.*
d. Remove *first.*

Choice A suggests removing the word *although* to form the following sentence: She found the coin first. This option removes the subordinating conjunction to make the clause independent. The resulting sentence is complete, so removing *although* is an acceptable way to correct the fragment. Choice A is incorrect.

Choice B forms the following sentence: Although she had found the coin first, she let her brother keep it. A comma and an independent clause have been added to the sentence fragment to form a complex sentence. The resulting sentence is complete and written correctly, so choice B is incorrect.

Choice C forms the following sentence: She let her brother keep the coin although she had found the coin first. An independent clause has been added before the sentence fragment to form a complex sentence. This sentence is correctly written and complete, so choice C is an acceptable way to correct the fragment. Choice C is incorrect.

Choice D removes the word *first*, leaving *Although she had found the coin.* This is still a sentence fragment, since it is a single dependent clause. Choice D does not correct the fragment, so D is correct.

Run-on Sentences

Run-on sentences consist of multiple independent clauses that have not been joined together properly. Run-on sentences can be corrected in several different ways:

Join clauses properly: This can be done with a comma and coordinating conjunction, with a semicolon, or with a colon or dash if the second clause is explaining something in the first clause.

Example:

> **Incorrect**: I went on the trip, we visited lots of castles.
>
> **Corrected**: I went on the trip, and we visited lots of castles.

Split into separate sentences: This correction is best to use when the independent clauses are very long or when they are not closely related.

Example:

> **Incorrect**: The drive to New York takes ten hours, my uncle lives in Boston.
>
> **Corrected**: The drive to New York takes ten hours. My uncle lives in Boston.

Make one clause dependent: This is the easiest way to make the sentence correct and more interesting at the same time. It's often as simple as adding a subordinating word between the two clauses or before the first clause.

Example:

> **Incorrect**: I finally made it to the store and I bought some eggs.
>
> **Corrected**: When I finally made it to the store, I bought some eggs.

Reduce to one clause with a compound verb: If both clauses have the same subject, remove the subject from the second clause, and you now have just one clause with a compound verb.

Example:

> **Incorrect**: The drive to New York takes ten hours, it makes me very tired.
>
> **Corrected**: The drive to New York takes ten hours and makes me very tired.

Note: While these are the simplest ways to correct a run-on sentence, often the best way is to completely reorganize the thoughts in the sentence and rewrite it.

Comma Splices

A comma splice is a specific error that may appear in a run-on sentence. When a sentence has two independent clauses, but the clauses are joined with only a comma, a **comma splice** is formed. Remember that if two independent clauses are joined with a comma, a coordinating conjunction is also needed. Most of the solutions for fixing run-on sentences can also be used to correct a comma splice.

Review Video: Fragments and Run-on Sentences
Visit mometrix.com/academy and enter code: 541989

EXAMPLE

Rick wants to go see a movie tomorrow he would miss his sister's recital.

Identify the change that would NOT correct this run-on sentence.

a. Add a comma after *tomorrow*.
b. Split it into two sentences between *tomorrow* and *he*.
c. Add a comma and *but* after *tomorrow*.
d. Add a subordinating conjunction to make one of the clauses dependent.

Choice A says to add a comma after *tomorrow*. This forms the following sentence: Rick wants to go see a movie tomorrow, he would miss his sister's recital. A comma has been used to join two independent clauses, but there is no coordinating conjunction. This choice forms a comma splice, so it is not an acceptable correction for this sentence. Choice A is the correct answer.

Choice B says to split the sentence into two sentences. This forms the following two sentences: Rick wants to go see a movie tomorrow. He would miss his sister's recital. Both of these sentences are complete. This is an acceptable way to correct the run-on sentence, so choice B is incorrect.

Choice C says to add a coordinating conjunction after *tomorrow*. This forms the following sentence: Rick wants to go see a movie tomorrow, but he would miss his sister's recital. A comma and a coordinating conjunction have been added between the two independent clauses. This is an acceptable way to correct a run-on sentence. Choice C is incorrect.

Choice D says to add a subordinating conjunction to make one of the sentences dependent. There are many new sentences that could be created by adding a subordinating conjunction. For example, consider the following sentence: Although Rick wants to go see a movie tomorrow, he would miss his sister's recital. Alternatively, the following sentence could also be created: Rick wants to go see a movie tomorrow even though he would miss his sister's recital. Both of these sentences have an independent clause and a dependent clause. These sentences are both complete and written correctly, so choice D is incorrect.

EXAMPLE

Identify the sentence that has a comma splice.

a. Tom stopped at the store to buy supplies and his family met him at the campsite.
b. The ball rolled into the living room quietly, but it still startled the dog.
c. Theresa brought her mom some flowers, her mom did not have a vase.
d. Sweet potatoes, pecans, and brown sugar are all ingredients in my cousin's sweet potato casserole.

Choice A has two independent clauses joined by a coordinating conjunction. This is incorrect because there should be a comma before the coordinating conjunction. While the sentence is written incorrectly, there is no comma, so this sentence does not have a comma splice. Choice A is incorrect.

Choice B has two independent clauses joined by a comma and a coordinating conjunction. This is the correct way to write a compound sentence, so there is no error here. Choice B is incorrect.

Choice C has two independent clauses joined by a comma. This is incorrect because independent clauses should be joined together by a comma and a coordinating conjunction. When the comma is present without a coordinating conjunction between two independent clauses, a comma splice is formed. This means that choice C is correct.

Choice D is a simple sentence that contains one independent clause. The only commas used in this sentence are used to separate items in a list. There are no clauses that need to be joined or errors related to commas, so choice D does not contain a comma splice. Choice D is incorrect.

The Eight Parts of Speech

Nouns

When you talk about a person, place, thing, or idea, you are talking about a **noun**. The two main types of nouns are **common** and **proper** nouns.

Common Nouns

Common nouns are generic names for people, places, and things. Common nouns are not usually capitalized.

Examples of common nouns:

> *People*: boy, girl, worker, manager
>
> *Places*: school, bank, library, home
>
> *Things*: dog, cat, truck, car

Proper Nouns

Proper nouns name specific people, places, or things. All proper nouns are capitalized.

Examples of proper nouns:

> *People*: Abraham Lincoln, George Washington, Martin Luther King, Jr.
>
> *Places*: Los Angeles, California; New York; Asia
>
> *Things*: Statue of Liberty, Earth, Lincoln Memorial

Note: When referring to the planet that we live on, capitalize *Earth*. When referring to the dirt, rocks, or land, lowercase *earth*.

Singular and Plural Nouns

Singular nouns name **one** person, place, thing, or idea. **Plural nouns** name **more than one** person, place, thing, or idea. Most nouns have both a singular and plural form. Many plural nouns are spelled like the singular noun with an *-s* at the end, but this is not true for all plural nouns. Singular nouns that already end in an *s*, *o*, *ch*, *sh*, or *x* usually end in *-es* when they are in the plural form. Singular nouns that end in a consonant followed by the letter *y* will usually lose the *y* and end in *-ies* in the plural form, and words that end with the letter *f* or *fe* will usually lose the *f* and end in *-ves*.

Some plural nouns have much different spellings than their singular form, and some plural nouns are spelled the same as their singular form. There are more rules for spelling plural nouns, but these are the most common spelling changes.

Examples of singular nouns:

> Typical nouns: dog, pencil, girl, store, hope, stingray
>
> Nouns ending in *s*, *o*, *ch*, *sh*, or *x*: mass, hero, lunch, polish, fox

Nouns ending in a consonant and *y*: puppy, baby, fairy, sky

Nouns ending in *f* or *fe*: self, life, calf, hoof

Examples of plural nouns:

Typical nouns: dogs, pencils, girls, stores, hopes, stingrays

Nouns ending in *s*, *o*, *ch*, *sh*, or *x*: masses, heroes, lunches, polishes, foxes

Nouns ending in a consonant and *y*: puppies, babies, fairies, skies

Nouns ending in a vowel and *f* or *fe*: selves, lives, calves, hooves

Collective Nouns

Collective nouns are the names for a group of people, places, or things that function like singular nouns. The following are examples of collective nouns: *class, company, dozen, group, herd, team,* and *public*. Collective nouns usually require an article, such as *a*, *an*, and *the*, which shows that the noun is a single unit. For example, a choir is a group of singers. Even though there are many singers in a choir, the word choir describes a single group. If we refer to the members of the group, and not the group itself, it is no longer a collective noun.

Incorrect: The *choir are* going to compete nationally this year.

Correct: The *choir is* going to compete nationally this year.

Incorrect: The *members* of the choir *is* competing nationally this year.

Correct: The *members* of the choir *are* competing nationally this year.

Pronouns

Pronouns are words that are used to stand in for nouns. There are several different types of pronouns, but the two main types are subjective and objective pronouns. **Subjective** nouns and pronouns that those that are the subject of a sentence. **Objective** nouns and pronouns are those that are an object in a sentence. Another important type of pronoun is the personal pronoun, which refers to people. Personal pronouns can be subjective or objective. **Possessive** nouns and pronouns show possession or ownership. Pronouns can also be singular or plural.

Singular

Subjective	Objective	Possessive
I	Me	My, Mine
You	You	Your, Yours
He	Him	His
She	Her	Her, hers
It	It	Its
Who	Whom	Whose

Plural

Subjective	Objective	Possessive
we	us	our, ours
you	you	your, yours
they	them	their, theirs

Reflexive: Reflexive pronouns are pronouns that function as the object of a sentence and refer to the subject. Examples of reflexive pronouns include *myself, yourself, himself, herself, itself, ourselves, yourselves*, and *themselves*.

Indefinite: Indefinite pronouns are used to refer to multiple nouns or an undefined noun. Examples of indefinite nouns include *all, any, each, everyone, either/neither, one, some*, and *several*.

Relative: Relative pronouns are used to connect relative clauses that specify or describe a noun to the rest of the sentence. Examples of relative pronouns include *which, who, whom*, and *whose*.

Review Video: Nouns and Pronouns
Visit mometrix.com/academy and enter code: 312073

VERBS

If you want to write a sentence, then you need a verb. Without a verb, you have no sentence. The verb of a sentence indicates action or being. In other words, the verb shows something's action or state of being or the action that has been done to something.

ACTION VERBS AND LINKING VERBS

Action verbs show what the subject is doing. In other words, an action verb shows action. **Linking verbs** link the subject of a sentence to a noun or pronoun. They can also link a subject to an adjective, so the linking verb helps create a description. You always need a verb if you want a complete sentence. However, linking verbs on their own cannot be a complete sentence. Any verb that shows a condition and connects to a noun, pronoun, or adjective that describes the subject of a sentence is a linking verb.

Action: He sings. | Run! | Go! | I talk with him every day. | She reads.

Linking:

Incorrect: I am.

Correct: I am John. | I smell roses. | I feel tired.

Review Video: Action Verbs and Linking Verbs
Visit mometrix.com/academy and enter code: 743142

VERB TENSES

A verb **tense** shows the different form of a verb to point to the time of an action. The present and past tense are indicated by the verb's form. An action in the present, *I talk*, can change form for the past: *I talked*. However, for future tense, an auxiliary, or helping, verb is sometimes needed to show the change in form. When writing a composition, it is important to use verb tenses consistently.

Choose the best tense for the composition and do not switch to a different tense unless it is necessary or appropriate for a particular sentence or paragraph.

Present: I talk
Past: I talked
Future: I will talk

Present: The action happens at the current time.

Example: He *walks* to the store every morning.

Past: The action happened in the past.

Example: He *walked* to the store an hour ago.

Future: The action is going to happen later.

Example: I *will walk* to the store tomorrow.

Review Video: Verb Tenses
Visit mometrix.com/academy and enter code: 269472

IRREGULAR VERBS

While most verbs gain the suffix -ed when used in the past tense, irregular verbs receive different spelling changes when they are written in the past tense. For example, *walk* is a regular verb, and it becomes *walked* when written in the past tense. However, *run* is an irregular verb because it becomes *ran* when written in the past tense.

EXAMPLE

My mother _____ me about the big nest of ants near the sandbox. I thanked her for telling me!

Which of the following verbs should go in the blank?

a. Warn
b. Warned
c. Will warn
d. Warns

First, look at the sentences. The first sentence does not have enough information to show which tense it is in. However, the second sentence says that the child thanked the mother. The verb here is *thanked*, which is the past-tense form of *thank*. Because the second sentence is in the past tense, it makes sense to say that the first sentence is also in past tense.

Choice A says that the missing verb is *warn*. *Warn* is a present-tense verb, but it can be used in the future tense if a helping verb is present. However, this sentence is in past tense, so it needs a past-tense verb. Choice A is wrong.

Choice B says that the missing verb is *warned*. *Warned* is a past-tense verb, and it logically completes the sentence. Choice B is correct!

Choice C says that the missing verb is *will warn*. *Will warn* is a future-tense verb, meaning that it describes an action that will occur in the future. However, since the speaker already thanked his or her mother for the warning, it is not logical to use a future-tense verb in the blank. Choice C is incorrect.

Choice D says that the missing verb is *warns*. *Warn* is usually used with plural subjects, and *warns* used with single subjects. *Warns* can be used in the future or present tense, but it cannot be used in the past tense. Since the sentence is in the past tense, it needs a past-tense verb, so D is incorrect.

ADJECTIVES

An **adjective** is a word that is used to modify a noun or pronoun. An adjective answers a question: *Which one? What kind?* or *How many?* Usually, adjectives come before the words that they modify, but they may also come after a linking verb.

> Which one? The *third* suit is my favorite.
>
> What kind? This suit is *navy blue*.
>
> How many? I am going to buy *four* pairs of socks to match the suit.

Review Video: Descriptive Text
Visit mometrix.com/academy and enter code: 174903

COMPARISON WITH ADJECTIVES

Some adjectives are relative, and other adjectives are absolute. Adjectives that are **relative** can show the comparison between things. **Absolute** adjectives can also show comparison, but they do so in a different way. Let's say that you are reading two books. You think that one book is perfect, and the other book is not exactly perfect. It is not possible for one book to be more perfect than the other. Either you think that the book is perfect, or you think that the book is imperfect. In this case, perfect and imperfect are absolute adjectives.

Relative adjectives will show the different **degrees** of something or someone to something else or someone else. The three degrees of adjectives include positive, comparative, and superlative.

The **positive** degree is the normal form of an adjective.

> Example: This work is *difficult*. | She is *smart*.

The **comparative** degree compares one person or thing to another person or thing.

> Example: This work is *more difficult* than your work. | She is *smarter* than me.

The **superlative** degree compares more than two people or things.

> Example: This is the *most difficult* work of my life. | She is the *smartest* lady in school.

Review Video: Adjectives
Visit mometrix.com/academy and enter code: 470154

ADVERBS

An **adverb** is a word that is used to **modify,** or describe, a verb, adjective, or another adverb. Usually, adverbs answer one of these questions: *When? Where? How?* and *Why?* The negatives *not* and *never* are considered adverbs. Adverbs that modify adjectives or other adverbs **strengthen** or **weaken** the words that they modify.

Examples:

He walks *quickly* through the crowd.

The water flows *smoothly* on the rocks.

Note: Adverbs are usually indicated by the suffix *-ly*, which has been added to the root word. For instance, *quick* can be made into an adverb by adding *-ly* to construct *quickly*. Some words that end in *-ly* do not follow this rule and can function as other parts of speech. Examples of adjectives ending in *-ly* include: *early, friendly, holy, lonely, silly*, and *ugly*. To know if a word that ends in *-ly* is an adjective or adverb, check your dictionary. Also, while many adverbs end in *-ly*, you need to remember that not all adverbs end in *-ly*.

Examples:

He is *never* angry.

You are *too* irresponsible to travel alone.

Types of Adverbs

Different types of adverbs are used to describe particular aspects of a verb, adjective, or other adverb. The following are examples of common types of adverbs:

Time: Some adverbs show when something was done, such as *yesterday*, *today*, or *in two days*.

Manner: Some adverbs show the way something was done, such as *hurriedly*, *neatly*, *grumpily*, or *loudly*.

Frequency: Some adverbs show how often something was done, such as *seldom*, *often*, *never*, or *often*.

Degree: Some adverbs show how much or to what degree something was done, such as *completely*, *barely*, *highly*, or *halfway*.

Conjunctive: Conjunctive adverbs are used similarly to conjunctions, as they connect different ideas, but they can connect ideas from different clauses or sentences. Some examples of conjunctive adverbs are *however*, *alternatively*, *likewise*, and *then*.

Comparison with Adverbs

The rules for comparing adverbs are the same as the rules for adjectives.

The **positive** degree is the standard form of an adverb.

> Example: He arrives *soon*. | She speaks *softly* to her friends.

The **comparative** degree compares one person or thing to another person or thing.

> Example: He arrives *sooner* than Sarah. | She speaks *more softly* than him.

The **superlative** degree compares more than two people or things.

> Example: He arrives *soonest* of the group. | She speaks the *most softly* of any of her friends.

Review Video: Adverbs
Visit mometrix.com/academy and enter code: 713951

Example

Identify the conjunctive adverb in the following sentences.

> Every night, Savannah's brother loudly gets up to get a glass of water. Consequently, she has started sleeping with earmuffs on so that he does not wake her up at night.

a. Every night
b. Loudly
c. Consequently
d. At night

Choice A says that *every night* is a conjunctive adverb. What does *every night* describe in this sentence? It describes how often Savannah's brother loudly gets a glass of water. This means that *every night* shows the frequency that Savannah's brother does this action. Since *every night* is an adverb that shows frequency, choice A is incorrect.

Choice B says that *loudly* is a conjunctive adverb. In this sentence, what does *loudly* describe? It describes the way that Savannah's brother gets a glass of water each night. This means that *loudly* is an adverb that shows manner. *Loudly* is not a conjunctive adverb, so choice B is incorrect.

Choice C says that *consequently* is a conjunctive adverb. What function does *consequently* have in this sentence? It shows the reason that Savannah started wearing earmuffs while she sleeps. It also shows a connection between the information in the first sentence and the information in the second sentence. Since *consequently* connects the ideas in these sentences, it is a conjunctive adverb. Choice C is correct.

Choice D says that *at night* is a conjunctive adverb. *At* and *night* work together to form an adverbial phrase. Which type of adverb do they form? In this sentence, *at night* shows when Savannah wants to avoid being woken up by her brother. This makes *at night* an adverb that shows time, meaning that *at night* is not a conjunctive adverb and choice D is incorrect.

Prepositions

A **preposition** is a word placed before a noun or pronoun that shows the relationship between an object and another word in the sentence.

Common prepositions:

about	before	during	on	under
after	beneath	for	over	until
against	between	from	past	up
among	beyond	in	through	with
around	by	of	to	within
at	down	off	toward	without

Examples:

The napkin is *in* the drawer.

The Earth rotates *around* the Sun.

The needle is *beneath* the haystack.

Can you find "me" *among* the words?

Prepositional Phrases

One important thing to know about prepositions is that they form special phrases, called prepositional phrases. A **prepositional phrase** begins with a preposition and ends with a noun or pronoun that is the object of the preposition. Normally, the prepositional phrase functions as an **adjective** or an **adverb** within the sentence.

Examples:

prepositional phrase
The picnic is on the blanket.

prepositional phrase
I am sick with a fever today.

prepositional phrase
Among the many flowers, John found a four-leaf clover.

Be careful not to mistake the object in a prepositional phrase as the subject of a sentence. The subject of the sentence will not be found in a prepositional phrase because a prepositional phrase is used to describe how an object is related to the subject. Prepositional phrases do not influence subject-verb agreement.

Review Video: Prepositions
Visit mometrix.com/academy and enter code: 946763

EXAMPLE

Which of the following could NOT complete the sentence?

She went ____ the cave.

a. Sadly
b. Into
c. From
d. Through

Choice A says that the missing word is *sadly*. The blank is between *went* and *the cave*, meaning that the missing word will connect these pieces of the sentence. While *sadly* could be used here to show how the girl felt, there would still be missing information. A preposition is needed here to show whether she entered, exited, or stood outside of the cave. *Sadly* is an adverb, so A is the correct answer.

Choice B says that *into* would complete the sentence. Does *into* complete the sentence without leaving missing information? To say *she went into the cave* is a logical, complete sentence. Choice B is incorrect.

Choice C says that the missing word is *from*. This creates the sentence *she went from the cave*. Since she could have left the cave to go somewhere else, this is also a logical, complete sentence. Choice C is incorrect.

Choice D says that *through* would complete the sentence. The sentence would read *she went through the cave*. Since she could have explored the whole cave or found an exit on the other side of it, *through* can logically complete the sentence. Choice D is incorrect.

EXAMPLE

Identify the prepositional phrase in the following sentence.

Mable visited the store to buy some vegetables.

a. To buy
b. Visited the store
c. The store to buy
d. To buy some vegetables

Remember the pieces of a prepositional phrase. Prepositional phrases should begin with a preposition and end with a noun or pronoun. Considering these rules, can any of the answer choices be eliminated? Choice B and choice C can be eliminated because neither choice begins with a preposition!

That leaves choices A and D. Choice A says that the prepositional phrase is *to buy*. This does start with a preposition, and it does give more information about Mable's trip to the store. However, it does not end with a noun or pronoun. Choice D says that the prepositional phrase is *to buy some vegetables*. Choice D begins with a preposition and ends with a noun, and it explains why Mabel went to the store.

Choice D is the only choice that has all of the pieces of a prepositional phrase, so D is correct!

Example

Read the sentence below and answer the following question.

A band with 15 members _____ performing at my restaurant tonight.

Identify the verb that best completes the sentence.

a. Were
b. Is
c. Are
d. Are not

This question is asking which verb should go in the blank. There are a couple of reasons why choosing the correct verb for this sentence may be confusing. First of all, there are two nouns that appear before the verb. Second, one of these nouns is singular and one is plural.

The first step is to determine which noun goes with the verb. The two nouns are *band* and *members*. While *members* is closest to the blank, it is part of a prepositional phrase that describes *band*. The subject of the sentence is *band*, so the verb must agree with *band*.

Is *band* singular or plural? The sentence says that the band has multiple members, but there is only one band. *Band* is a collective noun, meaning that it is a singular noun. This means that the correct verb will also be singular. With this in mind, can any of the answer choices be eliminated?

Choices A, C, and D are all plural verbs. Even though the blank appears after a plural noun, this noun is part of a prepositional phrase. The verb should match the singular subject *band*. The only choice with a singular verb is choice B, so B is the correct answer.

Conjunctions

Conjunctions join words, phrases, or clauses and they show the connection between the joined pieces. **Coordinating conjunctions** connect equal parts of sentences. Coordinating conjunctions can also be used to create compound subjects and compound predicates, in addition to compound sentences.

Coordinating Conjunctions

The **coordinating conjunctions** include: *and, but, yet, or, nor, for,* and *so*

Compound Subjects:

compound subject

Terry *and* Marissa went to the movies last Saturday.

compund subject

Either pumpkin pie *or* apple pie would be a good dessert to bring to Thanksgiving dinner.

compound subject

Neither the clownfish *nor* the goldfish liked the new fish food very much.

Compound Predicates:

compound predicate

Veronica left school *and* picked up her sister from soccer practice.

compound predicate

The cat did not take a nap *or* play with the dog yesterday.

Compound Sentences:

The rock was small, *but* it was heavy.

She drove in the night, *and* he drove in the day.

Bill dressed nicely today, *for* he must give an important presentation this afternoon.

Correlative Conjunctions

Some examples of **correlative conjunctions** are: *either...or* | *neither...nor* | *not only...but also*. When one correlative conjunction is used, its matching correlative conjunction will be used later in the sentence.

Examples:

Either you are coming *or* you are staying.

He *not only* ran three miles *but also* swam 200 yards.

Review Video: Coordinating and Correlative Conjunctions
Visit mometrix.com/academy and enter code: 390329

Subordinating Conjunctions

Subordinating conjunctions link dependent clauses, clauses with either a subject or a predicate, to independent clauses, clauses with both a subject and a predicate, to form a complex sentence. The subordinating conjunction will always be at the beginning of the dependent clause. When the dependent clause is at the beginning of the sentence, it will end with a comma. When the independent clause is at the beginning of the sentence, no comma is needed.

Common **subordinating conjunctions** include:

after	since	whenever
although	so that	where
because	unless	wherever
before	until	whether
in order that	when	while

Examples:

I am hungry *because* I did not eat breakfast.

He went home *when* everyone left.

While her brother ate dinner, she played his favorite video game.

Review Video: Subordinating Conjunctions
Visit mometrix.com/academy and enter code: 958913

EXAMPLE

Which of the following is a complex sentence?

a. Joseph went grocery shopping and put all of the groceries away at home.
b. Joseph went grocery shopping, and he put all of the groceries away at home.
c. Joseph went grocery shopping and put all of the groceries away when he got home.
d. Joseph went grocery shopping; he put all of the groceries away at home.

Choice A contains one subject and a compound predicate. Because there is only one subject, Joseph, there is only one clause. Since the sentence is made of one independent clause and a prepositional phrase, it is a simple sentence, and choice A is incorrect.

Choice B contains two clauses. The clauses are separated by a comma and a coordinating conjunction, and both are independent clauses. This sentence contains a prepositional phrase and two independent clauses, so it is a compound sentence. Choice B is incorrect.

Choice C contains two clauses. There are two subjects in the sentence, *Joseph* and *he*. Even though one clause is much shorter than the other, these subjects each go with a different clause. The first clause is independent. The second clause is dependent, as it begins with the word *when*. Since the sentence is made of one independent clause and one dependent clause, it is a complex sentence. Choice C is correct.

Choice D contains two clauses. They are both independent clauses, because they both contain a subject and a predicate, and they both form complete thoughts. Since there is no coordinating conjunction, they are linked by a semicolon. Since the sentence is made from two independent clauses, it is a compound sentence. Choice D is incorrect.

EXAMPLE

Identify the sentence that contains correlative conjunctions.

a. She can wait for her friend's letter to arrive, or she can call her now.
b. He must leave now, or he will end up in heavy traffic when he gets on the highway.
c. When your grandfather gets here, you can greet him with a handshake or a hug.
d. I can't decide whether to go to my brother's concert or to study for my test tomorrow.

Read the answer choices carefully. Remember that correlative conjunctions appear in pairs, so there will be at least two conjunctions in the sentence. Additionally, these conjunctions will go together. The information given immediately after the first conjunction will make little sense without the information that comes after the second conjunction.

Choice A contains the conjunction *or*. Though *or* can be a correlative conjunction, in this sentence, it is used by itself to connect two independent clauses. This means it is a coordinating conjunction. There are no correlative conjunctions in this sentence, so choice A is incorrect.

Choice B contains the conjunctions *or* and *when*. Again, *or* can be a correlative conjunction. However, the sentence could end after *traffic*. The information beginning with *when* is not needed to complete the thought, and *or* and *when* do not form a pair of correlative conjunctions. Choice B is incorrect.

Choice C contains the conjunctions *when* and *or*. *When* is used to begin a dependent clause. *Or* is used to form a compound object by linking *handshake* and *hug*. These conjunctions do not work together in this sentence, so they are not correlative conjunctions. Choice C is incorrect.

Choice D contains the conjunctions *whether* and *or*. *Whether* is used to introduce one choice the speaker can make, and *or* is used to introduce an alternative choice. If the sentence ended before *or*, it would be an incomplete thought. The conjunctions *whether* and *or* go together in this sentence, and they are correlative conjunctions. Choice D is correct.

End Punctuation

Periods

Use a period to end all sentences except direct questions and exclamations. Periods are also used for abbreviations.

Examples: 3 p.m. | 2 a.m. | Mr. Jones | Mrs. Stevens | Dr. Smith | Bill, Jr. | Pennsylvania Ave.

Note: An abbreviation is a shortened form of a word or phrase.

Question Marks

Question marks should be used following a **direct question**. A polite request can be followed by a period instead of a question mark.

Direct Question: What is for lunch today? | How are you? | Why is that the answer?

Polite Requests: Can you please send me the item tomorrow. | Will you please walk with me on the track.

Review Video: Question Marks
Visit mometrix.com/academy and enter code: 118471

Exclamation Marks

Exclamation marks are used after a word group or sentence that shows much feeling or has special importance. Exclamation marks should not be overused. They are saved for proper **exclamatory interjections**.

Example: We're going to the finals! | You have a beautiful car! | "That's crazy!" she yelled.

Review Video: Exclamation Points
Visit mometrix.com/academy and enter code: 199367

COMMAS

The comma is a punctuation mark that can help you understand connections in a sentence. Not every sentence needs a comma. However, if a sentence needs a comma, you need to put it in the right place. A comma in the wrong place or a missing comma will make a sentence's meaning unclear. These are some of the rules for commas:

Use Case	Example
Before a **coordinating conjunction** joining independent clauses in compound sentences	Bob caught three fish, and I caught two fish.
Between **items in a series**	I will bring the turkey, the pie, and the coffee.
After a **dependent clause** that **begins a complex sentence**	Before she left, Ashley turned off all of the lights in her house.
After **transition words**	Consequently, Joel's mother grounded him.
After an **introductory phrase**	After the final out, we went to a restaurant to celebrate.
After a **prepositional phrase** at the **beginning of a sentence**	At 10 in the evening, Georgia finally arrived home from work.
After an **adverbial clause**	Studying the stars, I was awed by the beauty of the sky.
Before and after **nonessential modifiers**	John Frank, who coaches the team, was promoted today.
Before and after **nonessential appositives**	Thomas Edison, an American inventor, was born in Ohio.
Before and after **nonrestrictive phrases** or **clauses**	His favorite movie, which premiered before he was born, is over three hours long.
After **absolute phrases**	Relieved the test was over, Leah dropped her pencil and slouched in her chair.

COMMAS FOR SETTING OFF NONESSENTIAL WORDS, PHRASES, AND CLAUSES

Identifying where to place commas for nonessential words, phrases, and clauses is sometimes tricky. If the word, phrase, or clause is necessary for the sentence to be complete or logical, then it is essential, or restrictive. Additionally, if the word, phrase, or clause cannot be removed without changing the meaning of the sentence, then it is essential. Nonessential words, phrases, and clauses are those that give unnecessary information or do not flow smoothly with the rest of the words in the sentence. These words usually can also be logically placed in more than one spot in the sentence. **Appositives** are often nonessential words or phrases. They are most often used to specify which person or thing is being discussed. An appositive is an additional name or description that may be essential or nonessential.

Review Video: When To Use a Comma
Visit mometrix.com/academy and enter code: 786797

EXAMPLE

Ella's favorite stuffed animal Rory used to be her mother's.

Which word in the sentence is nonessential and should be set off by commas?

a. Be
b. Stuffed
c. Her
d. Rory

Choice A says that *be* should be set off by commas. Since *be* is a verb, it is unlikely that it is a nonessential word. In this sentence, the subject is *stuffed animal*, and *be* is the verb that shows the subject's action. *Be* is essential to the sentence, so choice A is incorrect.

Choice B says that *stuffed* should be set off by commas. *Stuffed* is an adjective, so it may be nonessential. However, it affects the meaning of this sentence. The word *stuffed* shows that the sentence is about a toy, not a live animal. *Stuffed* is essential to the meaning of the sentence, so choice B is incorrect.

Choice C says that *her* should be set off by commas. *Her* is a personal pronoun, so it is unlikely that it is nonessential. This sentence uses the word *her* to identify whose mother previously owned the stuffed animal. *Her* is essential to show who is being discussed. Choice C is incorrect.

Choice D says that *Rory* should be set off by commas. *Rory* is a name, so it could be a nonessential word, or even an appositive. In this sentence, the word tells the reader the name of Ella's favorite stuffed animal. The sentence can only be about one stuffed animal, because Ella can only have one favorite. This means that the stuffed animal's name is extra, or nonessential, information. *Rory* is a nonessential appositive, so choice D is correct.

EXAMPLE

> The singer growing more exhausted with every song decided to stop dancing and stood still while singing.

Identify the nonrestrictive phrase that should be set off by commas in the above sentence.

a. The singer growing more exhausted
b. Decided to stop dancing
c. Growing more exhausted with every song
d. Stop dancing and stood still

Choice A says that *the singer growing more exhausted* is the nonrestrictive phrase. Is the sentence still a complete sentence without this phrase? No, because choice A includes the subject, *the singer*. Choice A is not the nonrestrictive phrase.

Choice B says that *decided to stop dancing* is the nonrestrictive phrase. Does the sentence make sense without this phrase? No, removing this phrase leaves the following sentence: The singer growing more exhausted with every song and stood still while singing. This is not a logical sentence, so choice B is not the nonrestrictive phrase.

Choice C says that *growing more exhausted with every song* is the nonrestrictive phrase. Removing this phrase leaves the following sentence: The singer decided to stop dancing and stood still while singing. This sentence makes sense and has the same meaning as the original sentence. This phrase gives extra information that is not essential to the sentence, so choice C is the nonrestrictive phrase. Choice C is correct.

Choice D says that *stop dancing and stood still* is the nonrestrictive phrase. Removing this phrase leaves the following sentence: The singer growing more exhausted with every song decided to while singing. This sentence is now missing important information. What did the singer decide to do while singing? The remaining sentence is now missing the verb. Removing choice D makes the sentence incomplete, so choice D is not the nonrestrictive phrase.

EXAMPLE

Where should a comma be added in the following sentence?

Though the mountain is very steep he is not afraid to scale it.

a. After *Though*
b. After *mountain*
c. After *steep*
d. After *afraid*

Choice A says there should be a comma after *though*. In this sentence, *though* is a subordinating conjunction that begins a dependent clause. Remember that a comma goes at the end of a dependent clause that appears at the beginning of a sentence. *Though* is at the beginning of the clause, and there is no other need for a comma right after it. Choice A is incorrect.

Choice B says there should be a comma after *mountain. Mountain* is the subject of the dependent clause in this sentence. The comma should go at the end of the dependent clause. *Mountain* appears in the middle of the dependent clause, not at the end of it. Choice B is incorrect.

Choice C says there should be a comma after *steep. Steep* is the last word in the dependent clause that begins the sentence. Adding a comma here would correctly separate the dependent clause from the following independent clause. This is the correct place for the comma, so choice C is correct.

Choice D says there should be a comma after *afraid. Afraid* is the verb in the independent clause, and there is no need to separate it from the rest of the sentence. Choice D is incorrect.

SEMICOLONS

The semicolon is used to connect major sentence pieces of equal value. Some rules for semicolons include:

Use Case	Example
Between closely connected independent clauses **not connected with a coordinating conjunction**	You are right; we should go with your plan.
Between independent clauses **linked with a transitional word**	I think that we can agree on this; however, I am not sure about my friends.
Between items in a **series that has internal punctuation**	I have visited New York, New York; Augusta, Maine; and Baltimore, Maryland.

Review Video: How to Use Semicolons
Visit mometrix.com/academy and enter code: 370605

EXAMPLE

Which of the following sentences is NOT written correctly?

a. My sister burned the lasagna we were going to eat for dinner; we went out to eat instead of cooking something else.
b. The ball rolled into the ditch, therefore, it was muddy and wet when he retrieved it.
c. She has lived in many cities, including Nashville, Tennessee; San Diego, California; and Salt Lake City, Utah.
d. He hung the picture in the wrong spot; now there is a distracting hole in the wall.

Choice A is a compound sentence. The semicolon is used to separate two independent clauses. There is no coordinating conjunction in the sentence. This sentence correctly uses a semicolon, so choice A is incorrect.

Choice B is a compound sentence. In a compound sentence, either a coordinating conjunction or a semicolon can be used to separate the independent clauses. This sentence includes a transitional word, but it uses neither a semicolon nor a coordinating conjunction. To revise this sentence, *therefore* can be replaced by a coordinating conjunction, or the first comma can be replaced with a semicolon This sentence is written incorrectly, so choice B is the correct answer.

Choice C is a sentence that includes a list. Remember that semicolons can be used to separate items in a list when at least one of the items includes a comma. In this sentence, a list of cities is given. Since a comma is required to separate the name of a city from the name of the state it is in, each of the items in the list contain a comma. This means that each full city name must be separated by a semicolon. This sentence is written correctly, so choice C is incorrect.

Choice D is a compound sentence and does not contain a coordinating conjunction. Semicolons can be used to separate independent clauses in a compound sentence instead of a coordinating conjunction. This sentence uses a semicolon correctly, so choice D is incorrect.

Quotation Marks

Use quotation marks to close off **direct quotations** of a person's written or spoken words, which are also called **dialogue**. Do not use quotation marks around indirect quotations. An indirect quotation gives someone's message without using the person's exact words. Use **single quotation marks** to close off a quotation inside a quotation.

> **Direct Quote**: Nancy said, "I am waiting for Henry to arrive."
>
> **Indirect Quote**: Henry said that he is going to be late to the meeting.
>
> **Quote inside a Quote**: The teacher asked, "Has everyone read Martin Luther King's 'I Have a Dream' speech?"

Quotation marks should be used around the titles of **short works**: newspaper and magazine articles, poems, short stories, songs, television episodes, and radio programs. Titles of **long works** should be italicized when they are part of a typed composition or underlined when they are part of a handwritten composition.

Examples:

> "Rip Van Winkle" (short story by Washington Irving)
>
> "O Captain! My Captain!" (poem by Walt Whitman)

Review Video: Quotation Marks
Visit mometrix.com/academy and enter code: 884918

APOSTROPHES

An apostrophe is used to show **possession** or the **deletion of letters in contractions**. An apostrophe is not needed with the possessive pronouns *his, hers, its, ours, theirs, whose*, and *yours*.

Singular Nouns: David's car | a book's theme | my brother's board game

Plural Nouns that end with -*s*: the scissors' handle | boys' basketball

Plural Nouns that end without -*s*: Men's department | the people's adventure

Review Video: Apostrophes
Visit mometrix.com/academy and enter code: 213068

Review Video: Punctuation Errors in Possessive Pronouns
Visit mometrix.com/academy and enter code: 221438

APOSTROPHES IN CONTRACTIONS

Contractions are combinations of words. Contractions involve taking two words, removing at least one letter from one of the words, putting an apostrophe in its place, and removing the space. For example, *does not* can be written as the contraction *doesn't*. The *o* is removed from *not* and is replaced with an apostrophe, which represents the removed letter, so it appears as *n't*. The space after does is then removed, turning *does not* into the contraction *doesn't*. Some more examples of contractions are listed below.

First Word	Second Word	Contraction
Can	Not	Can't
Do	Not	Don't
She	Will	She'll
They	Will	They'll
He	Is	He's
It	Is	It's
They	Are	They're
I	Am	I'm

Not all words can be used to form contractions, but many small, commonly used words can.

CAPITALIZATION

One important part of using correct grammar is properly capitalizing words. Usually, only nouns will be capitalized, but there are some exceptions. The most important capitalization rule is that the first word of every sentence, no matter what part of speech it is, should be capitalized. Another exception is that the pronoun *I* should always be capitalized.

Proper nouns are always capitalized, but sometimes it can be tricky to decide whether or not a noun is a proper noun. Some words that are usually common nouns may become proper nouns when used with other words or phrases. Also, when words that are not nouns are used with a noun, or when a group of words are used together as one noun, those words may also need to be capitalized.

Titles of Books, Stories, and Essays

Most of the words in titles of things like books, stories, and essays should be capitalized, but some should not. The very first word in a title should always be capitalized. Any other word in a title that is a noun, pronoun, adjective, verb or adverb should be capitalized. Articles, such as *a* or *the*, should not be capitalized. Short conjunctions and prepositions are usually not capitalized.

Abbreviations, Initials, and Acronyms

Abbreviations are shortened versions of other words. When an abbreviation shortens, or abbreviates, a word that should be capitalized, the abbreviation's first letter should also be capitalized. When the shortened word is a noun that is not capitalized, the abbreviation should be in lowercase. Initials are usually written using the first letter from multiple words. For example, John Fitzgerald Kennedy is commonly referred to by his initials, JFK. Acronyms also use the first letter from multiple words, but they are different from initials because they form words on their own. For example, NASA is an acronym for National Aeronautics and Space Administration. Some acronyms, like NASA, omit small words, such as *and*, *of*, and *for*. When initials and acronyms are used for proper nouns, each letter should be capitalized.

The types of words and phrases in the chart below are proper nouns and should always be capitalized:

	Description	Example
Historical Periods	A range of time in history that is related to specific events or circumstances	During the Romantic Period, many authors and poets wrote about their emotions.
Historical Events	Names of important events that happened in history	Napoleon Bonaparte led France after the French Revolution.
Historical Documents	Titles of important papers or compositions that are connected to historical events	The Mayflower Compact was written to create rules and expectations for the colony in Plymouth.
Languages	Names of the different languages that people speak	I want to learn to speak Cantonese, Spanish, and German.
Races and Ethnicities	Words often used to describe a person's heritage or cultural group	Malia taught her granddaughter how to hula so she could share a tradition of her Native Hawaiian heritage with her.
Nationalities	Words that describe which country a person is from	My teacher who moved to Canada last year is Romanian.
Organizations	Titles of official groups formed by people	Fewer than half of the states in America have a team in the National Basketball Association.

EXAMPLE

> Allison and Claire enjoy studying art from the beginning of the renaissance. They started a club so they and other students can learn more about it. Allison and Claire named the club Early Renaissance Art Club, which can be abbreviated to ERA Club. The students that joined elected Claire as the president and Allison as the vice president. The club's first meeting will take place after Christmas vacation.

Which of the following changes should be made in the passage?

a. In the first sentence, *Renaissance* should be capitalized.
b. In the third sentence, *ERA* should be written as *Era*.
c. In the fourth sentence, *president* and *vice president* should be capitalized.
d. In the last sentence, *Christmas* should be in lowercase.

Choice A says that *Renaissance* should be capitalized in the first sentence of the passage. The Renaissance is a historical period, so *Renaissance* is a proper noun that should always be capitalized. Choice A is correct.

Choice B says that *ERA* should be written as *Era*. In the third sentence of the passage, the word *era* is used as an acronym. Remember that all letters in an acronym should be capitalized. The correct capitalization is *ERA*, so choice B is incorrect.

Choice C says that *president* and *vice president* should be capitalized. Titles for people are capitalized when they are used as part of a person's name or in the place of a person's name. In this passage, these titles are not used as part of anyone's name or in place of anyone's name, so they should be in lowercase. Choice C is incorrect.

Choice D says that *Christmas* should be in lowercase. The passage says that the first meeting will be held after Christmas break. Even though *Christmas* is used to describe when the students are getting a vacation from school, it is the name of a holiday. Names of holidays are always capitalized, so choice D is incorrect.

WORD CONFUSION

TO, TOO, AND TWO

To can be an adverb or a preposition for showing direction, purpose, and relationship. A dictionary can also be used to see the many other ways to use *to* in a sentence.

> Examples: I went to the store. | I want to go with you.

Too is an adverb that means *also, as well, very,* or *in excess.*

> Examples: I can walk a mile too. | You have eaten too much.

Two is a number.

> Example: You have two minutes left.

THERE, THEIR, AND THEY'RE

There can be an adjective, adverb, or pronoun. Often, *there* is used to show a place or to start a sentence.

Examples: I went there yesterday. | There is something in his pocket.

Their is a pronoun that is used to show ownership.

Examples: He is their father. | This is their fourth apology this week.

They're is a contraction of *they are*.

Example: Did you know that they're in town?

ITS AND IT'S

Its is a possessive pronoun that shows ownership.

Example: The guitar is in its case.

It's is a contraction of *it is*.

Example: It's an honor and a privilege to meet you.

AFFECT AND EFFECT

There are two main reasons that *affect* and *effect* are so often confused: 1) both words can be used as either a noun or a verb, and 2) unlike most homophones, their usage and meanings are closely related to each other. Here is a quick explanation of the four usage options:

Affect (n): feeling, emotion, or mood that is displayed

Example: The patient had a flat *affect*. (i.e., his face showed little or no emotion)

Affect (v): to alter, to change, to influence

Example: The sunshine *affects* the plant's growth.

Effect (n): a result, a consequence

Example: What *effect* will this weather have on our schedule?

Effect (v): to bring about, to cause to be

Example: These new rules will *effect* order in the office.

EXAMPLE

Choose the correct spelling from each pair of homophones in the following passage.

I found a unique tree in the forest. (It's/Its) trunk is blue, and it has (two/too) many branches to count. I brought some of my friends to see it, but the tree did not seem to (affect/effect) them. While (their/they're) not fascinated by the strange tree, I am!

The first pair of homophones is *it's* and *its*. Remember that the contraction *it's* is used in place of *it is*. *Its* is a possessive pronoun that shows a thing's ownership or possession. An easy way to decide whether *it's* or *its* is correct is to see how the sentence sounds with *it is*, instead. *It is trunk is blue* does not make sense. *Its trunk is blue* means that the tree has a blue trunk, so *its* is the correct choice.

The next pair of homophones is *two* and *too*. *Two* only means the number two. *Too* can mean *also* or *in excess*. Which of these makes the most sense in this sentence? *Two many branches to count* or *too many branches to count*? The correct meaning is that there is an abundance of branches, so *too* is the correct choice for this pair.

The third pair of homophones is *affect* and *effect*. Since both of these words can be used as a noun or verb, identifying the correct part of speech is a helpful first step. The part of speech is a verb, since the correct word will show what *the tree* does to *them*. *Affect* as a verb means to change or influence. *Effect* as a verb means to lead to or cause something to happen. Replace the homophone with these synonyms. Seeing the tree cannot cause or lead the speaker's friends to exist, but it can change them or influence them. *Affect* is the correct choice for this pair.

The last pair of homophones is *their* and *they're*. *Their* is a possessive pronoun used to show that multiple people or things own something. *They're* is a contraction used in place of *they are*. Replace the homophone with *they are*. Does the sentence make sense? It does because they, the speaker's friends, are not fascinated by the tree. Saying *their not fascinated* does not make sense. *They're* is the correct choice for this pair.

Vocabulary

Word Roots and Prefixes and Suffixes

Affixes

Affixes in the English language are morphemes that are added to words to create related but different words. Derivational affixes form new words based on and related to the original words. For example, the affix *-ness* added to the end of the adjective *happy* forms the noun *happiness*. Inflectional affixes form different grammatical versions of words. For example, the plural affix *-s* changes the singular noun *book* to the plural noun *books*, and the past tense affix *-ed* changes the present tense verb *look* to the past tense *looked*. Prefixes are affixes placed in front of words. For example, *heat* means to make hot; *preheat* means to heat in advance. Suffixes are affixes placed at the ends of words. The *happiness* example above contains the suffix *-ness*. Circumfixes add parts both before and after words, such as how *light* becomes *enlighten* with the prefix *en-* and the suffix *-en*. Interfixes create compound words via central affixes: *speed* and *meter* become *speedometer* via the interfix *-o-*.

Review Video: Affixes
Visit mometrix.com/academy and enter code: 782422

Word Roots, Prefixes, and Suffixes to Help Determine Meanings of Words

Many English words were formed from combining multiple sources. For example, the Latin *habēre* means "to have," and the prefixes *in-* and *im-* mean a lack or prevention of something, as in *insufficient* and *imperfect*. Latin combined *in-* with *habēre* to form *inhibēre*, whose past participle was *inhibitus*. This is the origin of the English word *inhibit*, meaning to prevent from having. Hence by knowing the meanings of both the prefix and the root, one can decipher the word meaning. In Greek, the root *enkephalo-* refers to the brain. Many medical terms are based on this root, such as encephalitis and hydrocephalus. Understanding the prefix and suffix meanings (*-itis* means inflammation; *hydro-* means water) allows a person to deduce that encephalitis refers to brain inflammation and hydrocephalus refers to water (or other fluid) in the brain.

Review Video: Root Words in English
Visit mometrix.com/academy and enter code: 896380

Review Video: Determining Word Meanings
Visit mometrix.com/academy and enter code: 894894

PREFIXES

Knowing common prefixes is helpful for all readers as they try to determining meanings or definitions of unfamiliar words. For example, a common word used when cooking is *preheat*. Knowing that *pre-* means in advance can also inform them that *presume* means to assume in advance, that *prejudice* means advance judgment, and that this understanding can be applied to many other words beginning with *pre-*. Knowing that the prefix *dis-* indicates opposition informs the meanings of words like *disbar, disagree, disestablish,* and many more. Knowing *dys-* means bad, impaired, abnormal, or difficult informs *dyslogistic, dysfunctional, dysphagia,* and *dysplasia.*

SUFFIXES

In English, certain suffixes generally indicate both that a word is a noun, and that the noun represents a state of being or quality. For example, *-ness* is commonly used to change an adjective into its noun form, as with *happy* and *happiness, nice* and *niceness,* and so on. The suffix *–tion* is commonly used to transform a verb into its noun form, as with *converse* and *conversation or move* and *motion*. Thus, if readers are unfamiliar with the second form of a word, knowing the meaning of the transforming suffix can help them determine meaning.

PREFIXES FOR NUMBERS

Prefix	Definition	Examples
bi-	two	bisect, biennial
mono-	one, single	monogamy, monologue
poly-	many	polymorphous, polygamous
semi-	half, partly	semicircle, semicolon
uni-	one	uniform, unity

PREFIXES FOR TIME, DIRECTION, AND SPACE

Prefix	Definition	Examples
a-	in, on, of, up, to	abed, afoot
ab-	from, away, off	abdicate, abjure
ad-	to, toward	advance, adventure
ante-	before, previous	antecedent, antedate
anti-	against, opposing	antipathy, antidote
cata-	down, away, thoroughly	catastrophe, cataclysm
circum-	around	circumspect, circumference
com-	with, together, very	commotion, complicate
contra-	against, opposing	contradict, contravene
de-	from	depart
dia-	through, across, apart	diameter, diagnose
dis-	away, off, down, not	dissent, disappear
epi-	upon	epilogue
ex-	out	extract, excerpt

Prefix	Definition	Examples
hypo-	under, beneath	hypodermic, hypothesis
inter-	among, between	intercede, interrupt
intra-	within	intramural, intrastate
ob-	against, opposing	objection
per-	through	perceive, permit
peri-	around	periscope, perimeter
post-	after, following	postpone, postscript
pre-	before, previous	prevent, preclude
pro-	forward, in place of	propel, pronoun
retro-	back, backward	retrospect, retrograde
sub-	under, beneath	subjugate, substitute
super-	above, extra	supersede, supernumerary
trans-	across, beyond, over	transact, transport
ultra-	beyond, excessively	ultramodern, ultrasonic

Negative Prefixes

Prefix	Definition	Examples
a-	without, lacking	atheist, agnostic
in-	not, opposing	incapable, ineligible
non-	not	nonentity, nonsense
un-	not, reverse of	unhappy, unlock

Extra Prefixes

Prefix	Definition	Examples
for-	away, off, from	forget, forswear
fore-	previous	foretell, forefathers
homo-	same, equal	homogenized, homonym
hyper-	excessive, over	hypercritical, hypertension
in-	in, into	intrude, invade
mal-	bad, poorly, not	malfunction, malpractice
mis-	bad, poorly, not	misspell, misfire
neo-	new	Neolithic, neoconservative
omni-	all, everywhere	omniscient, omnivore
ortho-	right, straight	orthogonal, orthodox
over-	above	overbearing, oversight
pan-	all, entire	panorama, pandemonium
para-	beside, beyond	parallel, paradox
re-	backward, again	revoke, recur
sym-	with, together	sympathy, symphony

Below is a list of common suffixes and their meanings:

ADJECTIVE SUFFIXES

Suffix	Definition	Examples
-able (-ible)	capable of being	toler*able*, ed*ible*
-esque	in the style of, like	picturesque, grotesque
-ful	filled with, marked by	thankful, zestful
-ific	make, cause	terrific, beatific
-ish	suggesting, like	churlish, childish
-less	lacking, without	hopeless, countless
-ous	marked by, given to	religious, riotous

NOUN SUFFIXES

Suffix	Definition	Examples
-acy	state, condition	accuracy, privacy
-ance	act, condition, fact	acceptance, vigilance
-ard	one that does excessively	drunkard, sluggard
-ation	action, state, result	occupation, starvation
-dom	state, rank, condition	serfdom, wisdom
-er (-or)	office, action	teach*er*, elevat*or*, hon*or*
-ess	feminine	waitress, duchess
-hood	state, condition	manhood, statehood
-ion	action, result, state	union, fusion
-ism	act, manner, doctrine	barbarism, socialism
-ist	worker, follower	monopolist, socialist
-ity (-ty)	state, quality, condition	acid*ity*, civil*ity*, twen*ty*
-ment	result, action	Refreshment
-ness	quality, state	greatness, tallness
-ship	position	internship, statesmanship
-sion (-tion)	state, result	revi*sion*, expedi*tion*
-th	act, state, quality	warmth, width
-tude	quality, state, result	magnitude, fortitude

VERB SUFFIXES

Suffix	Definition	Examples
-ate	having, showing	separate, desolate
-en	cause to be, become	deepen, strengthen
-fy	make, cause to have	glorify, fortify
-ize	cause to be, treat with	sterilize, mechanize

Nuance and Word Meanings

Synonyms and Antonyms

When you understand how words relate to each other, you will discover more in a passage. This is explained by understanding **synonyms** (e.g., words that mean the same thing) and **antonyms** (e.g., words that mean the opposite of one another). As an example, *dry* and *arid* are synonyms, and *dry* and *wet* are antonyms.

There are many pairs of words in English that can be considered synonyms, despite having slightly different definitions. For instance, the words *friendly* and *collegial* can both be used to describe a warm interpersonal relationship, and one would be correct to call them synonyms. However, *collegial* (kin to *colleague*) is often used in reference to professional or academic relationships, and *friendly* has no such connotation.

If the difference between the two words is too great, then they should not be called synonyms. *Hot* and *warm* are not synonyms because their meanings are too distinct. A good way to determine whether two words are synonyms is to substitute one word for the other word and verify that the meaning of the sentence has not changed. Substituting *warm* for *hot* in a sentence would convey a different meaning. Although warm and hot may seem close in meaning, warm generally means that the temperature is moderate, and hot generally means that the temperature is excessively high.

Antonyms are words with opposite meanings. *Light* and *dark*, *up* and *down*, *right* and *left*, *good* and *bad*: these are all sets of antonyms. Be careful to distinguish between antonyms and pairs of words that are simply different. *Black* and *gray*, for instance, are not antonyms because gray is not the opposite of black. *Black* and *white*, on the other hand, are antonyms.

Not every word has an antonym. For instance, many nouns do not. What would be the antonym of *chair*? During your exam, the questions related to antonyms are more likely to concern adjectives. You will recall that adjectives are words that describe a noun. Some common adjectives include *purple*, *fast*, *skinny*, and *sweet*. From those four adjectives, *purple* is the item that lacks a group of obvious antonyms.

Review Video: Synonyms and Antonyms
Visit mometrix.com/academy and enter code: 105612

Denotative vs. Connotative Meaning

The **denotative** meaning of a word is the literal meaning. The **connotative** meaning goes beyond the denotative meaning to include the emotional reaction that a word may invoke. The connotative meaning often takes the denotative meaning a step further due to associations the reader makes with the denotative meaning. Readers can differentiate between the denotative and connotative meanings by first recognizing how authors use each meaning. Most non-fiction, for example, is fact-based and authors do not use flowery, figurative language. The reader can assume that the writer is using the denotative meaning of words. In fiction, the author may use the connotative meaning. Readers can determine whether the author is using the denotative or connotative meaning of a word by implementing context clues.

Review Video: Connotation and Denotation
Visit mometrix.com/academy and enter code: 310092

Nuances of Word Meaning Relative to Connotation, Denotation, Diction, and Usage

A word's denotation is simply its objective dictionary definition. However, its connotation refers to the subjective associations, often emotional, that specific words evoke in listeners and readers. Two or more words can have the same dictionary meaning, but very different connotations. Writers use diction (word choice) to convey various nuances of thought and emotion by selecting synonyms for other words that best communicate the associations they want to trigger for readers. For example, a car engine is naturally greasy; in this sense, "greasy" is a neutral term. But when a person's smile, appearance, or clothing is described as "greasy," it has a negative connotation. Some words have even gained additional or different meanings over time. For example, *awful* used to be used to describe things that evoked a sense of awe. When *awful* is separated into its root word, awe, and suffix, -ful, it can be understood to mean "full of awe." However, the word is now commonly used to describe things that evoke repulsion, terror, or another intense, negative reaction.

Review Video: Word Usage in Sentences
Visit mometrix.com/academy and enter code: 197863

Using Context to Determine Meaning

Context Clues

Readers of all levels will encounter words that they have either never seen or have encountered only on a limited basis. The best way to define a word in **context** is to look for nearby words that can assist in revealing the meaning of the word. For instance, unfamiliar nouns are often accompanied by examples that provide a definition. Consider the following sentence: *Dave arrived at the party in hilarious garb: a leopard-print shirt, buckskin trousers, and bright green sneakers.* If a reader was unfamiliar with the meaning of garb, he or she could read the examples (i.e., a leopard-print shirt, buckskin trousers, and bright green sneakers) and quickly determine that the word means *clothing*. Examples will not always be this obvious. Consider this sentence: *Parsley, lemon, and flowers were just a few of the items he used as garnishes.* Here, the word *garnishes* is exemplified by parsley, lemon, and flowers. Readers who have eaten in a variety of restaurants will probably be able to identify a garnish as something used to decorate a plate.

Review Video: Reading Comprehension: Using Context Clues
Visit mometrix.com/academy and enter code: 613660

Using Contrast in Context Clues

In addition to looking at the context of a passage, readers can use contrast to define an unfamiliar word in context. In many sentences, the author will not describe the unfamiliar word directly; instead, he or she will describe the opposite of the unfamiliar word. Thus, you are provided with some information that will bring you closer to defining the word. Consider the following example: *Despite his intelligence, Hector's low brow and bad posture made him look obtuse.* The author writes that Hector's appearance does not convey intelligence. Therefore, *obtuse* must mean unintelligent. Here is another example: *Despite the horrible weather, we were beatific about our trip to Alaska.* The word *despite* indicates that the speaker's feelings were at odds with the weather. Since the weather is described as *horrible*, then *beatific* must mean something positive.

Substitution to Find Meaning

In some cases, there will be very few contextual clues to help a reader define the meaning of an unfamiliar word. When this happens, one strategy that readers may employ is **substitution**. A good reader will brainstorm some possible synonyms for the given word, and he or she will substitute these words into the sentence. If the sentence and the surrounding passage continue to make sense, then the substitution has revealed at least some information about the unfamiliar word. Consider the sentence: *Frank's admonition rang in her ears as she climbed the mountain.* A reader unfamiliar with *admonition* might come up with some substitutions like *vow, promise, advice, complaint,* or *compliment.* All of these words make general sense of the sentence, though their meanings are diverse. However, this process has suggested that an admonition is some sort of message. The substitution strategy is rarely able to pinpoint a precise definition, but this process can be effective as a last resort.

Occasionally, you will be able to define an unfamiliar word by looking at the descriptive words in the context. Consider the following sentence: *Fred dragged the recalcitrant boy kicking and screaming up the stairs.* The words *dragged, kicking,* and *screaming* all suggest that the boy does not want to go up the stairs. The reader may assume that *recalcitrant* means something like unwilling or protesting. In this example, an unfamiliar adjective was identified.

Additionally, using description to define an unfamiliar noun is a common practice compared to unfamiliar adjectives, as in this sentence: *Don's wrinkled frown and constantly shaking fist identified him as a curmudgeon of the first order.* Don is described as having a *wrinkled frown and constantly shaking fist,* suggesting that a *curmudgeon* must be a grumpy person. Contrasts do not always provide detailed information about the unfamiliar word, but they at least give the reader some clues.

Words with Multiple Meanings

When a word has more than one meaning, readers can have difficulty determining how the word is being used in a given sentence. For instance, the verb *cleave,* can mean either *join* or *separate.* When readers come upon this word, they will have to select the definition that makes the most sense. Consider the following sentence: *Hermione's knife cleaved the bread cleanly.* Since a knife cannot join bread together, the word must indicate separation. A slightly more difficult example would be the sentence: *The birds cleaved to one another as they flew from the oak tree.* Immediately, the presence of the words *to one another* should suggest that in this sentence *cleave* is being used to mean *join.* Discovering the intent of a word with multiple meanings requires the same tricks as defining an unknown word: look for contextual clues and evaluate the substituted words.

Context Clues to Help Determine Meanings of Words

If readers simply bypass unknown words, they can reach unclear conclusions about what they read. However, looking for the definition of every unfamiliar word in the dictionary can slow their reading progress. Moreover, the dictionary may list multiple definitions for a word, so readers must search the word's context for meaning. Hence context is important to new vocabulary regardless of reader methods. Four types of context clues are examples, definitions, descriptive words, and opposites. Authors may use a certain word, and then follow it with several different examples of what it describes. Sometimes authors actually supply a definition of a word they use, which is especially true in informational and technical texts. Authors may use descriptive words that elaborate upon a vocabulary word they just used. Authors may also use opposites with negation that help define meaning.

Examples and Definitions

An author may use a word and then give examples that illustrate its meaning. Consider this text: "Teachers who do not know how to use sign language can help students who are deaf or hard of hearing understand certain instructions by using gestures instead, like pointing their fingers to indicate which direction to look or go; holding up a hand, palm outward, to indicate stopping; holding the hands flat, palms up, curling a finger toward oneself in a beckoning motion to indicate 'come here'; or curling all fingers toward oneself repeatedly to indicate 'come on', 'more', or 'continue.'" The author of this text has used the word "gestures" and then followed it with examples, so a reader unfamiliar with the word could deduce from the examples that "gestures" means "hand motions." Readers can find examples by looking for signal words "for example," "for instance," "like," "such as," and "e.g."

While readers sometimes have to look for definitions of unfamiliar words in a dictionary or do some work to determine a word's meaning from its surrounding context, at other times an author may make it easier for readers by defining certain words. For example, an author may write, "The company did not have sufficient capital, that is, available money, to continue operations." The author defined "capital" as "available money," and heralded the definition with the phrase "that is." Another way that authors supply word definitions is with appositives. Rather than being introduced by a signal phrase like "that is," "namely," or "meaning," an appositive comes after the vocabulary word it defines and is enclosed within two commas. For example, an author may write, "The Indians introduced the Pilgrims to pemmican, cakes they made of lean meat dried and mixed with fat, which proved greatly beneficial to keep settlers from starving while trapping." In this example, the appositive phrase following "pemmican" and preceding "which" defines the word "pemmican."

DESCRIPTIONS

When readers encounter a word they do not recognize in a text, the author may expand on that word to illustrate it better. While the author may do this to make the prose more picturesque and vivid, the reader can also take advantage of this description to provide context clues to the meaning of the unfamiliar word. For example, an author may write, "The man sitting next to me on the airplane was obese. His shirt stretched across his vast expanse of flesh, strained almost to bursting." The descriptive second sentence elaborates on and helps to define the previous sentence's word "obese" to mean extremely fat. A reader unfamiliar with the word "repugnant" can decipher its meaning through an author's accompanying description: "The way the child grimaced and shuddered as he swallowed the medicine showed that its taste was particularly repugnant."

OPPOSITES

Text authors sometimes introduce a contrasting or opposing idea before or after a concept they present. They may do this to emphasize or heighten the idea they present by contrasting it with something that is the reverse. However, readers can also use these context clues to understand familiar words. For example, an author may write, "Our conversation was not cheery. We sat and talked very solemnly about his experience and a number of similar events." The reader who is not familiar with the word "solemnly" can deduce by the author's preceding use of "not cheery" that "solemn" means the opposite of cheery or happy, so it must mean serious or sad. Or if someone writes, "Don't condemn his entire project because you couldn't find anything good to say about it," readers unfamiliar with "condemn" can understand from the sentence structure that it means the opposite of saying anything good, so it must mean reject, dismiss, or disapprove. "Entire" adds another context clue, meaning total or complete rejection.

SYNTAX TO DETERMINE PART OF SPEECH AND MEANINGS OF WORDS

Syntax refers to sentence structure and word order. Suppose that a reader encounters an unfamiliar word when reading a text. To illustrate, consider an invented word like "splunch." If this word is used in a sentence like "Please splunch that ball to me," the reader can assume from syntactic context that "splunch" is a verb. We would not use a noun, adjective, adverb, or preposition with the object "that ball," and the prepositional phrase "to me" further indicates "splunch" represents an action. However, in the sentence, "Please hand that splunch to me," the reader can assume that "splunch" is a noun. Demonstrative adjectives like "that" modify nouns. Also, we hand someone some*thing*—a thing being a noun; we do not hand someone a verb, adjective, or adverb. Some sentences contain further clues. For example, from the sentence, "The princess wore the glittering splunch on her head," the reader can deduce that it is a crown, tiara, or something similar from the syntactic context, without knowing the word.

Syntax to Indicate Different Meanings of Similar Sentences

The syntax, or structure, of a sentence affords grammatical cues that aid readers in comprehending the meanings of words, phrases, and sentences in the texts that they read. Seemingly minor differences in how the words or phrases in a sentence are ordered can make major differences in meaning. For example, two sentences can use exactly the same words but have different meanings based on the word order:

- "The man with a broken arm sat in a chair."
- "The man sat in a chair with a broken arm."

While both sentences indicate that a man sat in a chair, differing syntax indicates whether the man's or chair's arm was broken.

Review Video: Syntax
Visit mometrix.com/academy and enter code: 242280

Determining Meaning of Phrases and Paragraphs

Like unknown words, the meanings of phrases, paragraphs, and entire works can also be difficult to discern. Each of these can be better understood with added context. However, for larger groups of words, more context is needed. Unclear phrases are similar to unclear words, and the same methods can be used to understand their meaning. However, it is also important to consider how the individual words in the phrase work together. Paragraphs are a bit more complicated. Just as words must be compared to other words in a sentence, paragraphs must be compared to other paragraphs in a composition or a section.

Determining Meaning in Various Types of Compositions

To understand the meaning of an entire composition, the type of composition must be considered. **Expository writing** is generally organized so that each paragraph focuses on explaining one idea, or part of an idea, and its relevance. **Persuasive writing** uses paragraphs for different purposes to organize the parts of the argument. **Unclear paragraphs** must be read in the context of the paragraphs around them for their meaning to be fully understood. The meaning of full texts can also be unclear at times. The purpose of composition is also important for understanding the meaning of a text. To quickly understand the broad meaning of a text, look to the introductory and concluding paragraphs. Fictional texts are different. Some fictional works have implicit meanings, but some do not. The target audience must be considered for understanding texts that do have an implicit meaning, as most children's fiction will clearly state any lessons or morals. For other fiction, the application of literary theories and criticism may be helpful for understanding the text.

Resources for Determining Word Meaning and Usage

While these strategies are useful for determining the meaning of unknown words and phrases, sometimes additional resources are needed to properly use the terms in different contexts. Some words have multiple definitions, and some words are inappropriate in particular contexts or modes of writing. The following tools are helpful for understanding all meanings and proper uses for words and phrases.

- **Dictionaries** provide the meaning of a multitude of words in a language. Many dictionaries include additional information about each word, such as its etymology, its synonyms, or variations of the word.
- **Glossaries** are similar to dictionaries, as they provide the meanings of a variety of terms. However, while dictionaries typically feature an extensive list of words and comprise an entire publication, glossaries are often included at the end of a text and only include terms and definitions that are relevant to the text they follow.
- **Spell Checkers** are used to detect spelling errors in typed text. Some spell checkers may also detect the misuse of plural or singular nouns, verb tenses, or capitalization. While spell checkers are a helpful tool, they are not always reliable or attuned to the author's intent, so it is important to review the spell checker's suggestions before accepting them.
- **Style Manuals** are guidelines on the preferred punctuation, format, and grammar usage according to different fields or organizations. For example, the Associated Press Stylebook is a style guide often used for media writing. The guidelines within a style guide are not always applicable across different contexts and usages, as the guidelines often cover grammatical or formatting situations that are not objectively correct or incorrect.

Types of Essays

Essays

Essays usually focus on one topic, subject, or goal. There are several types of essays, including informative, persuasive, and narrative. An essay's structure and formality depend on the type of essay and its goal. While narrative essays typically do not include outside sources, other types of essays often require some research and the use of primary and secondary sources.

The basic format of an essay typically has three major parts: the introduction, the body, and the conclusion. The body is further divided into the writer's main points. Most essays will have at least three main points, but essays that go into more depth can have almost any number of main points.

An essay's introduction should answer three questions:

1. What is the **subject** of the essay?

   If an essay is about a book, the answer would include the title and author of the book, as well as any additional information needed, such as the subject or argument of the book.

2. How does the essay **discuss** the subject?

   To answer this, the writer briefly summarizes the main points and the evidence supporting them to let readers know how the essay is organized and what information they can expect to read.

3. What will the essay **prove**?

   This information is in the thesis statement, usually the opening paragraph's last sentence, which clearly states the writer's message.

The body elaborates on all the main points related to the thesis, introducing one main point at a time, and includes supporting evidence with each main point. Each body paragraph should state the point in a topic sentence, which is usually the first sentence in the paragraph. The paragraph should then explain the point's meaning, support it with quotations or other evidence, and then explain how this point and the evidence are related to the thesis. The writer should then repeat this procedure in a new paragraph for each additional main point.

The conclusion restates the content of the introduction, including the thesis, to remind the reader of the essay's main argument or subject. The essay writer may also summarize the highlights of the argument or description contained in the body of the essay, following the same organization originally used in the body. For example, a conclusion might look like: Point 1 + Point 2 + Point 3 = Thesis, or Point 1 → Point 2 → Point 3 → Thesis Proof. Good organization makes essays easier for writers to compose and provides a guide for readers to follow. Well-organized essays hold attention better and are more likely to get readers to believe or agree with the writer.

Using Sources in Essays

Sometimes writers use information from others in their work. This is most common in expository and persuasive writing. For an expository essay, a writer may not know all of the information that he or she needs to finish the composition. The writer may use other people's work to find the missing information and complete the composition. Persuasive writers may do research to find facts or statements from others that support their own beliefs and make their writing more persuasive. In both cases, research helps the writer find information that **supports** his or her **original work**.

Outside information must be relevant, true, and helpful to be appropriate for a composition. Writers must also be careful not to use too much outside information, since this can make the composition unoriginal. If a writer does use outside information, it is extremely important that the writer mention in the composition where the information came from. If the writer forgets or chooses not to say where the information came from, he or she has stolen someone else's work and presented it as their own. Doing this is called **plagiarism**.

Informational Texts

Informational texts, also called instructional or expository texts, are compositions written to inform the reader about a specific topic. An informational essay can inform readers in a variety of ways, such as giving them instructions, telling them facts about the topic, or teaching them why something happens. Informational texts should be logical, meaning that they should present information in an order that the reader can easily understand, and they should include the right amount of information so the writer successfully informs his or her audience of new information.

Informational texts should also focus on a **central idea**. In the introduction of an informational text, there may be a sentence or two that clearly state the essay's central idea. This sentence, or sentences, is called a **thesis statement**. The central idea should be clear throughout the composition. By emphasizing the central idea in the introduction, body, and conclusion, the writer can ensure that the central idea is clear. One way to make sure that the central idea is emphasized is to think about the purpose of each part of the essay. The introduction prepares the reader by telling them what the rest of the essay is about, so the central idea should be **introduced** in this section. The body tells the reader the information the writer wants to tell the audience, so this **explains** the central idea and facts about it to the reader. The conclusion is used to **remind** the reader of how the information in the body is related and **restates** the central idea one final time.

Structures or Organizational Patterns in Informational Texts

Informational text can be **descriptive**, meaning that it gives information that can be experienced through the five senses, or it answers the questions what, who, when, where, and why. One common method of organizing informational text is to put it in a certain sequence, or order. **Chronological** texts include events in the order that they occurred, from start to finish. **How-to**, or **instructional**, texts organize information into a series of instructions in the order in which the steps should be followed. **Comparison-contrast** structures of informational text describe different ideas to their readers by pointing out how things or ideas are similar and how they are different. **Cause and effect** structures of informational text describe events that occurred and the causes or reasons for those events. **Problem and solution** structures of informational texts introduce and describe problems and offer one or more solutions for each problem described.

Review Video: Organizational Methods to Structure Text
Visit mometrix.com/academy and enter code: 606263

Argumentative Writing

In argumentative writing, the writer expresses a belief or opinion that he or she wants to lead readers to agree with. When writing an argumentative composition, the writer should first identify the **topic** his or her opinion is about. The topic may be serious or fun, as long as there is one clear topic in the composition. The next step is for the writer to determine his or her opinion on the topic and determine why he or she holds that opinion. In order to persuade others to agree with their opinion, the writer must be able to give readers reasons to support the opinion. If the writer does not know why he or she has an opinion, it will be difficult to convince readers to agree. In addition to having reasons that support their opinion, writers should prepare examples that support each of these reasons in order to strengthen their composition.

Once the writer has determined his or her topic, opinion, and reasons for having the opinion, he or she is ready to begin writing an argumentative essay. In the introduction, the writer should capture the reader's interest, introduce the topic, and reveal his or her opinion about the topic. In the body of the composition, the writer should remind the reader of the opinion and give his or her reasons for holding the opinion. If the writer has any examples, facts, or other information that supports his or her opinion or reasons for believing it, these should also be included in the body. Writers may also use a body paragraph to mention opposing opinions or beliefs and explain why they disagree with them. As in other compositions, the conclusion should remind the reader of the essay's topic and purpose, as well as remind the reader how the opinion has been explained and supported. The conclusion should also invite the reader to continue thinking about the topic and writer's opinion. This can be done through questions or statements that lead readers to consider whether or not they agree with the author's opinion or what their own opinions are.

> **Review Video: Argumentative Writing**
> Visit mometrix.com/academy and enter code: 561544

Informative vs. Persuasive Writing

Informative writing, also called explanatory or expository writing, is written to show that something is true or factual, while **persuasive** writing is written to lead the reader to agree with something that may or may not be true or factual. While persuasive text is written to **persuade** readers to agree with the author's position, informative text simply **provides information** to readers. Informative writing **informs** readers about why or how something is as it is. This can include offering new information, explaining how a process works, or describing a concept for readers.

> **Review Video: Informational Text**
> Visit mometrix.com/academy and enter code: 924964

Facts and Opinions

Writers and readers must always be aware of the difference between fact and opinion. A **fact** can be tested and proven to be true. An **opinion**, on the other hand, is someone's personal thoughts or feelings. Opinions are often not changed by information. If an author writes that a newborn elephant is about five times taller than a newborn giraffe, then he or she is stating a fact. If the author writes that giraffes are more interesting than elephants, then he or she is giving an opinion because this cannot be proven to be true or false. Opinions are often supported by facts. For instance, the author might use a comparison between the way that giraffes eat and the way elephants eat as evidence of how giraffes are more interesting. An opinion supported by facts tends to be more convincing. On the other hand, when authors support their opinions with other opinions, readers should seriously think about and read the argument carefully to see whether it is logical and trustworthy.

> **Review Video: Distinguishing Fact and Opinion**
> Visit mometrix.com/academy and enter code: 870899

Narrative Writing

Put simply, **narrative** writing tells a story. Narratives should tell stories in such a way that the readers learn something or gain understanding about a related topic or idea. Personal narratives are narratives writers create about personal experiences that were meaningful to them. Narratives should start with the story's actions or events, rather than long descriptions or introductions. However, the narrative should still include descriptions at points where they will entertain the reader or help the reader visualize or better understand the scene. To write an effective description, writers should include sensory details, asking themselves what they saw, heard, felt or touched, smelled, and tasted during the experiences they describe. In narrative writing, the details should be **concrete** rather than **abstract**. Concrete details are those that can be experienced through one of the five senses, while abstract details are not able to be experienced in this way.

Using concrete details enables readers to imagine everything that the writer describes. Writers should make sure that there is a point to each story by describing what they learned from the experience they narrate.

Personal Narratives

A **personal narrative** is a story about something that happened to the writer. **Personal narrative essays** are structured the same as other types of essays, as they have an introduction, body paragraphs, and a conclusion. Like other essays, the introduction of a personal narrative should contain a hook, or an opening sentence that interests the reader and prompts them to read the rest of the narrative. The introduction may also provide context for the story told in the personal narrative. One significant difference between personal narratives and other essays is that the body paragraphs of a personal narrative should contain sensory details, or imagery. A good personal narrative will give the reader a clear picture of the events and engage their emotions, and sensory details are effective at achieving these goals. The body should describe the events in chronological order, and the story should be completed in the last body paragraph. The conclusion will summarize the main idea of the personal narrative and may include information such as the writer's brief reflection on the events, how the events taught or changed the writer, or any relevant events that have happened since the events in the narrative.

Sensory Details

Writers need to use vivid descriptions when writing descriptive essays. Narratives should also include descriptions of characters, things, and events. Writers should remember to describe not only the visual detail of what someone or something looks like, but details from other senses, as well. For example, they can contrast the feeling of a sea breeze to the feeling of a mountain breeze, describe how they think something inedible would taste, and compare sounds they hear in the same location at different times of day and night. Readers have trouble visualizing images or imagining sensory impressions and feelings from abstract descriptions, so concrete descriptions make these more real.

Informational Text Example

Below is a prompt for an informational text. There is also an example of an essay that addresses the prompt. There are multiple drafts of this essay to show what kinds of changes a writer may make during the writing process to improve his or her work.

PROMPT:

Do you ever dream of going to a new city, state, or even country? Write about one place you want to travel to on vacation. Be sure to share why you would like to visit that place.

Rough Draft

Imagine traveling into the city or the beach and being transported back in time. This is what it must be like to live in Greece. The old buildings, beautiful beaches, and Greek foods are reasons I want to visit Greece.

Several buildings from ancient Greece are still standing, and they can easily be enjoyed by visitors and the people of Greece today. Some of the most famous ones, like the Parthenon, are located throughout the capital. This means that even when you are sitting in an air-conditioned restaurant in Athens, you can still see what is left of history. There are also tours that teach visitors more about these structures and the events that happened at each one. Though seeing these structures is not the only reason I would like to visit Greece, they would be enough of a reason for me to visit.

In addition to the scenery, another reason to visit Greece is to try real Greek and Mediterranean foods. I have tried a few Greek foods, like baklava and pita bread, and I enjoyed them. While these foods are available in America, I think they are probably made a little differently in Greece. I am interested in seeing what the differences are and trying new things. I hope I can visit Greece soon, because I am getting hungry just thinking about the food there!

Greece has a variety of beaches, as some are small with rocky structures and some look like normal beaches. The water is also different from some American waters because Greece is next to the Mediterranean Sea. Also, many historical events and myths took place on some of the beaches. I would love to sit on one of those beaches and try to imagine ships or characters from myths coming to the shore! The beaches in Greece are beautiful, but I think they also sound fun and interesting!

Walking through historical structures, visiting unique beaches, and eating new foods there is my dream. If I only ever have the chance to go on one vacation, I hope it is to Greece!

Revised Draft

Imagine traveling into the city or the beach and being transported back in time. This is what it must be like to live in Greece. <u>The remaining historical sites that are still there allow visitors to see two cultures side by side.</u> The old buildings, beautiful beaches, and Greek foods are reasons I want to visit Greece.

Several buildings from ancient Greece are still standing, and they can easily be enjoyed by visitors and the people of Greece today. Some of the most famous ones, like the Parthenon, are located throughout the capital. This means that even when you are sitting in an air-conditioned restaurant in Athens, you can still see what is left of history. There are also tours that teach visitors more about these structures and the events that happened at each one. Though seeing these structures is not the only reason I would like to visit Greece, they would be enough of a reason for me to visit.

Greece has a variety of beaches, as some are small with rocky structures and some look like normal beaches. The water is also different from some American waters because Greece is next to the Mediterranean Sea. Also, many historical events and myths took place on some of the beaches. I would love to sit on one of those beaches and try to imagine ships or characters from myths coming to the shore! The beaches in Greece are beautiful, but I think they also sound fun and interesting!

In addition to the scenery, a third reason to visit Greece is to try real Greek and Mediterranean foods. I have tried a few Greek foods, like baklava and pita bread, and I enjoyed them. While these foods are available in America, I think they are probably made a little differently in Greece. I am interested in seeing what the differences are and trying new things. I hope I can visit Greece soon, because I am getting hungry just thinking about the food there!

<u>Greece is a special place where the old and the new come together.</u> Walking through historical structures, visiting unique beaches, and eating new foods there is my dream. If I only ever have the chance to go on one vacation, I hope it is to Greece!

Revised Draft Notes

Remember the purpose of the revising stage of the writing process. When revising, it is important to look at the whole composition. Do all of the paragraphs strengthen the composition? Do the introduction and conclusion help the reader understand the central idea and main points?

In this revision, nothing has been removed, but there are some additions. Look at the underlined words. In the introduction, a sentence has been added. Why? Previously, the introduction had only a hook and a thesis. The sentences were well written, but the writer did not provide a connection between the hook and the thesis. The new sentence connects the ideas in both sentences and introduces some of the main points the writer will discuss in the essay.

In the conclusion, another sentence has been added. This sentence strengthens the composition by creating a transition from the body to the conclusion. Before, the conclusion began abruptly by listing the three main points from the body of the essay. This sentence makes the essay flow better by giving the reader a transition from the body to the conclusion. This sentence reminds the reader of composition's central idea before repeating the writer's main points and sharing his or her hopes.

Finally, the third and fourth paragraphs have been switched. Why is that? Before, the writer discussed ancient buildings, then food, then the beaches. This revised draft discusses buildings, then beaches, then food. This new order puts the more closely related points, the scenery of the buildings and beaches, closer together in the essay. This helps the reader by making the organization of the essay more logical.

EDITED DRAFT

Imagine traveling into the city or the beach and being transported back in time. This is what it must be like to live in Greece, since the remaining historical sites ~~that are still there~~ allow visitors to see two cultures side by side. The ~~old~~ ancient buildings, beautiful beaches, and Greek foods are reasons I want to visit Greece.

Several buildings from ancient Greece are still standing, and they can easily be enjoyed by visitors and the people of Greece today. Some of the most famous ones, like the Parthenon, are located throughout the capital. This means that even when you are sitting in an air-conditioned restaurant in Athens, you can still see ~~what is left~~ glimpses of history. There are also tours that teach visitors more about these structures and the events that happened at each one. ~~Though seeing these structures is not the only reason I would like to visit Greece, they would be enough of a reason for me to visit.~~ Seeing these structures alone is enough of a reason for me to visit Greece!

Another reason I want to travel to Greece is to see the beaches there. There are a variety of beaches, as some are small with rocky structures and some look like ~~normal~~ typical beaches. The water is also different from some American waters because Greece is next to the Mediterranean Sea. Also, many historical events and myths took place on some of the beaches. I would love to sit on one of those beaches and try to imagine ships or characters from myths coming to the shore! The beaches in Greece are beautiful, but I think they also sound fun and interesting!

In addition to the scenery, a third reason to visit Greece is to try ~~real~~ authentic Greek and Mediterranean foods. I have tried a few Greek foods, like baklava and pita bread, and I enjoyed them. While these foods are available in America, I think they are probably made a little differently in Greece, so I am interested in seeing what the differences are and trying new things. I hope I can visit Greece soon, because I am getting hungry just thinking about the food there!

Greece is a special place where the old and the new come together. Walking through historical structures, visiting unique beaches, and eating new foods there is my dream. If I only ever have the chance to go on one vacation, I hope it is to Greece!

EDITED DRAFT NOTES

Since the writer has revised his or her work, the next step is to edit the composition. Remember that editing is very similar to revising, but editing usually includes paying attention to each paragraph, instead of the whole composition. Look at the changes that were made to each paragraph.

There are small changes throughout this draft. First, look at the introduction. Before, the introduction had four sentences that were about the same length. In this draft, the second and third sentences have been combined to make a longer sentence. This creates more sentence variety in the introduction, which makes the composition more entertaining for the writer's audience. A few words have been crossed out, as well. *That are still there* has been replaced with *remaining*. This change makes the writing more concise and formal. Also, *old* has been replaced with *ancient*. This clarifies what kind of buildings the writer is describing by using a word that more specifically describes the age of the buildings.

In the next paragraph, *what is left* has been replaced with *glimpses*. This change makes the writing more concise by using one word instead of three. Furthermore, this change makes the writing more interesting and entertaining by using a better vocabulary word. At the end of the paragraph, the last sentence has been condensed. Most of the sentences in this paragraph are long. Shortening this sentence adds sentence variety to this paragraph and makes the concluding sentence more concise. Overall, these changes make the paragraph easier to read by eliminating unnecessary words and using better vocabulary.

There are a few more changes left in the third and fourth paragraphs. A transition has been added to the beginning of the third paragraph. Now, the writer introduces the next main point before describing the beaches. This makes the essay flow better overall and making it easier for the writer's audience to read. *Normal* has been replaced with *typical*. Since there are so many different beaches in the world, there are not really any normal beaches. *Typical* is a much clearer word. Now, the reader knows that the writer is trying to distinguish the beaches in Greece from the type of beaches that he or she sees most often.

In the next paragraph, *real* has been replaced with *authentic*. The food the writer has tried in America has been real food, not fake food, so this is poor word choice. Now, *authentic* clarifies the writer's meaning that the food will be closer to its original Greek or Mediterranean style. These changes in word choice improve the clarity of the essay by using specific words that better communicate the writer's points. Finally, the third and fourth sentences have been joined together. This increases sentence variety by adding a longer sentence to this paragraph.

Final Draft

Imagine traveling into the city or the beach and being transported back in time. This is what it must be like to live in Greece, since the remaining historical sites allow visitors to see two cultures side by side. The ancient buildings, beautiful beaches, and Greek foods are reasons I want to visit Greece.

Several buildings from ancient Greece are still standing, and they can easily be enjoyed by visitors and the people of Greece today. Some of the most famous ones, like the Parthenon, are located throughout the capital. This means that even when you are sitting in an air-conditioned restaurant in Athens, you can still see glimpses of history. There are also tours that teach visitors more about these structures and the events that happened at each one. Seeing these structures alone is enough of a reason for me to visit Greece!

Another reason I want to travel to Greece is to see the beaches there. There are a variety of beaches, as some are small with rocky structures and some look like typical beaches. The water is also different from some American waters because Greece is next to the Mediterranean Sea. Also, many historical events and myths took place on some of the beaches. I would love to sit on one of those beaches and try to imagine ships or characters from myths coming to the shore! The beaches in Greece are beautiful, but I think they also sound fun and interesting!

In addition to the scenery, a third reason to visit Greece is to try authentic Greek and Mediterranean foods. I have tried a few Greek foods, like baklava and pita bread, and I enjoyed them. While these foods are available in America, I think they are probably made a little differently in Greece, so I am interested in seeing what the differences are and trying new things. I hope I can visit Greece soon, because I am getting hungry just thinking about the food there!

Greece is a special place where the old and the new come together. Walking through historical structures, visiting unique beaches, and eating new foods there is my dream. If I only ever have the chance to go on one vacation, I hope it is to Greece!

Final Draft Evaluation

The essay answers the prompt and is on topic throughout the composition. The central idea is clear and is stated in the introduction, supported in the body, and restated in the conclusion. The thesis statement restates parts of the prompt and gives the reader a preview of the rest of the essay. The body uses well-structured paragraphs to explain the supporting details and examples and connects them to the central idea. The conclusion also emphasizes the central idea and supporting details and invites the reader to consider what they have read.

The essay is also interesting and written with a variety of sentence types. It uses transitions and good paragraph structure to make the essay easy for the reader to understand. The introduction also uses a hook to get the reader's attention and help him or her relate to the information in the essay. Not only does this essay answer the prompt and have appropriate structure, but it also makes use of good, engaging, and interesting details.

Reading Practice Test #1

Refer to the passage "Fog" to answer questions 1-7.

Fog

Stealthy fog drifts through the air,
A dense, gray blanket everywhere.
It slowly seeps in from the sea,
Clutching rooftops, climbing trees.

Its eerie whisper fills the land—
"Catch me, catch me, if you can!"
It skims the sky and hugs the ground,
Distorts the vision, muffles sound.

It fills the mind and fools the feet
Like haunting shadows in the street.
It creeps across the alleyway
And dims the newborn light of day.

It smothers landscapes without shame
Then fades as quickly as it came.

1. What is the meaning of the word *distorts*, used in line 8?

a. Quiets
b. Sharpens
c. Changes
d. Stops

2. How does the poet use the metaphor in line 2 to describe a characteristic of the fog?

a. To show that fog can disappear like a ghost
b. To show that fog speaks like a person
c. To show that fog can be like a heavy covering
d. To show that fog can move like an animal

3. Based on lines 13 and 14, which of the following is most likely true about fog?

a. Fog can be dangerous
b. Only places near the water get fog
c. Fog is expected to happen every day
d. The effects of fog are temporary

4. Based on the theme of *Fog*, which of the following titles would be best for this poem?

a. Fog, the Mysterious Traveler
b. Dark Day on an Island
c. Types of Cloudy Weather
d. The Science Behind Fog

5. What does the poet show by ending "Fog" with two lines instead of four?

a. How boring fog can be
b. How quickly fog disappears
c. How thin fog really is
d. How much fog wants to leave

6. Which phrase from the poem shows that fog can make it difficult to see things?

a. Clutching rooftops, climbing trees
b. It fills the mind and fools the feet
c. Its eerie whisper fills the land
d. Distorts the vision, muffles sound

7. How does the poet's personification of fog in lines 5 and 6 affect the mood of the poem?

a. It describes the fleeting nature of fog and creates a mysterious mood
b. It describes the darkness of fog and creates a sad mood
c. It describes the friendly nature of fog and creates a hopeful mood
d. It describes the danger of fog and creates a warning mood

Refer to the passage "Geocaching" to answer questions 8-16.

Geocaching

(1) "Would you like to go geocaching with me this weekend, Tommy?" asked his father. "I have found a couple of new ones near the creek that I think would be fun. We could invite your friend Sam to join us."

(2) "Sure, Dad. I love geocaching," said Tommy. "Should we go on Saturday?" They agreed that they would leave Saturday morning to find the new geocaches, and Tommy ran to call Sam and invite him. Sam agreed to come with them. Although he wasn't sure what geocaching was, he always had fun with Tommy and his dad.

(3) Friday night, Tommy and his dad got their gear ready. They both had handheld GPS units, hiking boots with good wool socks, a backpack to carry first aid gear, water, and swag for the cache such as plastic soldiers, a water pistol, and some playing cards. Tommy's father made sure that they had a compass, a map, bug spray, and hats, and he printed out the coordinates for the geocaches. Tommy had given Sam a list of things to bring with him as well.

(4) Saturday morning, Tommy and Dad picked up Sam at his house, and off they went. "Mr. Jones, could you explain to me what geocaching is?" Sam asked as they were getting in the car.

(5) "Of course, Sam. Basically, it's like a giant worldwide treasure hunt. People hide geocaches, or containers, then take the coordinates with their GPS and enter the coordinates into a website where people like us can find them. Then, other people, like us, go hunting for these containers. Some of them are very tiny, just big enough to have a piece of paper for the date and your name. Some of them are large enough to hold books or toys and a logbook. Sometimes people even put disposable cameras in them so you can take a picture of yourself at the cache. There are even items in some caches that can be tracked so you can see how they move around the world."

(6) Tommy's dad could see that Sam was still a little confused, but he knew that the boy would catch on as they got going. Mr. Jones put the coordinates for the first cache into his GPS, and they headed off. "It looks like this first cache is only two miles from here," he told the boys.

(7) The GPS led the trio to a small parking area just inside the local park, where they stopped and got their backpacks on. They also sprayed themselves with bug spray and reset the GPS for off-road walking. "It looks like we have about 400 feet to go just that way," Mr. Jones said as they headed away from the car into the woods. When they arrived at the location, Sam looked around. "I don't see anything," he complained.

(8) Tommy laughed. "Our GPS is accurate to 15 feet, Sam, which means that the cache container is within 15 feet of Dad right now but in any direction. The way we do it is Dad stands still, and I walk 15 feet from him. Then we know how far in each direction to look. Why don't I walk 15 feet to his right and you go left? Then we know exactly where to search." Sam agreed, and the boys quickly marked off their search area. "The cache is medium sized, Sam, so be looking for something like the plastic boxes your mom puts leftovers in, okay?"

(9) Tommy, Sam, and Mr. Jones searched for about 10 minutes. They looked in tree branches, under rocks and leaves, and even inside a hollow log before Sam yelled, "I think I found it!" Sure enough, he had found the container under a pile of leaves beside the hollow log. Since this was Sam's first find, Tommy and his dad let Sam open the box and choose an item to trade. Sam chose to take a bouncy rubber ball and leave a water gun. Mr. Jones signed the logbook for all of them, and they hid the cache back where they found it.

(10) "That was so much fun, Tommy! I'm so glad you asked me to come along," Sam said excitedly.

(11) "Does that mean you boys are ready to find the next one?" Mr. Jones asked. The boys cheered, and the three of them set off for the car.

8. What will most likely happen during Tommy and Sam's next geocache hunt?

a. Tommy will find the next geocache since Sam found this one.
b. Mr. Jones will not need to use his GPS to help locate the geocache.
c. Sam will be upset if someone else finds the geocache.
d. The next geocache will have an item that gets traded.

9. Which event in "Geocaching" marks the climax of the story?

a. When Tommy and his dad pick up Sam
b. When Sam finds the cache under the leaves
c. When Mr. Jones inputs the GPS coordinates
d. When the group sets off to find the next cache

10. Part A: Based on paragraphs 7 and 8, what conclusion can the reader make about geocaching?

a. Only one cache was hidden in the park where the group searched.
b. All caches are the same size.
c. Caches are most often hidden in parks.
d. Using GPS coordinates may not take someone to the exact location of a cache.

Part B: Which of the following lines from the passage supports the answer to Part A?

a. "Our GPS is accurate to 15 feet, Sam, which means that the cache container is within 15 feet of Dad right now but in any direction."
b. The GPS led the trio to a small parking area just inside the local park, where they stopped and got their backpacks on.
c. "The cache is medium sized, Sam, so be looking for something like the plastic boxes your mom puts leftovers in, okay?"
d. They also sprayed themselves with bug spray and reset the GPS for off-road walking.

11. Which of the following gives the best summary of "Geocaching"?

a. Sam does not want to go geocaching because he does not know how, but Tommy convinces him to try it out. Mr. Jones explains geocaching to Sam on the drive to the park. Once Sam finds the first geocache, he is eager to find more.
b. Tommy invites Sam to go geocaching with him and his dad. Sam is new to geocaching and does not fully understand how it works at first, but he is excited after he finds the first cache. Sam gets to trade items in the cache, and the group sets off for the next one.
c. Tommy and his dad, Mr. Jones, pick up Sam on a Saturday morning for an adventure. Mr. Jones explains geocaching to Sam, who selects a water gun to place in the cache he finds and takes a rubber bouncy ball in return.
d. Sam, Tommy, and Mr. Jones walk through a local park with their backpacks and happen to find a treasure. The treasure was hidden under a pile of leaves by a log. They discover that it is a geocache and decide to try to find another one.

12. At the beginning of the passage, Sam is confused about what geocaching is. He complains that he does not see anything when the group arrives at the GPS coordinates. How do Sam's responses help develop the story's plot?

a. They give Sam a reason to be excited when he is the one to find the cache.
b. They show that Sam is reliant on the help of others when geocaching.
c. They highlight the value of the treasured items that Sam selects for the cache.
d. They explain why Sam has never been geocaching before.

13. Why did Mr. Jones and the boys hide the cache back where they found it in paragraph 9?

a. They did not have room in their packs to take the cache with them.
b. They did not like the treasure that was in the cache.
c. They wanted other geocachers to also have the chance to find the treasure.
d. They wanted to confuse other geocachers.

14. The word *geocaching* uses the prefix *geo-*, which comes from Greek and means *earth*. Based on this information and the passage, what is the meaning of the word *geocache*?

a. A container that is made from natural materials
b. An object that is hidden somewhere outdoors
c. A treasured object that is buried in the earth
d. An object that tells people where they are on Earth

15. Why would the passage "Geocaching" be best described as realistic fiction?

a. The story imagines how a historical event could have happened.
b. The story centers around an unexplained event.
c. The story could happen in real life to real people.
d. The story involves a crime that needs to be solved.

16. What does the third-person omniscient point of view allow the reader to understand?

a. There is a process to follow and gear needed for geocaching.
b. Sam became excited after finding the first cache of the day.
c. Sam was confused before the hunt, and Mr. Jones knew this.
d. It is valuable to use GPS coordinates to locate a cache.

Refer to the passage "Living on a Ranch" to answer questions 17-19.

Living on a Ranch

(1) Marcus Morgan lives in Laramie, Wyoming with his family. Laramie is between the Snowy Mountain Range and the Laramie Mountain Range, west of Cheyenne, Wyoming.

(2) Marcus and his family own a large cattle ranch outside of the city along U.S. Route 287. The Bar M Bar Ranch raises both beef and dairy cattle, along with a small herd of sheep. Mrs. Morgan keeps chickens and tends a small garden to feed the family. Marcus and his two brothers, James and Robert, have to help with chores and taking care of the animals.

(3) Life starts early on the ranch. Mrs. Morgan rings the bell to bring everyone in for breakfast at 4:30 am. The family eats breakfast with the ranch hands, and then the boys do their morning chores before heading off to school. When the boys return from school, they have more chores to complete before dinner and homework time.

(4) Everyone has a job on the ranch. Mr. Morgan supervises the ranch hands, oversees repairs, and takes care of all the vehicles on the ranch. Mrs. Morgan is in

charge of paying the bills and making sure everyone is fed. Marcus, at 15 years old, is the oldest child and has the most responsibility. He has to let the sheep out every morning and bring them back in every evening. He helps in the milking barn or with branding beef cattle when needed. He also takes care of the working dogs used all over the ranch. James gathers eggs, brings in a fresh pail of milk every morning, and cleans out horse stalls in the evenings. Robert, the baby of the family, helps his mom around the house and in the garden.

(5) Marcus especially likes working with the sheep. In the mornings, he and his favorite working dog, Shep, run the sheep out of their corral into the big pasture so they can graze. Marcus uses whistles and calls to tell Shep where he wants the sheep to go, and Shep herds them. In the evenings, Marcus and Shep round up the sheep from the pasture and return them to the corral. Then, Marcus must feed the sheep and check them for injuries. In the spring, Marcus and Shep help Mr. Morgan bring the sheep into the shearing shed one at a time to have their wool sheared.

17. Which two conclusions about the ranch are supported by the information in the passage? Select all that may apply.

a. People come to the ranch to buy cattle for beef and dairy.
b. The ranch is a family business.
c. There are more sheep than cattle on the ranch.
d. All the animals on the ranch are used for food.
e. Both people and animals have specific jobs on the ranch.

18. Which sentence best explains the role of the sheep on the Bar M Bar Ranch?

a. The Bar M Bar Ranch raises both beef and dairy cattle, along with a small herd of sheep.
b. He has to let the sheep out every morning and bring them back in every evening.
c. Then, Marcus must feed the sheep and check them for injuries.
d. In the spring, Marcus and Shep help Mr. Morgan bring the sheep into the shearing shed one at a time to have their wool sheared.

19. Which of the following describes the author's purpose for writing "Living on a Ranch"?

a. To explain Marcus' relationship with his brothers
b. To describe the hard work of living on a ranch
c. To argue that cows are the most useful animal on the ranch
d. To highlight the role of the working dogs on the ranch

Refer to the passage "Island Ponies" to answer questions 20-24.

Island Ponies

(1) Assateague Island is on the east coast. It is a long, thin island. It is so long that two-thirds of it is in Maryland and one-third in Virginia. The Maryland end of the island contains the majority of the Assateague National Seashore and Assateague Park. The southern end of the island, in Virginia, contains the Chincoteague National Wildlife Refuge.

(2) Two herds of wild ponies live on this island. The ponies that live in Maryland are called the Assateague horses, and the ponies that live in Virginia are called the Chincoteague ponies. Standing only an average of 13.2 hands high, or 54 inches, they are considered ponies because of how short they are. Both herds look alike, too. The

ponies can be either solid colored or pinto patterned. The two herds are the same breed of horse, but they are treated very differently.

(3) The Assateague horses are considered wild animals. Unless there is a dire need, they are left alone to survive on the poor habitat available on the Assateague National Seashore. The rangers do not give them veterinarian checkups, teach them to ride, or teach them to enjoy being around humans. They live as they have since the first ponies came to the island after a Spanish galleon sank off the coast in the 1500s.

(4) A veterinarian, however, checks the Chincoteague ponies twice a year. They are given shots that help keep them healthy despite the poor vegetation on the island. The Virginia ponies are used to people because of this treatment. The Chincoteague herd is managed by the Chincoteague Volunteer Fire Department, which holds a very special pony sale every year.

(5) Assateague Island isn't very large, so the herds have to be kept small so they have enough food and room. Both herds average 150 ponies. To keep the Chincoteague herd that small, the Fire Department rounds up the Chincoteague ponies every July by using bigger horses to drive them into the water for the 10-minute swim to Chincoteague Island. Veterinarians check the ponies, and then some of them are sold to spectators who want a pony of their own. The remainder of the herd is allowed to rest, and then they are pushed to swim back to their home island.

(6) The money from this sale helps the Fire Department buy new equipment and pays for the veterinarians who take care of the herd. It also helps to keep people interested in the ponies. So many people come to this sale and love the ponies that there is even a famous children's book about one of the first ponies sold.

20. Which key idea about the Assateague ponies is supported by paragraph 3?

a. The Assateague ponies are an endangered species.
b. The Assateague ponies are smaller than horses.
c. The Assateague ponies do not have much contact with humans.
d. The Assateague ponies are treated better than the Chincoteague ponies.

21. The author's purpose in the way that they organized the passage "Island Ponies" was most likely to:

a. Highlight the differences in the ways people view the two herds of ponies
b. Describe what it is like to encounter the island ponies when they are treated and sold
c. Use a narrative storyline about the ponies' history to entertain the reader
d. Present a solution to how the Chincoteague pony population should be managed

22. Which of the following ideas about the Chincoteague ponies is supported by paragraphs 4 through 6?

a. People think the Chincoteague ponies are special.
b. Buying a Chincoteague pony is expensive.
c. All of the Chincoteague ponies are always healthy.
d. Chincoteague ponies are not used to being around humans.

23. The main idea of "Island Ponies" is best shown in which sentence?

a. The southern end of the island, in Virginia, has the Chincoteague National Wildlife Refuge.
b. The two herds are the same breed of horse, but they are treated very differently.
c. A veterinarian, however, checks the Chincoteague ponies twice a year.
d. The Assateague horses are considered wild animals.

24. Which of the following describes the organizational pattern the author used in "Island Ponies"?

a. A descriptive pattern to show the step-by-step process veterinarians follow to care for the Chincoteague ponies
b. A cause-and-effect pattern to show how the treatment of the Assateague ponies had caused them to dislike humans
c. A compare-and-contrast pattern to show that the Assateague and Chincoteague ponies are similar but receive different treatment from humans
d. An advantage-and-disadvantage pattern to show the positive and negative effects of buying a Chincoteague pony

Refer to the passages "Living on a Ranch" and "Island Ponies" to answer questions 25-27.

25. How are the animals in "Life on a Ranch" different from the animals in "Island Ponies"?

a. None of the animals in "Life on a Ranch" are sold for money, but all of the animals in "Island Ponies" are.
b. All of the animals in "Life on a Ranch" spend time with humans, but none of the animals in "Island Ponies" do.
c. The animals in "Life on a Ranch" all have a specific purpose in the work of the ranch, but the animals in "Island Ponies" do not have a specific purpose on the island.
d. The animals in "Life on a Ranch" are all used for food, but the animals in "Island Ponies" are not.

26. In what way is the care of the sheep in "Life on a Ranch" similar to the care of the Chincoteague ponies in "Island Ponies"?

a. Both the sheep and the Chincoteague ponies are cared for every day.
b. Both the sheep and the Chincoteague ponies are given special food to eat.
c. Both the sheep and the Chincoteague ponies are usually left alone.
d. Both the sheep and the Chincoteague ponies are checked so they can stay healthy.

27. What is described by both paragraph 5 in "Life on a Ranch" and paragraph 5 in "Island Ponies"?

a. What it's like to own an animal
b. How each animal finds food
c. A yearly event involving the animals
d. Why the animals enjoy being around humans

Refer to the passage "Weather Can Be Dangerous" to answer questions 28-36.

Weather Can Be Dangerous

(1) Have you ever thought about just how powerful the weather can be? Well, for starters, consider this: weather helps you decide what to wear each day, what activities to participate in, and even when or if to travel.

(2) Think about your clothing. If the weather is going to be warm, you would probably dress in short sleeves. But if it's going to be cooler, you'd probably grab a jacket on your way out. If it's going to be rainy, you wouldn't wear your favorite shoes. And how about your daily activities? Would you go snow skiing in the middle of summer? Or swimming during a snowstorm? And how often do we hear of flights being canceled due to weather?

(3) At times, though, there is much more to the weather than deciding what shirt to wear. Weather can be destructive, dangerous, and deadly.

Floods

(4) Has it ever flooded in your area? According to statistics from flood experts, flooding occurs in all 50 states. It is the number one natural disaster in the country and accounts for many deaths per year across America. Flash floods can produce surges of water 10 to 20 feet high. However, it doesn't take 10 or 20 feet of water to be dangerous. In fact, just a few feet of water can easily sweep a car away, and even a few inches of water can cause major damage to your home.

Hurricanes

(5) A hurricane is another kind of natural disaster that can have staggering effects on people and their lives. The weather service began recording hurricanes in 1851 and continues to record them today. Hurricanes are destructive storms that begin over the ocean but often move over the land. They are marked by their vicious winds of 74 miles per hour or higher and torrential rains that can last for days. These terrible storms can cause flooding, power outages, and contamination of a city's drinking water. One of the worst hurricanes in history, known as "the Great

Storm of 1900," hit Galveston Island, Texas on September 8, 1900. This horrible storm was responsible for over 6,000 deaths.

Photograph of a house displaced during The Great Storm of 1900

Blizzards

(6) In many parts of the United States, blizzards can cause big problems. A blizzard is defined as a storm with driving snow, strong winds, and intense cold. These storms usually last for a prolonged time and affect a wide area. Blizzards can cause power outages, plumbing problems, and hazards from downed power lines. They can make driving, or even leaving your house, impossible. The extreme temperatures during a blizzard can be deadly for people or animals caught outside.

Tornadoes

(7) Have you ever heard of "Tornado Alley?" "Tornado Alley" refers to an area in the middle of the United States, including South Dakota, Nebraska, Kansas, Missouri, Oklahoma, Arkansas, Louisiana, and parts of North Dakota, Minnesota, Iowa, Ohio, Indiana, Illinois, Indiana, Kentucky, Tennessee, and Texas. In this "alley," conditions are often right for a tornado, a violent and destructive windstorm characterized by a funnel-shaped cloud that spins. Tornado winds can range in speed from around 50 to 300 miles per hour and can lift objects thousands of feet into the air and drop them miles away. One of the most dangerous things about tornadoes is that they often form with little or no warning, making getting to safety more difficult than with hurricanes.

(8) Weather can be very pleasant, like on lazy rainy days or when there's just enough snow that school gets canceled. However, we should never forget that it can also be very extreme and put people's lives in danger. It is important to know what is going on with the weather in your area and what to do to stay safe in extreme weather conditions. Don't ever underestimate how destructive the weather can be.

28. What did the author intend to show the reader by including the photograph following paragraph 5?

a. The amount of damage that was caused by the Great Storm of 1900
b. That the Great Storm of 1900 was even worse than described
c. How unprepared Galveston was for the Great Storm of 1900
d. The way that Galveston recovered from the Great Storm of 1900

29. Which of the above definitions (adapted from Merriam-Webster) matches the meaning of the word *sweep* as it is used in paragraph 4?

Sweep (*noun*) pronounced: swēp 1. to remove with a broom or a brush 2. to remove with a single, forceful action 3. to win an overwhelming victory 4. to extend in a wide curve or range

a. Definition 1
b. Definition 2
c. Definition 3
d. Definition 4

30. Based on the ideas in paragraph 8, what can the reader infer?

a. Taking safety measures can protect people from the effects of extreme weather.
b. Safety measures can keep people's houses from being destroyed during extreme weather.
c. Being aware of extreme weather is a safety measure that protects people and their homes.
d. The right safety measures can prevent extreme weather from developing in an area.

31. Which sentence from the passage shows that natural disasters can easily cause damage?

a. Well, for starters, consider this: weather helps you decide what to wear each day, what activities to participate in, and even when or if to travel.
b. In fact, just a few feet of water can easily sweep a car away, and even a few inches of water can cause major damage to your home.
c. They are marked by their vicious winds of 74 miles per hour or higher and torrential rains that can last for days.
d. However, we should never forget that it can also be very extreme and put people's lives in danger.

32. The details about hurricanes in paragraph 5 support which key idea of the passage?

a. Hurricanes are the most dangerous natural disaster.
b. A hurricane can only affect an isolated area.
c. Natural disasters can have a serious impact on an area.
d. Heavy rain is a common feature of natural disasters

33. What is the main theme of this article?

a. There are many different kinds of weather.
b. It's important to keep in mind how deadly natural disasters can be.
c. Hurricanes and tornadoes have a lot in common.
d. Though natural disasters are possible, they are uncommon.

34. Which two of the following sentences support the controlling idea that natural disasters can be dangerous? Select all that may apply.

a. This horrible storm was responsible for over 6,000 deaths.
b. According to statistics from flood experts, flooding occurs in all 50 states.
c. A hurricane is another kind of natural disaster that can have staggering effects on people and their lives.
d. The extreme temperatures during a blizzard can be deadly for people or animals caught outside.
e. In this "alley," conditions are often right for a tornado, a violent and destructive windstorm characterized by a funnel-shaped cloud that spins.

35. Based on the information in the passage, what can be concluded about natural disasters?

a. Natural disasters happen with no warning and in random areas.
b. Natural disasters develop due to normal, daily weather patterns.
c. Natural disasters do not occur every time rain, snow, or strong wind occurs.
d. Natural disasters occur at the same time in the same place every year.

36. What is the most likely reason that the author wrote this article?

a. To explain to readers how they can prepare for an upcoming extreme weather event
b. To tell readers why extreme weather events can be dangerous
c. To convince readers to make a plan for staying safe during extreme weather
d. To describe the effects of extreme weather events in America's history

Refer to the passage "A Call for Canines" to answer questions 37-42.

A Call for Canines

(1) Dogs truly are man's best friend, and getting one comes with a lot of responsibility. However, the responsibility that comes with dog ownership is not a bad thing. It is actually an opportunity for kids to learn how to be responsible. In fact, having a dog can teach a child many valuable lessons. More parents should allow their child to have a dog so that they can learn these lessons in a fun, safe way.

(2) The biggest lesson a child can learn through having a dog is responsibility. Dogs need food, water, exercise, attention, and a place to relieve themselves. A child must remember to provide these things for the dog so that the dog stays happy and healthy. Dogs must learn that they cannot bite people, eat things that are not good for them, or destroy things. A child must pay attention to the dog, and possibly train it, to help it learn to behave well and get used to a new environment. Overall, dogs can help children learn to be selfless and responsible because they require them to choose to care for a pet instead of doing other activities they may prefer.

(3) Another reason that children should be allowed to have dogs is that it is a safe way for children to learn to be responsible. If the child fails to give the dog what it needs, the child can see the real consequences of their actions. This can be an opportunity for parents to tell their child what they did wrong and help them learn the consequences in a safe way. For example, once when I was young, my brother was watching television and forgot to take his dog for a walk. The dog made a mess in the house because he needed exercise and attention. Once my brother learned what had happened, he had to clean up the mess. However, he never forgot to take the dog for a walk again after that day. The consequences of his poor choice were

easily fixed, and no one was hurt. He was able to learn a lesson without having to face serious consequences.

(4) Caring for a dog is also a fun and memorable way for children to learn how to be responsible. Dogs usually love to play and are often very affectionate, and most children enjoy petting and playing with dogs. Because children often enjoy and love their dogs, they are more likely to want to care for them. When a dog whines because it is hungry or wants attention, the child will want to make the dog happy by giving it what it needs. The child's love for the dog can also help them remember the lessons they learn as they care for it. Lessons about responsibility or uninteresting tasks that teach it are likely to be forgotten by a child. However, the child will remember both the good and bad memories they make with a beloved pet.

(5) Some may argue that getting a pet that is easier to care for, like a fish, will bring their child the same benefits with fewer risks. However, a fish will not love the child the way that a dog will. This means that the child will not bond with a fish the way he or she would with a dog. This can cause the child to be less invested in caring for the fish. The child will have a less memorable experience with the fish, so he or she may not remember the lessons that come with caring for it. Additionally, caring for a fish requires a lot less responsibility than caring for a dog. A fish will not teach a child the same lessons or make them as memorable as a dog will.

(6) Caring for a dog is one of the best ways to teach a child how to be responsible. Children must put forth effort to care for a dog, and they will see real consequences when they choose not to. They will also learn to be selfless because they will truly care for and love the dog. This will also help the child remember the lessons he or she has learned. Allowing a child to get a dog clearly has great benefits for the child's growth. Parents, what are you waiting for?

37. How does the author support the claims in paragraph 3?

a. By quoting an expert that agrees that children can learn from dogs
b. By telling a personal story that shows a child learning to be responsible
c. By providing statistics that show that adults remember their childhood dogs
d. By giving examples of lessons that children can learn from caring for a dog

38. Which sentence from the passage supports the idea that caring for a dog can be fun?

a. A child must pay attention to the dog, and possibly train it, to help it learn to behave well and get used to a new environment.
b. If the child fails to give the dog what it needs, the child can see the real consequences of their actions.
c. Dogs usually love to play and are often very affectionate, and most children enjoy petting and playing with dogs.
d. The child's love for the dog can also help them remember the lessons they learn as they care for it.

39. Which of the following best states the claim the author is making in "A Call for Canines"?

a. Dogs are the best pets because they are fun to play with and come with few risks.
b. Fish are only good pets for adults because children are easily bored by them.
c. Children should be allowed to have dogs so they can learn responsibility.
d. Responsibility must be learned using lessons and activities that are safe and fun.

40. Read the last sentence of the passage:

Parents, what are you waiting for?

Why did the author end the passage with this rhetorical question?

a. To invite parents to share their reasons for not getting their child a dog
b. To show parents that they have been convinced to get their child a dog
c. To help parents begin looking for a dog to get their child
d. To encourage parents to choose to get a dog for their child

41. In Latin, *bene* means *well*. Considering this, what is the meaning of the word *benefits* in paragraph 5?

a. Effects that are good for a person or thing
b. The possibility that something will go wrong
c. Actions that have no clear result
d. Pets that are healthy and well behaved

42. Which of the following sentences would be best to include in a summary of this essay?

a. Caring for a dog teaches children responsibility.
b. Dogs may need training to get used to a new space.
c. Most messes made by dogs can be cleaned up easily.
d. Fish do not need as much attention as dogs do.

Answers and Explanations for Reading Test #1

1. C: Fog can make it difficult to see things that are far away, and it can make nearby objects look different than they normally do. This means that, in line 8, the word *distorts* is most like the word *changes*. Choice C is correct. Because distorts is used to describe an effect on a person's vision, not hearing, choice A is incorrect. The fog's effects do not improve, or sharpen, a person's vision, so choice B is incorrect. The fog changes the way things look but does not stop a person from seeing everything, so choice D is incorrect.

2. C: The poet uses a metaphor in line 2 by calling fog a 'dense, gray blanket.' The poet says this because fog often looks like a thick layer, or like a covering over an area. It is also usually thick enough to make things hard to see. These characteristics of fog are similar to a dense blanket, so choice C is correct. While the poem describes the fog as eerie and haunting in lines 5 and 10, the metaphor in line 2 does not compare the fog to a ghost, so choice A is incorrect. The fog does have dialogue later in the poem. However, comparing the fog to a blanket does not describe the noises it can make, so choice B is incorrect. Line 2 does not describe the fog's movement, so choice D is incorrect.

3. D: The poem says that fog "fades as quickly as it came," which shows that the effects it has are not permanent. This means that choice D is correct. Although the poem says that fog "smothers landscapes," the poem does not suggest that fog is deadly. Additionally, the rest of the poem describes fog as sneaky, not dangerous, so choice A is incorrect. Since fog "smothers landscapes," it does not only occur near water, so choice B is incorrect. The poem does not explain how often fog appears, so choice C is incorrect.

4. A: The fog is described using multiple words that are associated with mystery, such as *eerie, haunting*, and *creeps*. The poem has a mysterious theme, and the fog is portrayed as a traveler, so choice A is correct. Though the poem says that fog "seeps in from the sea," the poem does not include details that suggest it takes place on an island, so choice B is incorrect. Choice C is incorrect because the poem describes fog, not any other type of cloudy weather. Choice D is incorrect because the poem only describes the qualities of fog. It does not give a scientific explanation of fog.

5. B: In the last line, the poet describes how quickly fog goes away. By using only two lines at the end of the poem, instead of four, the poet leads the reader to read the last stanza quickly. This illustrates how rapidly fog disappears, so choice B is correct. The poem does not suggest that fog is boring. Additionally, a poet would most likely use long lines or stanzas to show this, so choice A is incorrect. The fog is described as thick, not thin, so choice C is incorrect. The fog's desires are not described in the poem. Since the words in the poem do not support this idea, choice D is incorrect.

6. D: Something that "distorts the vision" would make it difficult to see things, so choice D is correct. The line "clutching rooftops, climbing trees" describes how fog appears to move, not how it affects a person's vision. This makes choice A incorrect. The line "it fills the mind and fools the feet" shows that fog can confuse people or cause them to get lost. While this may be caused by the fog's effect on a person's vision, it does not directly describe an impact on vision. Choice B is incorrect. The line "its eerie whisper fills the land" describes what sounds might come with fog but not how fog impacts vision, so choice C is incorrect.

7. A: Fog is not something that can be caught. The fog teases the readers by telling them to catch it, even though they cannot. This shows that the fog is fleeting, or temporary. Additionally, the poet says that the fog does this using an "eerie whisper." *Eerie* is similar to *mysterious* or *creepy*, so the fog's eerie whisper and its words create a tone of mystery. Choice A is correct. Choice B is incorrect because these lines do not show that fog looks or behaves in a dark way. The poem also does not have a sad tone. The fog's speech in these lines is not friendly since it taunts the readers. Also, the overall tone of the poem is not hopeful, so choice C is incorrect. Fog gives the reader an impossible task, but not a dangerous one. Additionally, the poem does not have a cautionary tone, so choice D is incorrect.

8. D: Paragraph 3 lists the items that Tommy and his dad packed to put in the geocaches. Paragraph 9 explains that Sam got to choose an item to trade since he found the first geocache. These events show that items are traded as part of each geocache hunt. Choice D is correct because it is reasonable to predict that another item will be traded when they find another geocache. There is no reason to predict that the boys will find an equal number of geocaches, so choice A is incorrect. In paragraph 5, Mr. Jones explains that coordinates for each geocache are input into a GPS. This is a necessary step for finding a geocache, so choice B is incorrect. The passage does not include information that suggests that Sam would be upset if someone else found the geocache. Additionally, paragraph 2 says Sam always has fun with Tommy and his dad. These facts show that choice C is incorrect.

9. B: Sam finding the cache is the highest point of the plot, or the climax. The events that lead up to this event, the rising action, build suspense and create conflict as Sam experiences geocaching for the first time. The result of the conflict occurs when Sam finds the cache, so choice B is correct. Tommy and his dad picking up Sam is part of the rising action, so choice A is incorrect. The GPS coordinates are part of the rising action, so they are not the climax of the story, and choice C is incorrect. Choice D is incorrect because the group sets off to find the next cache after the climax of the story has occurred.

10. Part A: D: In paragraphs 7 and 8, the GPS only takes Tommy, Mr. Jones, and Sam to the area the cache is in. It does not take them to the exact location. This shows that GPS coordinates may take geocachers near a cache, but not to its exact location, so choice D is correct. The reader cannot conclude that only one cache was hidden in the park where the group searched. At the beginning of the story, Mr. Jones explained to Tommy that he had found a couple of new geocaches to hunt for, so choice A is incorrect. The cache is described as "medium sized." This shows that other caches may be smaller or larger, so choice B is incorrect. Although the cache in the story was found in a park, these paragraphs do not support the idea that parks are the most common locations for geocaches, so choice C is incorrect.

Part B: A: Choice A is correct because it shows that the GPS is not completely accurate and that geocachers may have to look around for the cache. Choice B is incorrect because it simply describes the first place that the GPS led them to. In this sentence, the GPS is still leading them to the cache. So, this sentence does not show how close the GPS led them to the cache. Choice C is incorrect because it describes the size of the cache. This sentence does not give the reader any information about the accuracy of the GPS. Choice D is incorrect because it describes the trio's actions. It does not show the reader how close the GPS will get them to the cache.

11. B: The summary in choice B most accurately describes the story's events in the order that they happened, so it is correct. Choice A is incorrect because the passage shows that Sam wanted to go geocaching, even though he did not know what it was. Choice C is incorrect because it only includes minor details and does not accurately describe the main conflict of the story. Choice D is incorrect because it suggests that the trio was not looking for a geocache and only found it by accident.

12. A: Sam does not fully understand geocaching at first, and he is confused by the activity. When he finds the cache, he understands why the activity is fun and becomes excited, so choice A is correct. This event is the resolution of the story's conflict. While Mr. Jones and Tommy helped Sam understand how to find the cache, the story is not about Sam's reliance on others, so choice B is incorrect. Sam selecting an item for the cache is a minor detail in the story and does not affect the plot, so choice C is incorrect. The passage does not tell the reader why Sam has never been geocaching before, so choice D is incorrect.

13. C: Mr. Jones says that geocaching is "a giant worldwide treasure hunt" where containers are hidden for other people to find. Since Tommy, Mr. Jones, and Sam have found the container and left a prize in it, they want others to also be able to find it, so choice C is correct. The passage does not show that their packs are too full to take the geocache container with them. Additionally, geocaching does not involve taking the entire container, so choice A is incorrect. The passage also does not say that they did not like the treasure in the cache, so choice B is incorrect. Hiding the treasure back where it was found will not confuse others. It will allow other geocachers to use the same GPS coordinates to locate the cache, so choice D is incorrect.

14. B: Since *geo-* means *earth*, then the meaning of the word *geocache* must have something to do with the ground or the outdoors. In the story, Mr. Jones explains that geocaching takes place all over the world. Sam, Tommy, and Mr. Jones are looking for a geocache that is hidden outdoors. When they find it, it is a container with objects inside. Choice B describes the object that the trio in the story found. It also is related to the prefix *geo-* since it specifies that the object is outdoors, so choice B is correct. The material that the container is made of is not mentioned in the passage. The prefix *geo-* would only refer to materials that come from the ground, not all natural materials. For these reasons, choice A is incorrect. The object in the story was not buried underground, so choice C is incorrect. The trio was trying to find the location of the object. They did not use it to figure out where they were on Earth, so choice D is incorrect.

15. C: Realistic fiction includes events that could actually occur. Since the events and people in "Geocaching" are not out of the ordinary and could happen in real life, choice C is correct. This story does not imagine a historical event, so choice A is incorrect. A fictional story that involves an unexplained event is a mystery. "Geocaching" is not a mystery, since there are explanations for the events in the story, so choice B is incorrect. No crime occurs in the passage, so choice D is incorrect.

16. C: A third-person omniscient point of view allows the author to include each character's unspoken thoughts and feelings. For example, in paragraph 2, the author tells the reader that Sam does not understand what geocaching is. Additionally, in paragraph 6, the author tells the reader that Mr. Jones knows Sam is confused and thinks he will catch on, so choice C is correct. The process and gear needed for geocaching could be shown without a third-person omniscient point of view, so choice A is incorrect. Sam's excitement about the cache is shown through Sam's dialogue, so choice B is incorrect. Mr. Jones explains the value of GPS coordinates out loud, so this information would be known if the author had used a first-person point of view. This makes choice D incorrect.

17. B, E: The story describes the job of each Morgan family member on the ranch, and it mentions that the working dogs, such as Shep, also have jobs. Additionally, the passage says that Marcus's family owns the ranch. This information supports the conclusions in choices B and E, so they are correct. Beef and dairy cattle are raised on the ranch, but the passage does not say that people visit the ranch to buy them, so choice A is incorrect. The story also does not tell the reader the number of cattle or sheep at the ranch, only that the sheep herd is small, which makes choice C incorrect. While some of the animals are used for food, such as the cows and chickens, the passage does not suggest that the working dogs and sheep are used for food, so choice D is incorrect.

18. D: The sentence in choice D states that the sheep get their wool sheared every spring. This shows that the role of the sheep is to produce wool, so choice D is correct. Choice A says that sheep live on the ranch, but it is incorrect because it does not show the purpose of the sheep. Choices B and C explain how Marcus takes care of the sheep, but they do not explain the purpose that the sheep on the ranch serve. Choices B and C are incorrect.

19. B: The author provides details about living on a ranch that show the reader that it is hard work, so choice B is correct. These details include the daily jobs each family member has and the early time at which they wake up to start their chores. While the story tells the reader about Marcus' brothers, James and Robert, it does not describe their relationship, so choice A is incorrect. The passage describes the use and importance of other animals, like the sheep and the working dogs. The passage does not argue that cows are the most useful animals on the ranch, so choice C is incorrect. The working dogs' jobs are described in the passage, but the passage is not about the working dogs, so choice D is incorrect.

20. C: Paragraph 3 explains that the Assateague ponies do not have regular contact with rangers and that they live as wild animals. Choice C is correct. The passage does not suggest that the Assateague ponies are endangered, so choice A is incorrect. The size of the Assateague ponies is described in paragraph 2, not paragraph 3, which makes choice B incorrect. Paragraph 3 says the Assateague ponies are "left alone to survive," but it does not compare the treatment of the Assateague and Chincoteague ponies. This makes choice D incorrect.

21. A: The passage begins with general information about the ponies' island habitat and their similar appearances. It then gives specific information describing how the two herds of ponies are treated by humans. This structure shows the reader that even though the ponies are very similar, they are treated differently, so choice A is correct. Choice B is incorrect because the passage does not describe the experience of being near the ponies. The story gives facts about the ponies and is not meant to entertain the reader, so choice C is incorrect. While the Chincoteague pony sale is described in the passage, the author gives information about the Assateague ponies, too, so choice D is incorrect.

22. A: Paragraphs 4 through 6 explain that the Chincoteague ponies can be bought at a special sale, which many people attend each year to see the ponies. This supports choice A, so it is correct. While some details about the sale are described in these paragraphs, the price of the ponies is not described, so choice B is incorrect. While these paragraphs do say that veterinarians check on the ponies and try to keep them healthy, they do not suggest that the ponies never become ill. This makes choice C incorrect. Choice D is incorrect because these paragraphs state that the Chincoteague ponies are used to being around humans because of the visits from veterinarians.

23. B: The passage shows that, even though the ponies live on the same island and look alike, the Assateague ponies are left alone and the Chincoteague ponies are treated by veterinarians. This is summarized in choice B, so it is the correct answer. While Assateague Island is where both types of ponies live, the island itself is not the main topic of the passage, so choice A is incorrect. The fact that the Chincoteague ponies receive checkups from a veterinarian shows how they are cared for, but it is not the main idea of the passage, so choice C is incorrect. The passage is about both groups of horses, not just the Assateague horses, so choice D is incorrect.

24. C: The author describes the similarities between the two herds and the differences in how they are treated. This is done using a compare-and-contrast structure, so choice C is correct. The author describes how the Chincoteague ponies are cared for but does not include a step-by-step process, so choice A incorrect. The passage says that humans have left the Assateague ponies alone. However, the passage does not say that this has caused the Assateague ponies to dislike humans, so choice B is incorrect. Choice D is incorrect because the passage discusses buying a pony but does not describe the advantages and disadvantages of having one.

25. C: In "Life on a Ranch," each animal has a purpose. For example, the sheep provide wool, the cows provide beef and dairy, and the working dogs herd sheep. In "Island Ponies," neither type of pony has a specific purpose on the island, so choice C is correct. Choice A is incorrect because "Life on a Ranch" does not explain whether or not the animals are sold for money. Additionally, in "Island Ponies," the Assateague ponies are not sold for money, only the Chincoteague ponies are. The reader can infer that the animals in "Life on a Ranch" all spend time with humans because the animals belong to the Morgan family and are cared for by the family. The Chincoteague ponies are similar, as many people come to the pony sale to look at and buy them, so choice B is incorrect. Choice D is incorrect because not all of the animals in "Life on a Ranch" are used for food, such as the working dogs.

26. D: In "Life on a Ranch," Marcus checks the sheep for injuries as part of his chores every evening. In "Island Ponies," the Chincoteague ponies get checkups from a veterinarian twice a year, so choice D is correct. While the Chincoteague ponies receive care, they do not receive care every day, so choice A is incorrect. Choice B is incorrect since neither passage mentions the type of food that is given to the sheep nor the Chincoteague ponies. Choice C is incorrect because only the Assateague ponies are usually left alone, not the Chincoteague ponies or the sheep.

27. C: Paragraph 5 of "Life on a Ranch" says that the sheep are sheared for their wool every spring. Paragraph 5 of "Island Ponies" states that the ponies are available at a yearly sale every July. This means that choice C is correct. Paragraph 5 of "Island Ponies" does not describe what it is like to own one of the Chincoteague ponies, so choice A is incorrect. Neither passage provides any information about how the animals in the passage find food, so choice B is incorrect. Paragraph 5 of both passages tells the reader about some interaction of the animals with humans. However, paragraph 5 of "Life on a Ranch" does not say that the sheep enjoy being around humans, so choice D is incorrect.

28. A: The image after paragraph 5 is included to give the reader a visualization of the amount of damage that was caused by the Great Storm of 1900. Choice B is incorrect because the photo shows no indication of the storm being worse than it was described. Choice C is incorrect because the photo does not demonstrate how unprepared Galveston was for the storm. Choice D is incorrect because the photo does not show Galveston's recovery process after the storm.

29. B: The previous sentence mentions how even small amounts of water can be "dangerous." This indicates to the reader that the word "sweep" should be used in a negative context. Definition 2 is the only option that is used in such a context.

30. A: Paragraph 8 indicates that it is important to be constantly aware of the weather conditions in your area in order to stay safe. This suggests that knowing how to prepare for certain weather conditions will allow individuals to keep safe and protect themselves in times of extreme weather.

31. B: Choice B states that even the smallest amounts of water in your home can cause costly damage and just a few feet of it can sweep your car completely away. This indicates how easily natural disasters can cause damage to property. Choice A is incorrect because it doesn't mention how natural disasters can cause damage. Choices C and D are incorrect because they are examples of more extreme weather circumstances, so they don't demonstrate that disasters can "easily" cause damage.

32. C: Paragraph 5 explains that hurricanes can cause flooding, power outages, and even contamination of a city's water supply. The author also uses the example of the Great Storm of 1900 to demonstrate that hurricanes may even be deadly. These consequences demonstrate that natural disasters can have serious impacts on an area.

33. B: The article spends time discussing how each type of natural disaster can be dangerous in its own way and emphasizes the importance of being prepared for any natural disaster you may face. Choice A is incorrect because it is not the main topic of the article. Choices C and D are incorrect because the article does not insinuate either statement is true.

34. A, D: Choice A says that a hurricane caused thousands of deaths, which shows that a hurricane can be dangerous. Choice D demonstrates exactly how dangerous natural disasters can be by explaining that if one should get caught out in a blizzard, it could be deadly. Choices B, C, and E do not demonstrate the dangerous effects a natural disaster can have.

35. C: The passage describes the effects of extreme weather conditions that accompany natural disasters. The passage also shows that destruction and danger usually accompany natural disasters. Rainy, snowy, and windy days happen often, but such conditions do not often cause much destruction or danger. Because these conditions can happen without the occurrence of a natural disaster, choice C is correct.

36. B: Throughout the article, the author explains the nature of several natural disasters and describes the negative and dangerous effects they can have on the communities in which they take place. Choices A and C are incorrect because the article fails to provide instructions for how to prepare for a natural disaster. Choice D is incorrect because the article only uses one historical event in paragraph 5 to support its main premise that natural disasters are dangerous.

37. B: In paragraph 3, the author summarizes an event that he or she personally experienced and uses it to support the claims in the paragraph. This means that choice B is correct since the author included a personal story. There are no quotes from experts or statistics included in the passage, so choices A and C are incorrect. The author does not list specific lessons that children can learn from caring for a dog. The author only mentions one lesson in the personal story, so choice D is incorrect.

38. C: The sentence in choice C says that dogs like to play and that children enjoy playing with them. Most children would say that playing with a dog is fun, so choice C is correct. Choice A only describes a couple of responsibilities that come with owning a dog. These are not clearly fun activities, so choice A is incorrect. Choice B explains why owning a dog can teach children about consequences. This is not an example of having fun with a pet dog, so choice B is incorrect. Choice D explains why a child's love for the dog can impact how well they learn responsibility. This does not describe the activities that are part of caring for a dog, so choice D is incorrect.

39. C: The author uses the information in this essay to prove that owning a dog can help children learn how to be responsible. This is stated in choice C, so it is the correct answer. The author does say that dogs can help children learn responsibility better than other pets can. However, the author does not say that dogs are the best pets in general. The author's claim is also related to how dogs help children learn, not how fun or easy they are to care for, so choice A is incorrect. The essay only mentions fish in paragraph 5, and this paragraph presents a counterargument. This is not the author's claim, so choice B is incorrect. The claim is related to how owning a dog teaches responsibility, not responsibility in general, so choice D is incorrect.

40. D: This rhetorical question asks parents why they have not allowed their child to have a dog yet. This implies that parents know the reasons that they should allow their child to have a pet dog. The question is meant to encourage parents to decide that their child can have a pet dog, so choice D is correct. The author is not truly asking parents why they have not allowed their child to have a dog. Rhetorical questions are not meant to be answered, so choice A is incorrect. Some parents may read the essay and still not be convinced to allow their child to have a dog, so choice B is incorrect. The essay does not include information about how to search for a dog. The author also does not use the rhetorical question to offer to help parents find a dog for their child, so choice C is incorrect.

41. A: *Well* is a synonym of *good* or *right*. In paragraph 5, the author says that some parents think owning a fish can have the same benefits as owning a dog. It also says that owning a fish has fewer risks than owning dogs. This shows that benefits and risks are opposites. Benefits are something parents want to have, and risks are something they do not want to have. The Latin root in *benefit* and the way it is used in the passage show that a benefit is a good effect. Choice A is correct. Benefits are positive. Something going wrong is usually bad, or negative, and an action with no clear result is neither good nor bad, and neither positive nor negative. This means that choices B and C are incorrect. Benefits are something that can come from owning a pet, but they are not pets, so choice D is incorrect.

42. A: A summary of this passage should mention the author's claim and the main reasons the author gives to support this claim. Choice A restates the author's claim, so it would be an appropriate sentence to include in a summary of this essay. Choices B and C are details that are related to possible problems that may come with owning a dog. These details do not directly support the claim, and they are not among the main reasons the author uses to support the claim. Choices B and C are incorrect. Choice D is a detail from the author's counterargument. This should not be included in a summary of the essay because it does not help the reader understand what the essay is about. Choice D is incorrect.

Language Practice Test #1

Questions 1 – 7 pertain to the following passage:

Masters of the Seas

(1) Pirates have been sailing the seas for thousands of years. (2) The first recorded pirate raids occurred in 735 B.C. (3) During the middle ages, pirates lived mostly in Europe. (4) Later, pirates moved into the Caribbean, the South China Sea, and any other place with ships.

(5) Sometimes noblemen became pirates. (6) Some pirates were escaped slaves or criminals hiding from the law, others were gamblers, rebels, or people seeking adventure. (7) Even a few women were pirates!

(8) In spite of their different backgrounds; all pirates were looking for treasure. (9) They looked for real treasure such as gold, silver, and jewels. (10) They also looked for trading items such as spices, cloth, and tobacco. (11) In addition, pirates looked for useful items like tools, maps, and food.

(12) While many people think of pirates as part of history, there were still pirates on the seas today. (13) Modern pirates sail mostly near the coast of Africa, and they attack tanker ships and merchant ships. (14) Instead of treasure, today pirates ask for ransom money. (15) As long as there are ships sailing. (16) Pirates always will be around.

1. In sentence 3, what change, if any, should be made to the capitalization?

a. No change is necessary
b. Change middle ages to Middle ages
c. Change middle ages to Middle Ages
d. Change middle ages to middle Ages

2. Which sentence is the best choice for the first sentence of paragraph 2?

a. Sometimes noblemen became pirates
b. Although they all raided ships, pirates came from many different backgrounds
c. There were many ships on the seas, especially in the 1700s and 1800s
d. Pirates were very knowledgeable in geography, and they were all excellent sailors

3. What revision, if any, is needed in sentence 6?

a. No revision is necessary
b. Remove the comma between law and others
c. Change the comma between law and others to a semicolon followed by the word and
d. Change the comma between law and others to a period

4. Which change, if any, is needed in sentence 7?

a. No change is necessary
b. Change were to was
c. Change women to woman
d. Change few to several

5. Which of the following choices is the most correct version of sentence 8?

a. In spite of their different backgrounds; all pirates were looking for treasure
b. In spite of their different backgrounds, all pirates were looking for treasure
c. In spite of their different backgrounds. All pirates were looking for treasure
d. In spite of their different backgrounds; and all pirates were looking for treasure

6. Which change, if any, works best in sentence 12?

a. No change is necessary
b. Change were to was
c. Change were to are
d. Change were to is

7. Which revision, if any, is needed in sentences 15 and 16?

a. No revision is necessary
b. As long as there are ships sailing; pirates always will be around
c. As long as there are ships sailing. I think pirates always will be around
d. As long as there are ships sailing, pirates always will be around

Questions 8 – 14 pertain to the following passage:

Alicia wrote this report all about volcanoes. She would like your help revising her report. Read the report and look for places where Alicia could make revisions or improvements. When you are finished reading, answer the questions that follow.

The Power of Volcanoes

(1) The word *volcano* comes from *Vulcan*, the name of the ancient Roman god of fire. (2) A volcano occurs when hot, melted rock called magma breaks through the earth's crust. (3) I once saw a volcano erupt when I was on vacation in Hawaii. (4) When magma comes out on the surface of the earth and it is called lava. (5) Hot lava and ash often explode out of volcanoes, sometimes causing a lot of destruction.

(6) There are four basic types of volcanoes. (7) Shield volcanoes have broad, gentle slopes. (8) Cindercone volcanoes are pointed, kind of like pyramids. (9) Strato-volcanoes have many lairs of rock formed by hardened lava and ash from previous eruptions. (10) Dome volcanoes were shaped like steep mounds and are the result of slow-flowing lava.

(11) Whatever the type, volcanoes happen in places where the plates of the earth's crust touch each other. (12) There are many active volcanoes all over the world. (13) Some is in the United States, in places like Washington, Colorado, and Hawaii. (14) Some volcanoes are even under water, far below the surface of the ocean.

(15) When volcanoes erupt, they can change many things. (16) They can add height to mountains and even form new islands. (17) In Iceland, the island of Surtsey was formed by an erupting volcano in 1963. (18) Volcanoes can also collapse mountains. (19) At Crater Lake in Oregon, where a volcano collapsed a mountain, forming the deepest lake in the United States. (20) No matter their type or effects, everyone must agree that volcanoes are very powerful.

8. In sentence 1, what change, if any, should be made in capitalization?

a. No change is necessary
b. Change ancient Roman god to Ancient Roman God
c. Change ancient Roman god to ancient Roman God
d. Change ancient Roman god to ancient roman god

9. Which sentence does not belong in paragraph 1?

a. Sentence 1
b. Sentence 4
c. Sentence 3
d. Sentence 5

10. What revision, if any, is needed in sentence 4?

a. No revision is needed
b. Replace and with a comma
c Insert a comma before and
d. Replace and with a semicolon

11. Which spelling change is needed in sentence 9?

a. Change volcanoes to volcanos
b. Change previous to pervious
c. Change eruptions to erupshuns
d. Change lairs to layers

12. What revision, if any, is necessary in sentence 10?

a. No revision is necessary
b. Change were to are
c. Change were to was
d. Change were to is

13. Which of the following is the best version of sentence 13?

a. Some is in the United States, in places like Washington, Colorado, and Hawaii
b. Some were in the United States, in places like Washington, Colorado, and Hawaii
c. Some was in the United States, in places like Washington, Colorado, and Hawaii
d. Some are in the United States, in places like Washington, Colorado, and Hawaii

14. Which change, if any, is needed in sentence 19?

a. No change is needed
b. Remove the comma after Oregon
c. Remove the word where
d. Replace the comma after Oregon with a semicolon

Questions 15 – 21 pertain to the following passage:

Down on thc Farm

(1) On the day of the field trip, our classroom was buzzing with excitement. (2) Finally, the time came to get on the bus. (3) I watched out the window as big buildings slipped by, then houses and then fields. (4) The bus turned down a long, gravel driveway and stopped by a big red barn. (5) We were at the farm!

(6) We learned that Farmer Jones and his wife grew corn and pumpkins and raised cows and chickens. (7) First, we took a tour of the farm. (8) They had several farm workers to help take care of the farm. (9) Farmer Jones and his wife also have a small market where they sold there crops and some crops from other farmers who lived nearby.

(10) I loved walking through the cornfield with the dry stalks rustling above my head. (11) Farmer Jones also let me feed a calf from a bottle, and I loved feeling it suck and tug to get at the milk. (12) When we were done seeing the farm. (13) Farmer Jones took us all up to the market for some fresh, hot corn on the cob. (14) It was so yummy!

(15) When the time came to get back on the bus, no one wanted to leave. (16) We thanked Farmer Jones and headed back to town. (17) I loved visiting the farm and seeing how Farmer Jones lived maybe I will decide to be a farmer someday.

15. What spelling change, if any, is needed in sentence 1?

a. No change is needed
b. Change classroom to class room
c. Change buzzing to buzing
d. Change excitement to excitment

16. Which of the following choices is the best version of sentence 3?

a. I watched out the window as big buildings slipped by, then houses and then fields
b. I watched out the window as big buildings slipped by, then houses; and then fields
c. I watched out the window as big buildings slipped by, then houses, and then fields
d. I watched out the window as big buildings slipped by, then houses; then fields

17. Which sentence is the best choice for the first sentence of paragraph 2?

a. Sentence 6
b. Sentence 7
c. Sentence 8
d. Sentence 9

18. Which revision, if any, is needed in sentence 9?

a. No revision is needed
b. Change have to had
c. Change have to has
d. Change have to having

19. Which of the following choices is the proper spelling choice for sentence 9?

a. They're
b. There
c. Thier
d. Their

20. What revision, if any, is needed in sentences 12 and 13?

a. No revision is needed
b. Change the period to a semicolon
c. Add Then at the beginning of sentence 13
d. Change the period to a comma

21. What change, if any, is necessary in sentence 17?

a. No change is necessary
b. Insert a comma after lived
c. Insert a period after lived
d. Insert a semicolon and and after lived

Questions 22 -28 pertain to the following passage:

Some People Never Learn

(1) One lazy Sunday afternoon, all the boys in our neighborhood decide to play football in the big field on the corner. (2) There used to be a gas station there, but a construction company knocked it down. (3) My brother, Seth, went to play, so I went along to watch. (4) It had rained all morning. (5) So the field was muddy and slick. (6) On the second play of the game, a big boy crashed into Seth and knocked him to the ground.

(7) I rushed over to Seth. (8) He was pale and shaking, and he was holding his arm. (9) He told me to run home and get Mom. (10) Mom came with the car, and we help Seth get in and buckle his seatbelt. (11) Then we did drive him to the hospital.

(12) In the emergency room, the doctors and nurses began working on Seth. (13) They sent him for x-rays and gave him some pills to make the pain better. (14) Then a doctor came in and said Seth broke his upper arm. (15) Seth's arm would have to be in a sling for six weeks to help it heal.

(16) For six long weeks, I helped Mom take care of Seth he needed help with almost everything. (17) Lucky for him, he didn't have to do chores for six weeks, and he even got to skip some of his schoolwork. (18) Finally Seth's arm was better, and he could take off the sling. (19) The very next day, Seth was back out in the field playing football. (20) Some people never learn!

22. What change, if any, is needed in sentence 1?

a. No change is needed
b. Change decide to decides
c. Change decide to decided
d. Change decide to deciding

23. Which sentence does not belong in this essay?

a. Sentence 1
b. Sentence 2
c. Sentence 6
d. Sentence 9

24. What revision, if any, is needed in sentences 4 and 5?

a. No revision is needed
b. Replace the period with a comma
c. Replace the period with a semicolon
d. Insert and at the beginning of sentence 5

25. Which change, if any, is needed in sentence 6?

a. No change is needed
b. Insert a comma after Seth
c. Remove the comma after game
d. Insert a semicolon after Seth

26. Which of the following is the most correct version of sentence 11?

a. Then we did drive him to the hospital
b. Then we drived him to the hospital
c. Then we would drive him to the hospital
d. Then we drove him to the hospital

27. What revision, if any, is necessary in sentence 16?

a. No revision is necessary
b. Insert a comma after Seth
c. Remove the comma after weeks
d. Insert a period after Seth

28. What change, if any, is needed in sentence 18?

a. No change is needed
b. Remove the comma after better
c. Insert a comma after Finally
d. Insert a semicolon after better

Answers and Explanations for Language Test #1

1. C: The term *Middle Ages* refers to a specific period in history, and the name of a specific historical period always should be capitalized. Options A, B, and D all offer improper capitalization, making these choices incorrect.

2. B: The topic sentence of a paragraph should introduce the main idea of the paragraph. Option B begins with a transition from paragraph 1 by mentioning that all pirates raid ships. It then introduces the topic of paragraph 2, which discusses the diverse background of pirates. Option A, the current topic sentence, discusses one possible background for pirates, but it does not represent fully the main idea of the paragraph. Options C and D are similar, both discussing an aspect of pirates, but these options do not introduce the overall main idea of paragraph 2.

3. D: Sentence 6 is a type of run-on sentence called a comma splice. It contains two complete sentences joined only by a comma. The best option for correcting this sentence is to replace the comma with a period, creating two separate sentences. Options A and B retain the run-on structure of the sentence, making them incorrect options. Option C uses a semicolon to separate the independent clauses, but it unnecessarily adds the word *and* to the sentence, making it an incorrect option.

4. A: Sentence 7 is correct as it is written. Option B is incorrect because the subject of the sentence is plural, so a plural verb is necessary. Option C is incorrect because the sentence discusses more than one woman, making *women* the correct word choice. Option D is incorrect because changing *few* to *several* creates an awkward and improper sentence.

5. B: The first part of sentence 8 is an introductory phrase, which is dependent, so it cannot stand on its own. A comma is the most appropriate punctuation to join an introductory phrase with its associated independent clause. Options A and D are not correct because a semicolon is not an appropriate punctuation choice for joining an introductory phrase with its associated independent clause. Option C is incorrect because the introductory phrase cannot be followed by a period, since it cannot stand on its own as a sentence.

6. C: Sentence 12 is written in present tense and has a plural subject, so the present tense, plural verb *are* is the best choice for this sentence. Option A is incorrect because it uses a past tense verb when the sentence is written in present tense. Option B is incorrect because it uses a past tense, singular verb when the sentence is written in present tense and the subject is plural. Option D is incorrect because it uses a singular verb when the subject of the sentence is plural.

7. D: Sentence 15 is a sentence fragment. Careful reading shows that the best correction option connects the fragment of sentence 15 to sentence 16 with a comma, creating a single, strong sentence. Option A is incorrect because it retains sentence 15 as a fragment. Option B is incorrect because a semicolon cannot connect a dependent clause to an independent clause. Option C is incorrect because it only adds the words *I think*, retaining sentence 15 as a fragment.

8. A: is the best choice because the current capitalization is correct, since the only proper noun in the sentence is *Roman*. B is not the best choice because it capitalizes *Ancient* and *God*, neither of which are proper nouns in this context. C is not the best choice because it capitalizes *God*, which is not a proper noun in this context. D is not the best choice because it does not capitalize *roman*, which is a proper noun.

9. C: is the best choice because sentence 3 describes a personal experience that does not belong in a factual essay about volcanoes. A, B, and D are not the best choices because sentences 1, 4, and 5 all are essential to develop factual information about volcanoes.

10. B: is the best choice because the sentence contains a dependent introductory clause, and a dependent introductory clause always should be separated from the main clause of the sentence with a comma. A and C are not the best choices because they both create a sentence fragment. C is not the best choice because a semicolon cannot join a dependent clause to an independent clause.

11. D: is the best choice because *layers* is a better word choice than *lairs* in this sentence. A, B, and C are not the best choices because they all change properly spelled words to misspelled versions.

12. B: is the best choice because the subject of the sentence is plural and the essay is written in present tense, making *are* the right choice. A is not the best choice because *were* is a past-tense verb, and this passage is written in present tense. C is not the best choice because *was* is a singular, past-tense verb, and this sentence has a plural subject and is written in present tense. D is not the best choice because *is* is a singular verb, and the subject of this sentence is plural.

13. D: is the best choice because this sentence has a plural subject, and this essay is written in present tense, so *are* is right choice. A is not the best choice because *is* is a singular verb, and the subject of this sentence is plural. B is not the best choice because *were* is a past-tense verb, and this essay is written in present tense. C is not the best choice because *was* is a singular, past-tense verb, and this sentence has a plural subject and is written in present tense.

14. C: is the best choice because removing *where* changes the sentence from a dependent clause to a complete sentence. A, B, and D are not the best choices because they all retain the dependent clause, making the sentence a fragment—thus unable to stand on its own.

15. A: is the best choice because there are no misspelled words in the sentence. B, C, and D are not the best choices because they all change properly spelled words to misspelled versions.

16. C: is the best option because items in a series always should be separated by commas, including a comma just before the conjunction. A is not the best choice because it omits the comma before the conjunction. B and D are not the best choices because they both improperly use a semicolon to separate items in a series when those items contain no internal commas.

17. B: is the best choice because it clearly establishes the overall topic of the paragraph, which is what the topic sentence of a paragraph should do. A, C, and D are not the best choices because they all offer details and specifics instead of establishing a broad overview of the paragraph.

18. B: is the best choice because this essay is written in past tense. A and C are not the best choices because *have* and *has* are both present-tense verbs, and this essay is written in past tense. D is not the best choice because *having* is a gerund form of the verb and is inappropriate for this sentence.

19. D: is the best choice because *their* is the proper spelling for a plural personal pronoun showing ownership. A is not the best choice because *they're* is a contraction for *they are*, which does not fit in the sentence. B is not the best choice, because *there* refers to location, which does not fit in the sentence. C is not the best choice because it is misspelled.

20. D: is the best choice because sentence 12 actually is a dependent clause that should function as an introductory element to the independent clause in sentence 13, and an introductory dependent clause should be joined to the corresponding independent clause with a comma. A and C are not the best choices because they retain sentence 12 as a sentence fragment. B is not the best choice because a semicolon should not join a dependent clause to an independent clause.

21. C: is the best choice because adding a period eliminates the run-on sentence by creating two complete sentences. A is not the best choice because it retains the run-on sentence structure. B is not the best choice because it creates a comma splice, another type of run-on sentence. D is not the best choice because a semicolon should not be used with a conjunction to join two independent clauses.

22. C: is the best choice because *decided* is a past-tense verb, and this passage is written in past tense. A is not the best choice because *decide* is a present-tense verb, and this passage is written in past tense. B is not the best choice because *decides* is a singular, present-tense verb, and this sentence has a plural subject and is written in past tense. D is not the best choice because *deciding* is a gerund form of the verb, which is not appropriate in this sentence.

23. B: is the best choice because sentence 2 gives unnecessary details unrelated to the progression of this story. A, C, and D are not the best choices because sentences 1, 6, and 9 all offer relevant information important to the development of the story.

24. B: is the best choice because sentence 5 is a dependent clause that needs to be combined with sentence 4 through the use of a comma to form a complete sentence. A and D are not the best choices because they both retain sentence 5 as a sentence fragment. C is not the best choice because a semicolon should not join an independent clause to a dependent clause.

25. A: is the best choice because the sentence is correct as written. B is not the best choice because it inserts an unnecessary and incorrect comma. C is not the best choice because it deletes the necessary comma after the introductory phrase. D is not the best choice because it inserts an unnecessary and incorrect semicolon.

26. D: is the best choice because it uses the simple past-tense verb *drove*, which is appropriate for this story, since it is written in past tense. A and B are not the best choices because they both use awkward and incorrect verb forms. C is not the best choice because *would drive* is a future-tense verb, and this story is written in past tense.

27. D: is the best choice because it eliminates the run-on sentence and creates two complete sentences. A and C are not the best choices because they both retain the run-on sentence structure. B is not the best choice because separating two independent clauses with only a comma creates a comma splice, a type of run-on sentence.

28. C: is the best choice because *Finally* is an introductory word in this sentence, so it should be separated from the rest of the sentence with a comma. A is not the best choice because it does not separate the introductory word from the rest of the sentence. B is not the best choice because it removes the necessary comma separating two independent clauses joined by a coordinating conjunction. D is not the best choice because a semicolon should not be used with a coordinating conjunction to join two independent clauses.

Reading Practice Test #2

Refer to the passage "The Talent Show" to answer questions 1-4.

The Talent Show

(1) The first notes floated from the piano. Megan smiled, warm and excited beneath the glaring stage lights. This was her moment. She had practiced. She had prepared. She was ready. As the introduction ended, Megan opened her mouth and began to sing.

(2) The song flowed along, and Megan relaxed, scanning the faces of the audience. But somewhere in the middle of the second verse, her mind suddenly went blank. The music went on, but the words were gone. Megan's smile faded. She stood silently with her mouth hanging open. When the music finally trickled to a stop, Megan ran from the stage.

(3) In a cramped dressing room backstage, Megan buried her face in her hands. She had wanted so much to win this talent show. Tears seeped between her fingers. Her confidence, pride, and excitement had been replaced by utter disappointment. She felt a hand on her shoulder and lifted her damp face.

(4) "Ella and Kaylee are here," Megan's mom said, giving her shoulder a quick squeeze.

(5) Ella and Kaylee, Megan's two best friends, pulled folding chairs over to face Megan. She looked at them forlornly.

(6) "I'm a total failure," she moaned.

(7) Ella and Kaylee exchanged glances. Kaylee reached out and squeezed Megan's hand.

(8) "What are you talking about?" Kaylee said. "That first verse was some of your best singing ever."

(9) "Thanks," Megan said. "But the problem is that the first verse is all I sang. Then I totally bombed. I can't believe I forgot the words after all that practice."

(10) "You didn't totally bomb," Ella said. "You just forgot the words. That happens to everybody. Besides, don't the pros say you should leave your audience wanting more?"

(11) "I guess so," Megan admitted.

(12) "Well, trust me," Ella said. "I guarantee they wanted more—like the rest of the song! You probably did, too."

(13) Megan smiled a little. "So, you guys don't think I'm a total dork for forgetting the words?"

(14) "Of course not," Kaylee said. "Forgetting the words doesn't make you a dork. It just makes you human. And you're still the most talented person I know."

(15) Ella nodded in agreement. Megan pulled Ella and Kaylee into a quick hug. Then she wiped her eyes and managed to give a genuine smile.

(16) "I'm so lucky to have best friends like you two," Megan said. "It's nice to know that you'll be my friends forever, no matter what!"

1. What is the main theme of this story?

a. Real friends support you, no matter what.
b. It is easy to forget the words of a song.
c. Performing in a talent show can be embarrassing.
d. Megan feels like a failure.

2. Why does Kaylee say what she says in paragraph 8?

a. To cheer Megan up by making a joke about her performance
b. To make Megan feel better about what she did sing
c. To distract Megan from the fact that she did not finish the song
d. To help Megan forget that she did not finish the song

3. Which of the following facts about the story shows that it is realistic fiction?

a. The story's setting is not described using many details.
b. All of the story's main characters have dialogue.
c. The story has a beginning, a middle, and an end.
d. The events in the story are possible and likely to happen.

4. How do the events in paragraph 2 contribute to the conflict of the story?

a. They show why Megan thought she would win the talent show.
b. They show why Megan became upset and hid backstage.
c. They show why Megan was avoiding Ella and Kaylee.
d. They show why Megan forgot the words to the song she was singing.

Refer to the passage "The Tournament" to answer questions 5-7.

The Tournament

(1) Looking for a hole in the defense, Scott dribbled the ball, shifting it from hand to hand. A trickle of sweat ran down his back. No one was open. There were only seconds left on the clock, and Scott knew he had a difficult decision to make.

(2) The other team was leading by two points, and Scott was just outside the three-point line. If he could make the shot, the Eagles would be state champions again. But if he missed ... Scott didn't want to think about that. He knew what he had to do.

(3) It was a classic jump shot. The ball left his hands and sailed toward the basket in a perfect arc. The crowd, the other players, and the whole stadium seemed frozen in time. All eyes were on the ball as it struck the rim and bounced off. The buzzer blared. The game was over. Scott had missed, and the Eagles had lost.

(4) Scott became a statue on the court as people surged around him. Elated family members swarmed the winning team. Teammates hugged and slapped each other on the back. Even Scott's teammates joined in the celebration.

(5) Suddenly, Scott felt himself being hoisted unsteadily onto the shoulders of his friends. Over the loudspeaker, the announcer proclaimed that Scott had been named the most valuable player of the championship game. Everyone cheered, and the Eagles took a victory lap with Scott on their shoulders. Finally, Scott's friends put him back on solid ground.

(6) Scott was bewildered. He was the one who missed the most important shot of the game. How could anyone call him the most valuable player? He didn't feel very valuable at the moment. Scott approached Coach Travis.

(7) "Coach," Scott said, "there must be some mistake. I can't be the most valuable player."

(8) "There's no mistake," Coach Travis said. "You had 26 points, 11 rebounds, and 8 assists. I'd say that makes you a very valuable player."

(9) "But I missed that last shot," Scott said. "We lost the game because of me."

(10) "I don't know about that," said Coach Travis. "Everybody misses a shot from time to time. Don't be so hard on yourself. It's all about perspective."

(11) "What do you mean?" Scott asked.

(12) "Well," Coach Travis answered, "you could say you are the reason we lost the game because you missed that last shot. On the other hand, you could say you are the reason we almost won because of your awesome performance throughout the game. How you look at it is up to you."

(13) Scott's teammates came running over and surrounded Coach Travis. They jostled one another playfully, talking and laughing.

(14) "Hey, Coach," one player called out, "how about treating your team to pizza?"

(15) "I don't know," said Coach Travis. "Do you think you deserve pizza?"

(16) Scott piped up. "Of course we do! After all, we almost won the game."

(17) Coach Travis smiled. "You're right, Scott. We did almost win. Okay, pizza for everyone!"

5. Why does the author use a metaphor to describe Scott's actions in the first sentence of paragraph 4?

a. To show how alarming the crowd was to Scott
b. To show how proud Scott was of his performance
c. To show how focused Scott was at the end of the game
d. To show how dismayed Scott was that they had lost

6. Which of the following is the best summary of this story?

a. At the buzzer, Scott misses an important basket because he isn't a very good basketball player.
b. Coach Travis feels Scott is the most valuable player in the game because he scored 26 points.
c. When Scott misses an important shot, he is disappointed, but Coach Travis shows him there are different ways to look at the situation.
d. The Eagles lose the state championship because of Scott, but Coach Travis sees things differently and makes Scott the most valuable player.

7. How is Scott's attitude most likely to be different at the beginning of the next basketball season?

a. Scott will be more focused on doing his best than trying to win.
b. Scott will no longer think that winning is a good goal.
c. Scott will become more concerned with having fun than winning.
d. Scott will lose interest in basketball and not care if his team wins.

Refer to the passages "The Talent Show" and "The Tournament" to answer questions 8-9.

8. Part A: In what ways are Scott and Megan most similar in these stories?

a. They are both skilled performers.
b. They are both very active athletes.
c. They are both disappointed in themselves.
d. They both have good friends that help them.

Part B: What pieces of evidence from the stories support this claim?

a. *The Talent Show*, Paragraph 3: "Her confidence, pride, and excitement had been replaced by utter disappointment."
   The Tournament, Paragraph 9: "We lost the game because of me."
b. *The Talent Show*, Paragraph 8: "That first verse was some of your best singing ever."
   The Tournament, Paragraph 8: "I'd say that makes you a very valuable player."
c. *The Talent Show*, Paragraph 10: "Besides, don't the pros say you should leave your audience wanting more?"
   The Tournament, Paragraph 15: "Do you think you deserve pizza?"
d. *The Talent Show*, Paragraph 15: "Megan pulled Ella and Kaylee into a quick hug."
   The Tournament, Paragraph 4: "Teammates hugged and slapped each other on the back."

9. What general theme is evident in both stories?

a. Winning is important, but it isn't everything.
b. Good friends are the most valuable thing in life.
c. Coaches can offer a good perspective on tough situations.
d. When you try your best, you shouldn't be disappointed in yourself.

Refer to the passage "Summer Afternoon" to answer questions 10-16.

Summer Afternoon

Golden sunlight bathes the meadow
In brilliant midday glory.
Slim green pillars bow in homage[1]
To a gentle summer breeze.
Flowers turn their eager faces
Upward to an azure[2] sky.
All is quiet, calm, and peaceful,
Dozing in the pleasant heat.

Just across the sleepy meadow
A lazy stream meanders through,
Sauntering between the banks
Of hardened, sun-baked earth.
Dragonflies flit to and fro
Like scattered thoughts and fleeting dreams.
Bright light glistens on the water
Like sparkling, molten silver.

The meadow rests in tacit glow
As minutes turn to hours.
The sun sinks lower in the sky,
And shadows slowly lengthen.
Daylight, dappled by the trees,
Spreads across the open landscape
Like a dim and dusky cloak,
And—in silence—evening falls.

[1] to honor
[2] blue

10. What is the meaning of the word *dozing*, as it is used in line 8?

a. Cheering up
b. Singing
c. Working
d. Sleeping

11. Based on lines 1 through 6, what can be concluded about the flowers?

a. The flowers are the only plants that can turn their heads.
b. The flowers were sad until the Sun started shining.
c. The flowers want to face the Sun and receive its sunlight.
d. The flowers do not see the Sun, but they do see the blue sky.

12. Which lines from the poem show that different areas of the environment have different responses to the Sun rising?

a. Slim green pillars bow in homage/To a gentle summer breeze.
b. Just across the sleepy meadow/A lazy stream meanders through,
c. Bright light glistens on the water/Like sparkling, molten silver.
d. Daylight, dappled by the trees,/Spreads across the open landscape

13. What does the line break signify between lines 16 and 17?

a. That the poet is talking about a third area beyond the stream
b. That the tone is changing from cheerful to sorrowful
c. That the last stanza was written by a different poet
d. That the afternoon is ending and the Sun is going down

14. What does the poet's word choice show about the mood in stanzas 1 and 3 compared to the mood in stanza 2?

a. Stanza 2 has an active mood, while stanzas 1 and 3 both have a calm mood.
b. Stanza 2 has an upbeat mood, while stanzas 1 and 3 both have a gloomy mood.
c. Stanza 2 has an exhausted mood, while stanzas 1 and 3 both have a silly mood.
d. Stanza 2 has a fun mood, while stanzas 1 and 3 both have a serious mood.

15. Why does the poet use a compare-and-contrast structure for stanzas 1 and 2?

a. To explain that the events in the meadow caused the events at the stream.
b. To tell why the events in the meadow happened before the events at the stream
c. To show the difference between the events in the meadow and the events at the stream.
d. To present the events in the meadow as the answer for correcting the events at the stream.

16. What is most likely the reason that the poet used a third-person omniscient point of view in this poem?

a. To show what the Sun saw as it shined in the afternoon and set in the evening
b. To describe what happened in different areas and at different times during the day
c. To explain why the dragonflies think the stream and plants in the meadow are lazy
d. To illustrate what can be seen in the meadow in the afternoon and evening

Refer to the passage "A World of White: The Iditarod Trail" to answer questions 17-25.

A World of White: The Iditarod Trail

(1) Imagine clinging desperately to your sled as brutal winds batter your body. The path ahead appears and disappears like a mirage, frequently obscured by blowing curtains of snow. You are freezing and sweating at the same time. Your throat burns with thirst, and your body aches with fatigue. You know your dogs must feel it too, so you encourage them to press on to the next checkpoint. All around you, the world is endless, empty, and white. Welcome to the Iditarod Trail.

(2) Alaska's Iditarod Trail is the world's most famous sled dog racing venue. But the trail is older than the sport of sled dog racing. In fact, the Iditarod Trail was first established in the early 1900s, during the Alaskan gold rush. In those days, sled dogs were used for work, hauling thousands of pounds of gold from the landlocked Iditarod to the port of Anchorage. But in faraway Nome, also known for gold, six-year-old George Allen had the idea to put together a race to see whose sled dogs were fastest, and the sport of sled dog racing was born.

(3) Though the Iditarod Trail Race is the most famous race in the sport of sled dog racing, the first race along the trail was actually a race to save lives. In 1925, a diphtheria outbreak began in Nome. To prevent an epidemic that could kill thousands, doctors desperately needed the vaccine serum, but the closest supply of serum was in Anchorage. A train ran from Anchorage to the village of Nenana, but that was still 674 miles from Nome. A cry for help was sent by the doctors, and in the midst of the blizzards and windstorms of January, the call was answered. Twenty brave mushers drove their dogs in a frantic relay, carrying 300,000 bottles of serum from Nenana to Nome. They followed the Iditarod Trail.

(4) Dog sledding, or "mushing," became quite popular after that heroic journey, but by the 1960s, it had lost popularity, and the Iditarod Trail had been largely forgotten. There were a few lovers of mushing, however, who worked tirelessly to reestablish the Iditarod Trail and create a new sled dog race that followed the trail. The first official race was held in 1967 to celebrate the centennial of the purchase of Alaska from Russia. The race involved 58 drivers who mushed 56 miles in two days. This race was a success, but the popularity and future of the Iditarod Trail was still in question.

(5) In March of 1973, the first Anchorage to Nome Iditarod Trail Race was organized and held. This race was much longer than previous races, covering more than 1,000 miles—the entire Iditarod Trail. Thirty-four mushers began the race, but only 22 were able to finish. After the 1973 race, the popularity of the Iditarod Trail finally grew and was firmly established. In 1978, the Iditarod Trail became a National Historic Trail.

(6) The modern Iditarod Trail Race is open to mushers over 18 years old who have qualified in a recognized race of 200 miles or more. For younger mushers between 14 and 18 years old, the Junior Iditarod offers a 130-mile version of the race. Many Junior Iditarod participants go on to compete in the Iditarod Trail Race, as the Junior Iditarod is good practice for the grueling trek of the main race. All mushers must prepare for the race extensively, often for months before. Many mushers run their

dogs more than 1,500 miles in preparation, giving them experience in all types of weather and terrain.

(7) To enter the Iditarod Trail Race, participants must pay an entrance fee. Then, they must travel to Anchorage with their dogs. In Anchorage, they attend a mushers' banquet where they are given their racing order numbers. Afterward, all participating dogs are checked by a veterinarian and marked by race officials to prevent participants from switching dogs mid-race, which is not allowed. The dogs are even drug tested at the beginning and at checkpoints throughout the race to prevent cheating! Finally, the sleds and equipment are checked, and participants are ready to start the race.

(8) On the morning of the Iditarod Trail Race, mushers leave Anchorage in their assigned racing order. They are sent out one at a time, at two-minute intervals. For more than a week—sometimes up to three weeks—they travel throughout Alaska, stopping at designated checkpoints along the Iditarod Trail as they make their way to Nome. When all participants have reached Nome, another mushers' banquet is held. Awards are given, and everyone is applauded for their achievement. Win or lose, the mushers know that only the toughest of the tough have what it takes to finish the race and conquer the great Iditarod Trail.

17. How does the introduction of this passage support the reader's understanding of the Iditarod Trail Race?

a. It shows how intense the race can be for participants.
b. It explains what inspired the race.
c. It describes how hard it is to prepare for the race.
d. It describes the events of the first race on the Iditarod Trail.

18. Why does the author use the simile in the following sentence in paragraph 1?

The path ahead appears and disappears like a mirage, frequently obscured by blowing curtains of snow.

a. To show how heavy the snow is falling
b. To show how difficult it is to see the path
c. To show how cold the mushers must be
d. To show how hard the dogs are running

19. In paragraph 3, which words best convey the feelings of the doctors in Nome in 1925?

a. The words "epidemic" and "diphtheria" show how seriously the doctors took their work.
b. The words "blizzards" and "windstorms" show how scared the doctors were to be in Alaska during winter.
c. The words "brave" and "frantic relay" show how determined the doctors were to cure their patients.
d. The words "desperately" and "cry for help" show how anxious the doctors were to get the serum quickly.

20. Which of the following is the best summary of the history of the Iditarod Trail Race given in paragraphs 4 and 5?

a. After the Iditarod Trail became a National Historic Trail, the race became more popular, and today many mushers participate each year.
b. After a slow start in 1967, the Iditarod Trail Race became firmly established in 1973, and it has grown in popularity.
c. In the first race in 1973, 34 mushers began the race but only 22 finished, proving that the race was too hard.
d. Mushers between 14 and 18 years of age can race in the Junior Iditarod, while those over 18 can participate in the main race if they qualify.

21. Part A: What is the meaning of the word *epidemic*, used in paragraph 3?

a. A natural disaster
b. Uncontrollable pollution
c. A widespread disease
d. A severe infection

Part B: Which of the following sentences from paragraph 3 helps the reader understand the meaning of *epidemic*?

a. A cry for help was sent by the doctors, and in the midst of the blizzards and windstorms of January, the call was answered.
b. Though the Iditarod Trail Race is the most famous in the sport of sled dog racing, the first race along the trail was actually a race to save lives.
c. In 1925, a diphtheria outbreak began in Nome.
d. A train ran from Anchorage to the village of Nenana, but that was still 674 miles from Nome.

22. What is the author's main purpose in writing this article?

a. To encourage mushers to race on the Iditarod Trail
b. To inform the reader about the 1925 diphtheria outbreak
c. To describe the terrain of Alaska
d. To educate the reader about the Iditarod Trail

23. Which sentence from the passage shows that the sled dogs must also train for the Iditarod Trail Race?

a. In those days, sled dogs were used for work, hauling thousands of pounds of gold from the landlocked Iditarod to the port of Anchorage.
b. Twenty brave mushers drove their dogs in a frantic relay, carrying 300,000 bottles of serum from Nenana to Nome.
c. Many mushers run their dogs more than 1,500 miles in preparation, giving them experience in all types of weather and terrain.
d. Afterward, all participating dogs are checked by a veterinarian and marked by race officials to prevent dog switching mid-race, which is not allowed.

24. Which of the following sentences from the passage supports the central idea that the Iditarod Trail Race has had an eventful history?

a. The path ahead appears and disappears like a mirage, frequently obscured by blowing curtains of snow.
b. Dog sledding, or "mushing," became quite popular after that heroic journey, but by the 1960s, it had lost popularity, and the Iditarod Trail had been largely forgotten.
c. The modern Iditarod Trail Race is open to mushers over 18 years old who have qualified in a recognized race of 200 miles or more.
d. Win or lose, the mushers know that only the toughest of the tough have what it takes to finish the race and conquer the great Iditarod Trail.

25. The supporting details in paragraph 6 support which key idea?

a. Mushers and their dogs should be prepared for the intense conditions they will encounter during the Iditarod Trail Race.
b. There are many stages to preparing for the Iditarod Trail Race since it is one of the most physically-intense competitions.
c. Children and teenagers should not participate in the Iditarod Trail Race because they cannot properly prepare for it.
d. Dog teams must get used to different terrains and weather conditions before beginning the Iditarod Trail Race so they do not get lost.

Refer to the passage "Notes of Mystery" to answer questions 26-29.

Notes of Mystery

Cast of Characters
• Marla: A ninth-grade student, Matthew's sister • Matthew: A eleventh-grade student, Marla's brother • Madison: A ninth-grade student

SCENE 1

[In the school parking lot. MATTHEW is sitting in the driver's seat of his car. MARLA slumps in the passenger's seat.]

MATTHEW: What's wrong with you?

MARLA: I found out that the chess team may not happen this year. The coach is moving to another school, and no other teachers want to coach it.

MATTHEW: Oh. [pause] Have you thought about joining another team or club?

MARLA: No, I— [MARLA begins crying.] I'm not good at anything else! All of my friends are in sports or band, but I don't like either of those! High school has already been hard enough! There are so many older kids, and the classes are so difficult. And now the one thing that I was already comfortable with is gone.

[MATTHEW begins to speak, but MARLA cries harder. MATTHEW drives in silence.]

SCENE 2

[MARLA and MADISON are walking up to MARLA'S locker. MADISON is talking nonstop about band. MARLA opens her locker, and a piece of paper falls out. MARLA picks up the paper.]

MADISON: What does it say?

MARLA: It says, "Remember when you won the spelling bee in fourth grade? You were the only nine-year-old who could spell *conscientious*."

MADISON: What a weird note!

MARLA: Yeah, it is. [pause] Who could have written it? And why?

[MADISON shrugs. MARLA closes the locker and stares at the note as they exit.]

SCENE 3:

[In the cafeteria. MARLA and MADISON are eating lunch together.]

MADISON: I don't understand. We've asked all our friends, compared the notes to other people's handwriting, and even watched your locker before school. Five more notes, but no clues or leads!

MARLA: I know! And look at the one I got this morning. It says, "Remember when you were into magic tricks in sixth grade? I'm still not sure how you did some of those tricks!" [pause] Wait, I only did those at home. [MARLA's eyes grow wide.] I think I know who wrote these!

[MARLA exits.]

SCENE 4:

[In the library. MATTHEW is writing at a table. MARLA enters and hands him the note.]

MARLA: You're the one writing the notes!

MATTHEW: What notes?

MARLA: Don't pretend! Look, the handwriting in the notes matches your handwriting on the paper right in front of you!

MATTHEW: Fine, you got me.

MARLA: Aha! [pause] Alright, well, why have you been writing them?

MATTHEW: Because I wanted you to remember that you're good at plenty of things besides chess. You can do lots of other activities or join other teams without having to do band or sports. Honestly, I think you can do anything.

MARLA: [stunned] Wow, Matt, that's really nice! Thank you! But why didn't you just tell me that?

MATTHEW: I wasn't sure you'd believe it coming from your brother. Now, a lot of the club sign ups close this week, so you better act soon if you want to—

[MARLA hugs MATTHEW, then begins to run off.]

MATTHEW: Where are you going?

MARLA: [running offstage and calling back] To sign up for the spelling team!

[MARLA exits and MATTHEW smiles and continues writing.]

THE END

26. Based on the passage, what can be inferred about Marla and Matthew?

a. Matthew gets annoyed when Marla is upset.
b. Marla does not pay attention to Matthew.
c. Marla relies on Matthew for guidance.
d. Matthew genuinely cares about Marla.

27. How did the setting of scene 2 impact the plot?

a. It allowed Matthew to deliver the note to Marla without her knowing it came from him.
b. It allowed Madison to be present when Marla found the first anonymous note.
c. It allowed Marla to easily find the note and immediately read it.
d. It allowed Marla to quickly find Matthew after realizing that he had written the notes.

28. Which elements of this play show that it is a mystery?

a. The events in the story each take place in a different location.
b. The plot is centered around a question that the characters want to answer.
c. The events that occurred in the story could happen to anyone.
d. The plot explains the cause of an event that happened several years ago.

29. Read the following line from the play:

MARLA: [running offstage and calling back] To sign up for the spelling team!

What does this dialogue suggest about how Marla has changed?

a. She has been studying dictionaries to learn new spelling words
b. She has gotten more comfortable with being a high school student.
c. She has taken the notes to heart and gained confidence in her abilities.
d. She has learned all she can from Matthew and is ready to practice it.

Refer to the passage "Building the New Nest" to answer question 30-33.

Building the New Nest

(1) One summer night, a mother robin and her chicks were resting in their nest when a violent storm began. The wind blew hard, and heavy rain drops fell all around them. In the morning, when things were still, the mother robin inspected the nest. It was intact, but the tree it rested in had not fared well in the storm. Most of its branches had snapped off, and only a few of its leaves remained. The tree was no longer a safe home for the mother robin and her chicks, so she told them she would need to find a new tree and build a new nest.

(2) Her youngest chick excitedly asked, "Mama, may I build the new nest? It would be so fun! I do love to build things."

(3) The mother robin laughed and said, "No, you are quite young. You can certainly help me build it—"

(4) "No, Mama, I can do it myself! Let me show you!"

(5) The mother robin laughed again and said, "Okay. I'll go with you to the new tree and give you three days to build it. If it isn't complete in three days, then you can help me finish it."

(6) The next day, the mother robin and her youngest chick flew to the new tree. The mother robin watched as her chick flew to and fro, finding twigs for the nest. However, the young bird grew tired quickly. As he rested before they flew back to the others, he said, "I did not know I would have to fly so far to find materials!"

(7) "Well, I can help you—" the mother robin began.

(8) "No, I can do it alone!" the young chick insisted.

(9) That night, when he and the other chicks were asleep, the mother robin quietly got up and flew to the new tree. She found materials for the nest and dropped them nearby. Then, she returned to her chicks before morning.

(10) The next day, the young chick finished half of the nest. He was surprised at how much closer the materials were. When he asked his mother about this, she simply told him that the wind blew them over to the tree.

(11) That night, the mother robin left to move more items to the new tree. However, as she left, the youngest chick woke up! He flew after her and saw what she was doing. When she returned, he was awake and waiting for her.

(12) "Mama, why did you help me?"

(13) The mother robin responded, "Because you will hurt yourself by flying and working so much! I could not convince you to ask for help, but I did not want you to be hurt."

(14) The young bird thought about this and thanked his mother for helping him. The two then set out for the new tree. Together, they finished the nest in no time, faster than either could have on their own. That evening, all of the birds were able to move into their new, safe nest.

30. What is the young chick likely to do next time there is a big task to complete?

a. Rest and let others complete it since he helped build the nest
b. Complete it all by himself since he can now fly farther without getting tired
c. Secretly help his siblings complete it since he wants them to think they did it alone
d. Allow others to help him since he has learned that having help is better than working alone

31. Which of the following themes can be seen in this passage? Select all the apply.

a. Independence must be earned.
b. Parents should encourage curiosity.
c. Asking for help is not a bad thing.
d. Wisdom comes with experience.
e. Bird nests must be protected.

32. How does the young chick's performance in paragraph 6 impact the plot?

a. It causes the mother robin's concern for the young chick to grow.
b. It helps the mother robin see that the young chick will not finish the nest on time.
c. It shows the mother robin that the young chick needs help.
d. It reveals that the mother robin will not allow the chick to continue building the nest.

33. Why does the author use a third-person omniscient narrator in this story?

a. To show the thoughts and emotions of both the mother robin and the young chick
b. To show how the rainstorm destroyed the tree that the birds were living in
c. To show why the mother robin chose to help her young chick after his first day of work
d. To show what the young chick and mother robin did when the other was not looking

Refer to the passages "Notes of Mystery" and "Building the New Nest" to answer questions 34-36.

34. What is one difference between Matthew in "Notes of Mystery" and the mother robin in "Building the New Nest"?

a. Matthew was not caught putting notes in Marla's locker. The mother robin was caught moving materials closer to the tree.
b. Matthew lied about who put the notes in Marla's locker. The mother robin did not lie about who put the materials closer to the tree.
c. Matthew helped Marla because he wants to cheer her up. The mother robin helped the chick because she wanted the nest to be done faster.
d. Matthew wanted Marla to know he was helping her. The mother robin did not want the young chick to know she was helping him.

35. Which of the following themes is supported by both passages?

a. Siblings do not always have the same talents.
b. Helping is one way to show family members love.
c. A person being helped should never know who helped them.
d. Adults should always help the children in their family.

36. How do Marla in "Notes of Mystery" and the young chick in "Building the New Nest" respond to help differently?

a. Marla is disappointed that Matthew is the one helping her. The young chick rejects his mother's help because he wants help from his siblings.
b. Marla rejects Matthew's help because she wants to handle things herself. The young chick thanks his mother for her help when she offers it.
c. Marla is embarrassed by Matthew's help and must learn to appreciate it. The young chick asks for help and is thankful for it.
d. Marla appreciates Matthew's help and thanks him for it. The young chick protests his mother's help but learns to be thankful for it.

Refer to the passage "Everybody's Problem" to answer questions 37-42.

Everybody's Problem

(1) I used to think homeless people were dirty and lazy and mean. I thought they were all old men with scraggly beards and mangy dogs. I thought they lived on the street because they wanted to. I thought they were all drug addicts and alcoholics who ate from garbage cans and slept in boxes. I used to think homelessness wasn't my problem. Then I met Chris, and he showed me I was wrong—about everything. Homelessness is everybody's problem.

(2) The sun was climbing into the bright blue sky as we loaded up the bus at the youth center. It was a crisp, cold Thanksgiving morning, and our youth group was headed down to a local shelter called The Lighthouse. We were going to serve Thanksgiving dinner to more than a hundred homeless people. It seemed like an appropriate way to spend Thanksgiving Day.

(3) When we arrived at the shelter, we were each given a job to do. My job was peeling potatoes. The shelter director gave me a peeler and a garbage can and sat me down in front of a giant pile of potatoes. I had never seen so many potatoes in one place before. They rose from the tray like Mt. Everest. By the time I had peeled them all, my hands and arms and shoulders ached.

(4) When the kitchen work was done, we were given our serving stations. The director explained that this was the only meal many of the homeless people would eat that day, and for some, it was the only hot meal they would have that week. Even so, there wasn't a lot of food for so many people. We were supposed to give each person one slice of turkey, one scoop of mashed potatoes, one scoop of stuffing, a small drizzle of gravy, a few green beans, and a sliver of pumpkin pie.

(5) I was plodding along, dishing up mashed potatoes with an ice cream scoop, when I happened to look up at the person I was serving. He wasn't a dirty, bearded old man. He was a boy about my age, with brown hair and brown eyes and a patched green jacket.

(6) "Hi," the boy said. "I'm Chris."

(7) "I'm Ben," I said as I scooped some potatoes onto his plate. "Happy Thanksgiving."

(8) "Thanks," Chris said, and then he was gone.

(9) As Chris moved down the line, I began to look around, really seeing things for the first time. Very few of the homeless people fit my stereotype. There were men and women, old and young. Children played in a corner of the dining room. At one table, teenagers talked in a tight group. People chatted and smiled. A few were even laughing. This was not what I had pictured a homeless shelter would be like.

(10) When everyone had been served, I began to help clean up. I couldn't help watching Chris as I cleared the tables and wiped them down. He was playing peek-a-boo with a little girl in a high chair. I wondered if it was his little sister.

(11) I was so lost in thought that I jumped when the shelter director tapped my shoulder. She laughed.

(12) "I'll finish cleaning up here," she said. "Why don't you go talk to Chris? He's very nice."

(13) As I approached the table where Chris was sitting, I felt nervous. What would I say? Could we possibly have anything to talk about? Would he even want to talk to me? I sat cautiously beside him.

(14) "Hi, Ben," he said.

(15) "Hi, Chris. Is that your little sister?"

(16) Chris smiled. "Yep. This is Sophia. And over there is my little brother, Dane." Chris motioned toward the corner where the smaller children were playing. Then he pointed to a dark-haired woman at a nearby table. "That's my mom."

(17) "Are you all homeless?" I asked.

(18) "Yep," answered Chris. "We've been here at The Lighthouse for almost two months now. It's okay here, but I miss my old school and my friends. I hope we can move back to a real house soon."

(19) "I didn't know there was such a thing as homeless kids," I admitted.

(20) "Me neither," said Chris. "At least, not until I became one."

(21) "How did it happen?" I asked. Then I had second thoughts. "I mean, you don't have to tell me if you don't want to. I was just wondering."

(22) "It's okay," Chris said. "I don't mind talking about it. About a year ago, my dad got really sick. He was in the hospital for a few months. Then he died. We didn't have any insurance or anything, and my mom couldn't get a job. Besides, she was really sad, and she was trying to take care of me and Dane and Sophia."

(23) "So, how did you end up homeless?" I wondered.

(24) "Mom says there were just too many bills and not enough money. First, we got our lights turned off. Then we couldn't pay our rent, so we had to move out of our house. We stayed with friends for a while, but eventually there was nobody left to stay with. So, we came here."

(25) "Will you stay here forever?" I asked.

(26) "No," Chris said. "My mom is in a program to give her training and help her get a job. When she finds a job, we can get a new place to live. Then things can be normal again."

(27) I heard my youth leader calling for us to load the bus. I wanted to talk to Chris more and ask him more questions, but I knew I had to leave. I stood up.

(28) "I have to go," I said. "I'm glad I got to meet you, Chris. I hope you get a new house soon."

(29) "Thanks, Ben," Chris said. "It was nice to meet you, too. Thanks for hanging out with me for a while. Happy Thanksgiving."

(30) "Happy Thanksgiving," I echoed as I headed toward the door. When I looked back, Chris waved. Then he started playing peek-a-boo with Sophia again.

(31) I will probably never see Chris again, but I have thought of him many times since that day. In just a few minutes together, he taught me so much about the problem of homelessness. It isn't just a problem that affects lazy, mean old men. It affects men and women of all ages. It affects children. It affects whole families. It affected Chris. And because I got the chance to see homelessness through his eyes, it affects me now, too. I think I'll go back again next Thanksgiving ... or maybe sooner. After all, now I know that homelessness is everybody's problem.

37. What is the setting for this story?

a. A youth center
b. A homeless shelter
c. A community center
d. A school

38. If you were describing this story, what classification would you use?

a. Memoir
b. Biography
c. Autobiography
d. Fiction

39. What point of view is used to tell this story?

a. First person
b. Second person
c. Third person
d. All of the above

40. What is the main theme of this story?

a. Kids can be homeless
b. Potatoes are difficult to peel
c. Serving at a homeless shelter is a good Thanksgiving project
d. Homelessness is everybody's problem

41. What major event in the life of Chris's family led to their homelessness?

a. Their house burned down
b. Chris's mom lost her job
c. They had to live in their car
d. Chris's dad got sick and died

42. How does meeting Chris change Ben's mind about homelessness?

a. It doesn't change Ben's mind at all
b. It makes Ben afraid of being homeless
c. It helps Ben see that homelessness affects everyone
d. It keeps Ben from ever helping in a homeless shelter again

Answers and Explanations for Reading Test #2

1. A: The main theme of the story is about the support that real friendship provides. Megan's friends comfort her after her performance, leading to Megan's conclusion in paragraph 16 that everything will be okay because of her supportive friends. While the other three answer choices did occur in the story, they are simply supportive details rather than the main idea.

2. B: Kaylee points out that Megan should focus on what she did sing rather than what she didn't sing because the part of the song she was able to sing was great. Kaylee did not make a joke about Megan's performance (A). Kaylee also didn't want to simply distract Megan from (C) or help her forget (D) the fact that she didn't finish the song; she wanted Megan to focus on the good aspects of her performance.

3. D: Realistic fiction is a genre in which the events of the story did not actually happen but could have potentially happened in real life. The events in this story could have taken place in real life. Choices A, B, and C are incorrect because they describe aspects that could be in any story, not just realistic fiction.

4. B: Paragraph 2 describes the moment Megan forgot the words to the song and ran backstage. This is the point where the story's conflict begins. Choice A is incorrect because Megan does not mention thinking she would win the talent show in the paragraph. Choice C is incorrect because there was no mention of Megan wanting to avoid her friends. Choice D is incorrect because it is never explained why Megan forgot the words to the song.

5. D: A metaphor is a nonliteral comparison between two things. Scott is compared to a statue in the metaphor in paragraph 4 to demonstrate how dismayed he was that his team lost the game. Choice A is incorrect because the crowd did not alarm Scott. Choice B is incorrect because Scott was not proud of his performance, as he had missed the game's winning shot. Choice C is incorrect because Scott was no longer focused, as the game had already ended.

6. C: This choice effectively sums up the main points expressed within the story. Choice A is incorrect because Scott's lack of skill isn't implied within the story at all. Choices B and D focus more on supporting details than the main ideas, so they are incorrect.

7. A: In paragraphs 10-12, Coach Travis helps Scott understand that, as long as he did his best, winning doesn't matter. Choice B is incorrect because, although Scott may be less focused on winning, it is still important to him. Choice C is incorrect because the story's focus was on the effort Scott put into winning, not on how much fun he had. Choice D is incorrect because the story clearly shows that winning is important to Scott.

8. Part A: C: Scott gets disappointed in himself for missing the winning shot, while Megan gets disappointed in herself for forgetting the words to her song. Choices A and B are incorrect because Scott is not a performer (A), and Megan is not an athlete (B). Choice D is incorrect because Scott's story does not mention his relationship with his friends.

Part B: A: Scott gets disappointed in himself for missing the winning shot, while Megan gets disappointed in herself for forgetting the words to her song. Choice A is the only option that displays these emotions from the text.

9. D: Both Scott and Megan show disappointment with themselves within their stories. Choice A is incorrect because, although both characters had a desire to win, that was not the main theme in either story. Choice B is incorrect because friendship was not a theme in Scott's story. Choice C is incorrect because Megan did not have a coach in her story.

10. D: *Dozing* is another word for *sleeping*, so choice D is correct. This meaning is supported by the other descriptions in the poem. In line 9, the speaker says that the meadow is sleepy. Additionally, the words *gentle*, *quiet*, *calm*, and *peaceful* in stanza 1 show that there is not much activity in the meadow. The poem does not suggest that the things in the meadow are upset, gloomy, or sad. This shows that the poem does not support the idea that dozing would mean *cheering up*, so choice A is incorrect. The meadow is described as quiet, so the things in it would not be singing. Therefore, choice B is incorrect. There are no details in the poem that suggest that the things in the meadow have tasks to complete or are working, so choice C is incorrect.

11. C: When the Sun is high in the sky and light falls on the meadow, lines 5 and 6 say that the "flowers turn their eager faces" toward the Sun. *Eager* means that someone or something is excited or ready for something. This supports the idea that the flowers are glad to face the Sun and that they want to do so. Choice C is correct. Lines 1 through 6 only mention one other plant: the grass. While the grass does not turn, this does not mean that other, unmentioned plants cannot turn their heads. Choice A is incorrect. The flowers were facing the ground before the Sun came up. However, the poem does not suggest that the flowers were sad. The speaker is simply describing the flowers sitting up and opening when the Sun comes up. Choice B is incorrect. The poem says that the Sun "bathes the meadow," which means that its light covers the whole meadow. The poem also does not mention anything that would block the flowers' view of the Sun, so choice D is incorrect.

12. B: The poem describes what happens in the meadow and the area near the stream during the middle of the day. The meadow and area near the stream are different areas of the environment. Choice B shows that, in response to the Sun rising to its peak in the sky, the meadow is sleepy and the stream is lazily moving. These lines show that the things in the meadow are still and calm, and the things near the stream are active and moving. This means choice B is correct. The lines in choice A simply describe the grass bowing to the breeze. This describes one area and its response, so choice A is incorrect. The lines in choice C only describe the stream, so choice C is also incorrect. The lines in choice D describe what happens when the Sun descends. They do not describe a response to the Sun rising, so choice D is incorrect.

13. D: Line breaks are often used to show a change in idea or focus in a poem. Stanzas 1 and 2 describe what happens in the middle of the day when the Sun is high in the sky. Stanza 3 describes what happens in the evening when the Sun is going down. This means that the line break between the stanzas signifies that time has passed, so choice D is correct. The third stanza mentions the meadow in line 17, and it does not introduce a new area, so choice A is incorrect. The tone does not become sorrowful in stanza 3, so choice B is incorrect. One poet wrote the entire poem, and there is nothing to signal that the writer has changed. This means that choice C is incorrect.

14. A: Stanza 2 describes the stream moving through the area, the dragonflies quickly moving around, and the water sparkling. Stanza 2 also includes words like "sauntering," "flit," "scattered," "fleeting," and "sparkling." These elements and words create an active mood in stanza 2. Stanzas 1 and 3 describe plants that stay in their places, enjoy the rising sun, and rest as it sets. These stanzas have a calm mood. The plants in the meadow are not described as being gloomy or serious. They are glad and restful, so choices B and D are incorrect. The stream and dragonflies in stanza 2 are not exhausted, so choice C is incorrect.

15. C: Stanza 1 describes the meadow during midday, and stanza 2 describes the area near the stream during midday. The events that happen in these areas are different, so the poet contrasts them by describing them in different stanzas. This means choice C is correct. The events in the meadow and near the stream are both caused by the Sun rising, so choice A is incorrect. The events in the meadow and the events near the stream happen at the same time. This means that choice B is incorrect. There is not a problem created by the events near the stream, so choice D is incorrect.

16. B: The use of a third-person omniscient narrator allowed the poet to describe events that occurred in different places at the same time. Choice B is correct. The Sun is not the narrator of the poem, and the poem does not describe the environment from the Sun's perspective, so choice A is incorrect. The dragonflies' thoughts are not described in the poem, so choice C is incorrect. The second stanza of the poem describes what happens outside of the meadow. Also, a first-person narrator could describe what can be seen in the meadow during the afternoon and evening. This makes choice D incorrect.

17. D: The introductory paragraph describes the experience of a participant in the Iditarod Trail Race, which supports the reader's understanding of the conditions the racers endure. This makes choice A correct. Choices B and C are incorrect, as the inspiration of the race is described in paragraph 3, and preparation techniques are described in paragraph 5. The passage does not indicate that paragraph 1 is describing the first Iditarod Trail Race, so choice D is incorrect.

18. B: The author compares the path appearing and disappearing to a mirage. This indicates how difficult it is to see the path. Choice A is incorrect because, although the author describes how hard the snow is falling, no comparison is being made, so it is not a part of the simile. Choices C and D are incorrect because there is no mention of how cold it is or how hard the dogs are running.

19. D: The words "desperately" and "cry for help" demonstrate the urgency of the situation and how anxious the doctors were to get it resolved. The words in the other answer choices do not effectively indicate how the doctors were feeling.

20. B: This is the best summary for paragraphs 4 and 5 as it effectively sums up the main points the author was trying to make. The other answer choices are incorrect because they only state supporting details provided within the paragraphs.

21. Part A: C: The previous sentence mentions a "diphtheria outbreak," which shows the reader that the passage is describing a disease that has spread wildly. Choices A and B are incorrect, as the paragraph is talking about a disease outbreak, not a natural disaster or pollution. Choice D is incorrect because the word "epidemic" is describing how much the disease has spread, not its severity.

Part B: C: Diphtheria is a disease, and an outbreak is when a very contagious disease spreads to a lot of people in an area. The doctors wanted to prevent an epidemic that the diphtheria outbreak could have caused. This shows that the sentence in choice C helps the reader understand the definition of *epidemic*. Choice A is incorrect because it tells the reader that the doctors needed help, and despite the weather, they received it. This sentence does mention doctors, but it does not show that the doctors were trying to prevent the spread of a disease. Choice B is incorrect because it states that the trail was first used to save lives. This sentence does not mention a disease or the spread of illness. Choice D is incorrect because it tells the reader why it was difficult to get to Nome. It does not show the reader what the problem in Nome was.

22. D: This passage gives the reader information on the Iditarod Trail. Choice A is incorrect because, although information is given on how to participate in races on the trail, no encouragement is provided. Choices B and C are incorrect because they are just minor supporting details.

23. C: Choice C is correct because it describes the preparation that sled dogs go through in order to get ready for the race. Choices A and B are incorrect because they only explain what the dogs were used for before the creation of the race. Choice D is incorrect because it only describes how the dogs are evaluated to ensure they are medically ready to participate in the race.

24. B: They key words "heroic journey" help to support the idea that the history of the Iditarod Trail Race was an eventful one. The remaining answer choices focus on other details of the trail, such as its harsh conditions (A and D) and the requirements one must meet to participate in the race (C) instead of the trail's history.

25. A: Paragraph 6 describes how mushers and their dogs run more than 1,500 miles in preparation for the race. It also states that they practice running in all kinds of weather and terrain. This evidence supports the key idea that mushers and their dogs should be prepared for the intense conditions of the Iditarod Trail.

26. D: Matthew shows that he cares about his sister by encouraging her to be more confident in her abilities, so choice D is correct. Matthew is not annoyed that Marla is upset. He is only quiet on the way home because Marla is very upset, and he does not think she will listen to him. Choice A is incorrect. Marla is only around Matthew in scenes 1 and 4 of the play. She originally does not suspect that he is leaving the notes, but this does not show that she does not pay attention to her brother. The events in the drama do not support choice B, so it is incorrect. Marla does not ask Matthew for advice, and it takes a while for her to accept his suggestion in scene 1. This shows that Marla likely does not rely on Matthew for advice or guidance, so choice C is incorrect.

27. A: Scene 2 is set at Marla's locker at the characters' high school. The locker is in a place where many people pass by at different times. Since Matthew can go to Marla's locker when she is not there, he is able to put the notes in Marla's locker without her seeing him. This makes choice A correct. Madison could have been present at other locations where Matthew could have left the note for Marla. This makes choice B incorrect. There are many places where Marla could have easily found the note and read it immediately. The specific location did not impact this part of the plot, so choice C is incorrect. Marla was not at her locker when she realized Matthew was the one writing the notes, so choice D is incorrect.

28. B: The plot revolves around Marla receiving notes from an unknown person and working with Madison to figure out who is writing them. This means that the characters are working to answer a question that is important to the plot. This is a common characteristic of mysteries, so choice B is correct. Choices A and C are characteristics found in multiple genres, not just mysteries, so they are incorrect. Choice D is a characteristic that is common in historical fiction and myths. It is not limited to mysteries. This element is also not present in this drama, so choice D is incorrect.

29. C: At the beginning of the play, Marla is crying because she thinks that chess is the only thing she is good at. The first note she receives from Matthew reminds her of a time that she won a spelling bee. This line at the very end of the play shows that the reminder has encouraged Marla to try out for the spelling team. At first, she doubted her abilities and skills, but now she is ready to try new things and improve old skills. This makes choice C correct. No other details in the play suggest that Marla has been studying spelling words, so choice A is incorrect. The details also do not suggest that she is more comfortable being a high-school student or that she has nothing else to learn from Matthew. This means that choices B and D are also incorrect.

30. D: In "Building the New Nest," the young chick learns to accept help from his mother. He and his mother are able to build the nest much quicker than either of them could have by themselves. This change supports the prediction in choice D since this choice describes the lesson that the chick learned. The chick was eager to help build the new nest, and even when he was tired, he wanted to keep working on it himself. This shows that he would be likely to help with a new task rather than rest and let others do it. Choice A is incorrect. Choice B would show that the chick did not learn a lesson in the story. Also, the chick has not gained the ability to fly farther without tiring, so choice B is incorrect. There is no information in the story that show that the chick thought helping in secret was a good idea. Choice C is not supported by the passage, so it is incorrect.

31. C, D: The young chick did not want to ask for help because he wanted to build the nest by himself. However, at the end of the story, he realized that it was better to work with his mother instead of alone. This supports the idea that asking for help is not bad, so choice C is correct. Choice D is also correct because the chick realizes that wisdom comes with experience. His mother has more experience with nest building, and, therefore, she has more knowledge about what all it entails than he does. The young chick does not become more independent in this story, so choice A is incorrect. The young chick did not display curiosity in this passage. He already knew that he liked building things, so he was not trying anything new. Choice B is unsupported by the passage, so it is incorrect. Choice E is incorrect because the story is not about the safety of the birds' nest.

32. A: In paragraph 6, the young chick grows tired after flying to pick up materials for the nest. He refused to accept help, and his mother grows concerned that he will hurt himself. This means choice A is correct. The events in paragraph 6 did not show how quickly the chick would finish the nest, so choice B is incorrect. The mother robin knew that the young chick would need help before he began working on the nest, so choice C is incorrect. The mother robin did let the chick continue to build the nest, so choice D is incorrect.

33. D: The author shows what the mother robin does while the young chick is sleeping. The author also shows what the young chick does when the mother robin is away. The actions of both main characters can be shown when the other is not watching because the story is told by a third-person omniscient narrator. Choice D is correct. The internal thoughts of the mother robin are not told in the story, so choice A is incorrect. The way that the rainstorm destroyed the tree is not described, so choice B is incorrect. The mother robin's dialogue shows why she decided to help the young chick. This information would also be available if the story were told by a first-person narrator, so choice C is incorrect.

34. A: Marla figured out that Matthew was the one putting notes in her locker, but she did not catch him doing so. The young chick woke up at night and caught his mother moving the materials. This matches the difference described in choice A, so it is correct. The mother robin did lie by saying that the wind blew the materials closer to the tree, so choice B is incorrect. The mother robin helped the chick because she did not want him to hurt himself. She did give him a certain amount of time to build the nest. However, she also suggested that if he did not finish it in time, they would finish it together. The mother robin does not appear worried about when the nest will be built, so choice C is incorrect. Matthew gave Marla the notes in secret. He also told her that he was not sure she would listen if she knew they came from him. This shows that choice D is incorrect.

35. B: In "Notes of Mystery," Matthew helps his sister because he loves her and wants her to have more confidence in her abilities. In "Building the New Nest," the mother robin helps the young chick because she loves him and wants to keep him from getting hurt. Both stories support the idea that helping family members can show them love, so choice B is correct. Matthew's talents are not described in "Notes of Mystery." Similarly, the other chicks' talents are not described in "Building the New Nest." Since neither story supports the idea in choice A, it is incorrect. In both stories, the character receiving help discovers who was helping them, and this has a positive outcome. Choice C is not supported by the passage, so it is incorrect. Matthew in "Notes of Mystery" is not an adult, so the story does not support the theme in choice D.

36. D: Marla appreciates Matthew's encouragement and thanks him for it. The young chick does not want his mother's help, at first, but later realizes that he needs it. This matches the description in choice D, so it is the correct answer. Marla does not show that she is disappointed or embarrassed by Matthew's help, so choices A and C are incorrect. The young chick does not accept his mother's help when she offers it. He only thanks her for her help after she has already given it, so choice B is incorrect.

37. B: This story is set at a homeless shelter.

38. A: This story is written in the style of a memoir, as evidenced by the first-person, reflective tone.

39. A: This story is written in first person. That means the author is involved in the events of the story and is telling it from his point of view.

40. D: The main theme of the story is that homelessness is everybody's problem. One clue that this is the main point of the story is that the author clearly states it in the last line of the story. It's not always true that the last line of a short piece contains the main point, but that is often the case.

41. D: The death of Chris's dad was the major problem the family had to deal with that eventually led to their homelessness.

42. C: After meeting Chris, Ben had a completely different view of homelessness. Prior to the Thanksgiving meal, Ben thought homeless people were nothing but a bunch of old, filthy drunks and drug addicts. Meeting Ben and his family helped him understand that homelessness can happen to all kinds of people.

Language Practice Test #2

Questions 1 – 7 pertain to the following passage:

Clara Barton: A Heart for Helping

(1) Clara barton was born on Christmas in 1821. (2) She lived in North Oxford, Massachusetts, and was the youngest of five children. (3) Although she loved sports, reading, and horseback riding, Clara mostly enjoyed helping people. (4) In fact, when she was only 11. (5) Clara spent two years caring for her brother after he suffered a serious injury.

(6) Clara becomes a teacher while she was still a teenager because she loved to help so much. (7) After teaching for many years, Clara moved to Washington D.C. to work in the Patent Office, where she gave permits to new inventors. (8) In 1861, the Civil War began, and Clara used her free time to gather supplies for soldiers.

(9) In 1862, Clara started traveling to battlefields to help wounded soldiers and deliver food and supplies. (10) Even though she was not a nurse, Clara saved the lives of many soldiers. (11) Nurses were in great demand during the Civil War. (12) When the war ended, she continued to give speeches to people about the bad conditions on battlefields. (13) Many people heard Clara speak.

(14) In 1869, Clara traveled to Switzerland to visit some friends. (15) While there, she learned about a new organization called the International Red Cross, Clara began working with them. (16) In 1881, she returned to the United States and established the American Red Cross. (17) Then Clara spends the rest of her life doing what she loved best: helping people.

1. Which version of sentence 1 has the most correct capitalization?

a. Clara barton was born on Christmas in 1821
b. Clara Barton was born on Christmas in 1821
c. Clara Barton was born on christmas in 1821
d. Clara barton was born on christmas in 1821

2. What revision, if any, is needed in sentences 4 and 5?

a. No revision is needed
b. Remove the period
c. Replace the period with a semicolon
d. Replace the period with a comma

3. What change, if any, is necessary in sentence 6?

a. No change is necessary
b. Change loved to loves
c. Change becomes to became
d. Change was to were

4. What spelling correction, if any, is needed in sentence 9?

a. No correction is needed
b. Change traveling to travelling
c. Change battlefields to battlefeilds
d. Change soldiers to souldiers

5. Which sentence does not belong in this essay?

a. Sentence 4
b. Sentence 7
c. Sentence 11
d. Sentence 15

6. What revision, if any, is needed in sentence 15?

a. No revision is needed
b. Replace the comma after Cross with a period
c. Remove the comma after Cross
d. Replace the comma after there with a semicolon

7. What change, if any, is necessary in sentence 17?

a. No change is necessary
b. Replace helping with helped
c. Replace loved with loves
d. Replace spends with spent

Questions 8 – 14 pertain to the following passages:

Amazing Pandas

(1) When a baby panda is born, it is about the size of a breakfast sausage. (2) Tiny and almost furless, it snuggled close to its mother. (3) The baby panda stays very near its mother for the first two months of life. (4) Because until it is two months old, the panda's eyes cannot open. (5) It relies on its mother for everything.

(6) Even when the baby panda's eyes are open, it still needs its mother for food. (7) Baby pandas nurse from their mothers up to eight times a day until they are 18 months old. (8) During this time they also chew on bamboo but this is just for fun. (9) Their teeth are not strong enough to really eat the bamboo.

(10) Bamboo does not have many vitamins and calories, though, so pandas must spend up to 14 hours a day eating just to stay full! (11) Sometime between 12 and 18 months of age, pandas begin really eating bamboo. (12) Even so, they do not wander far from home; pandas stay with their mothers until they are full grown.

(13) When a full grown panda is about five feet long and weighs about 200 pounds. (14) They live in the forests of China, although many now live in zoos and other places. (15) In fact, there were only about 1600 pandas left in the wild because their habitats have been destroyed to build cities. (16) People need to care for pandas so these amazing animals will always be with us.

8. What change, if any, is needed in sentence 2?

a. No change is needed
b. Change furless to fur-less
c. Change snuggled to snuggles
d. Change its to it's

9. What revision, if any, is necessary in sentences 3 and 4?

a. No revision is necessary
b. Replace the period with a comma
c. Replace the period with a semicolon
d. Remove the period

10. What change, if any, is needed in sentence 8?

a. No change is needed
b. Insert a period after bamboo
c. Insert a comma after bamboo
d. Insert a semicolon after bamboo

11. Which sentence is the best choice for the first sentence of paragraph 3?

a. Sentence 10
b. Sentence 12
c. Sentence 9
d. Sentence 11

12. What revision, if any, is necessary in sentence 12?

a. No revision is necessary
b. Replace the semicolon with a comma
c. Remove the comma after so
d. Change the period to an exclamation point

13. What change, if any, is needed in sentence 13?

a. No change is needed
b. Remove the period to combine sentence 13 with sentence 14
c. Insert a comma after long
d. Remove the word When

14. What revision, if any, is necessary in sentence 15?

a. No revision is necessary
b. Change were to are
c. Change 1600 to sixteen hundred
d. Change their to there

Questions 15 – 21 pertain to the following passage:

Niagara Falls

(1) Last Summer, my family went on a trip to Niagara Falls in New York. (2) Niagara Falls is a famous waterfall that flows between the United States and Canada. (3) When I first saw the falls. (4) I couldn't believe it. (5) It was huge! (6) I had never seen so much water in my life.

(7) To get a better look at the falls, we decided to take a boat ride to the base of the falls, where the waterfall crashes into the river. (8) We got on a boat with a lot of other people. (9) Every person was given a blue plastic rain poncho. (10) As we got closer to the bottom of the falls, I knew why. (11) The water sprayed up like it was raining, and the crashing is so loud I couldn't even hear myself yell.

(12) We saw another boat, far below us, headed for the base of Niagara Falls. (13) When the boat ride was over, we drove back to the top of the falls and walked along the sidewalk. (14) The falls was so big it made the boat look like a toy and the people look like tiny insects.

(15) Before we left Niagara Falls, I bought some postcards at a gift shop. (16) When we got home, I used the post cards to make a new page for my scrapbook. (17) I also wrote down some of my memories from the trip. (18) Then I will always remember my trip to Niagara Falls.

15. Which of the following versions of sentence 1 contains proper capitalization?

a. Last Summer, my family went on a trip to Niagara Falls in New York
b. Last summer, my family went on a trip to niagara falls in New York
c. Last summer, my family went on a trip to Niagara Falls in New York
d. Last Summer, my family went on a trip to Niagara Falls in new york

16. What revision, if any, is necessary in sentences 3 and 4?

a. No revision is necessary
b. Replace the period with a comma
c. Remove the period
d. Replace the period with and

17. What change, if any, is needed in sentence 11?

a. No change is needed
b. Change sprayed to sprays
c. Change was to is
d. Change is to was

18. Which sentence is the best choice as the first sentence of paragraph 3?

a. Sentence 12
b. Sentence 13
c. Sentence 11
d. Sentence 14

19. Which revision, if any, is necessary in sentence 14?

a. No revision is necessary
b. Insert a comma after big
c. Insert a semicolon after toy
d. Insert a comma after tiny

20. Which of the following reflects the correct spelling?

a. Niagra Falls
b. Nyagra Falls
c. Niagara Falls
d. Niagira Falls

21. What change, if any, is needed in sentence 18?

a. No change is needed
b. Change remember to remembered
c. Change will to would
d. Change Then to Now

Questions 22 – 28 pertain to the following passage:

A Night to Be Remembered

(1) At the beginning of the year, my teacher announced that our school was going to have a speech contest. (2) It sounded like fun. (3) So I decided to enter. (4) I thought and thought about what to say in my speech. (5) Then I go to the library and did some research.

(6) I decided to write my speech about the life and accomplishments of Dr. Martin Luther King Jr. (7) He is one of my favorite people, and I wrote the best speech ever. (8) When I was done, I read the speech to my parents. (9) My dad once gave a speech to the city council. (10) They loved it!

(11) On the night of the speech contest, I was very nervous. (12) My stomach was flip-flopping even through I knew my speech by heart. (13) When it was my turn, I took a deep breath, stood up, and gave my speech perfectly. (14) Everyone clapped, and I sat down. (15) Then I had to wait for the judges' decision.

(16) After what seemed like forever, the head judge stood up and said it was a close concert and everyone did well. (17) Then he announced that I won first place! (18) I was so surprised that my head was spinning and my knees were wobbly. (19) After everyone cheered, and my parents took me out for ice cream. (20) It was a night I will never forget.

22. What revision, if any, is needed in sentences 2 and 3?

a. No revision is needed
b. Replace the period with a comma
c. Remove the period
d. Insert And at the beginning of sentence 3

23. What change, if any, is necessary in sentence 5?

a. No change is necessary
b. Change go to did go
c. Change go to went
d. Change did to done

24. Which version of sentence 6 reflects correct capitalization?

a. I decided to write my speech about the life and accomplishments of Dr. Martin Luther King Jr.
b. I decided to write my speech about the life and accomplishments of dr. Martin Luther King Jr.
c. I decided to write my speech about the life and accomplishments of Dr. Martin luther King jr.
d. I decided to write my speech about the life and accomplishments of Dr. Martin Luther King jr.

25. Which sentence does not belong in this story?

a. Sentence 2
b. Sentence 7
c. Sentence 9
d. Sentence 15

26. What spelling correction, if any, is needed in sentence 12?

a. No correction is needed
b. Change stomach to stomache
c. Change flip-flopping to flipflopping
d. Change through to though

27. Which revision, if any, is necessary in the wording of sentence 16?

a. No revision is necessary
b. Change head to heard
c. Change well to good
d. Change concert to contest

28. What change, if any, is needed in sentence 19?

a. No change is needed
b. Remove the word After
c. Remove the comma after cheered
d. Replace the comma after cheered with a semicolon

Answers and Explanations for Language Test #2

1. B: is the best choice because *Clara Barton* and *Christmas* both are proper nouns and should be capitalized. A is not the best choice because *Clara Barton* is a proper noun and both parts of the name should be capitalized. C is not the best choice because *Christmas* is a proper noun and should be capitalized. D is not the best choice because *Clara Barton* and *Christmas* all are proper nouns and should be capitalized.

2. D: is the best choice because sentence 4 actually is an introductory, dependent clause for sentence 5, and an introductory clause links to the corresponding independent clause with a comma. A is not the best choice because it retains sentence 4 as a sentence fragment. B is not the best choice because it omits the necessary comma after the introductory dependent clause. C is not the best choice because a semicolon should not link a dependent clause with an independent clause.

3. C: is the best choice because this passage is written in past tense and *became* is the past-tense verb form. A is not the best choice because *becomes* is a present-tense verb, and this passage is written in past tense. B is not the best choice because *loves* is a present-tense verb, and this passage is written in past tense. D is not the best choice because *were* is a plural verb, and the subject of the sentence is singular.

4. A: is the best choice because all words in the sentence currently are spelled correctly. B, C, and D are not the best choices because they all change properly spelled words to misspelled versions.

5. C: is the best choice because sentence 11 offers a fact that is irrelevant to this essay about Clara Barton. A, B, and D are not the best choices because sentences 4, 7, and 15 all are necessary for the development of this essay.

6. B: is the best choice because it eliminates the run-on sentence by creating two separate, complete sentences. A, C, and D are not the best choices because they all retain the run-on sentence structure.

7. D: is the best choice because it replaces the present-tense verb *spends* with the past-tense verb *spent*, and this passage is written in past tense. A is not the best choice because *spends* is a present-tense verb, and this passage is written in past tense. B is not the best choice because it replaces the gerund *helping* with *helped*, and the gerund form is required in this sentence. C is not the best choice because *loves* is a present-tense verb, and this passage is written in past tense.

8. C: is the best choice because *snuggles* is a present-tense verb and this passage is written in present tense. A is not the best choice because *snuggled* is a past-tense verb and this passage is written in present tense. B and D are not the best choices because they both replace appropriate words with wrong word forms.

9. B: is the best choice because sentence 4 is a dependent clause that should link to the independent clause in sentence 3 with a comma to create a complete sentence. A is not the best choice because it retains sentence 4 as a sentence fragment. C is not the best choice because a semicolon should not join an independent clause to a dependent clause. D is not the best choice because a comma is necessary when joining a dependent clause to an independent clause.

10. C: is the best choice because a comma should be used just before a coordinating conjunction that connects two independent clauses. A is not the best choice because it omits the necessary comma before the conjunction. B is not the best choice because a period is unnecessary in this sentence. D is not the best choice because a semicolon should not be used with a coordinating conjunction to join two independent clauses.

11. D: is the best choice because sentence 11 gives broad information about the topic of the paragraph, making it the best choice as the first sentence of the paragraph. A, B, and C are not the best choices because sentences 10, 12, and 9 all offer specific details about the eating habits of pandas, but they are not broad enough to serve as the topic sentence of the paragraph.

12. A: is the best choice because the sentence is correct as written. B is not the best choice because replacing the semicolon with a comma creates a comma splice, a type of run-on sentence. C is not the best choice because it omits a necessary comma after the introductory phrase. D is not the best choice because the sentence is a declarative statement, not an exclamation.

13. D: is the best choice because removing *When* allows the sentence to stand on its own as a proper sentence. A and C are not the best choices because they both retain sentence 13 as a sentence fragment. B is not the best choice because sentence 13 and sentence 14 are not closely related enough to be combined.

14. B: is the best choice because *are* is a present-tense verb, and this passage is written in present tense. A is not the best choice because *were* is a past-tense verb, and this passage is written in present tense. C is not the best choice because numbers over ten should be written in numeric form instead of in words. D is not the best choice because *there* is the proper form for this sentence.

15. C: is the best choice because summer is not a proper noun, but Niagara Falls and New York are proper nouns and require capitalization. A is not the best choice because summer is not a proper noun and should not be capitalized. B is not the best choice because Niagara Falls is a proper noun and should be capitalized. D is not the best choice because New York is a proper noun and should be capitalized.

16. B: is the best choice because sentence 3 is an introductory, dependent clause that needs to be joined with a comma to the independent clause in sentence 4. A is not the best choice because it retains sentence 3 as a sentence fragment. C is not the best choice because it omits the necessary comma after the introductory clause. D is not the best choice because it turns the combined sentence 3 and 4 into a long sentence fragment.

17. D: is the best choice because *was* is a past-tense verb, and this passage is written in past tense. A is not the best choice because *is* is a present-tense verb, and this passage is written in past tense. B and C are not the best choices because they both change appropriate past-tense verbs to inappropriate present-tense verbs.

18. B: is the best choice because sentence 13 introduces the broad, overall topic of the paragraph. A and D are not the best choices because sentences 12 and 14 offer details that build on the main topic of the paragraph, making them unsuited as topic sentences. C is not the best choice because sentence 11 belongs in paragraph 2 rather than in paragraph 3.

19. A: is the best choice because the sentence is correct as written. B is not the best choice because it breaks up the sentence with an unnecessary comma. C is not the best choice because it separates a compound subject with an unnecessary semicolon. D is not the best choice because it inserts a comma between an adjective and the noun it modifies.

20. C: is the best choice because it reflects the correct spelling of Niagara Falls. A, B, and D are not the best choices because they all are spelled incorrectly.

21. D: is the best choice because *Now* is in present tense and fits the tone and present tense of the sentence. A and C are not the best choices because they both use future-tense words, and this sentence is written in present tense. B is not the best choice because *remembered* is a past-tense verb, and this sentence is written in present tense.

22. B: is the best choice because sentence 3 is a dependent clause that should be joined to the independent clause in sentence 2 with a comma. A and D are not the best choices because they both retain sentence 3 as a sentence fragment. B is not the best choice because a comma is necessary to separate two clauses joined by a coordinating conjunction.

23. C: is the best choice because *went* is a past-tense verb, and this passage is written in past tense. A is not the best choice because *go* is a present-tense verb, and this passage is written in past tense. B and D are not the best choices because they use improper verb forms.

24. A: is the best choice because it contains the most appropriate capitalization. B is not the best choice, because Dr. is a title and should be capitalized. C is not the best choice because Luther is a proper noun and Jr. is a suffix, both of which should be capitalized. D is not the best choice because Jr. is a suffix and should be capitalized.

25. C: is the best choice because sentence 9 contains information irrelevant to the story. A, B, and D are not the best choices because sentences 2, 7, and 15 all contribute important information to the development of this story.

26. D: is the best choice because *though* is the most appropriate word for this sentence. A is not the best choice because *through* is not the most appropriate word for this sentence. B and C are not the best choices because they both change properly-spelled words to misspelled words.

27. D: is the best choice because *contest* is the best word choice for this sentence. A is not the best choice because *concert* is not the best word choice for this sentence. B and C are not the best choices because they both change appropriate word choices to inappropriate word choices.

28. B: is the best choice because removing the word *After* allows the sentence to stand on its own as a complete sentence. A is not the best choice because it retains sentence 19 as a sentence fragment. B and C are not the best choices because they both make unnecessary punctuation changes and retain sentence 19 as a sentence fragment.

How to Overcome Test Anxiety

Just the thought of taking a test is enough to make most people a little nervous. A test is an important event that can have a long-term impact on your future, so it's important to take it seriously and it's natural to feel anxious about performing well. But just because anxiety is normal, that doesn't mean that it's helpful in test taking, or that you should simply accept it as part of your life. Anxiety can have a variety of effects. These effects can be mild, like making you feel slightly nervous, or severe, like blocking your ability to focus or remember even a simple detail.

If you experience test anxiety—whether severe or mild—it's important to know how to beat it. To discover this, first you need to understand what causes test anxiety.

Causes of Test Anxiety

While we often think of anxiety as an uncontrollable emotional state, it can actually be caused by simple, practical things. One of the most common causes of test anxiety is that a person does not feel adequately prepared for their test. This feeling can be the result of many different issues such as poor study habits or lack of organization, but the most common culprit is time management. Starting to study too late, failing to organize your study time to cover all of the material, or being distracted while you study will mean that you're not well prepared for the test. This may lead to cramming the night before, which will cause you to be physically and mentally exhausted for the test. Poor time management also contributes to feelings of stress, fear, and hopelessness as you realize you are not well prepared but don't know what to do about it.

Other times, test anxiety is not related to your preparation for the test but comes from unresolved fear. This may be a past failure on a test, or poor performance on tests in general. It may come from comparing yourself to others who seem to be performing better or from the stress of living up to expectations. Anxiety may be driven by fears of the future—how failure on this test would affect your educational and career goals. These fears are often completely irrational, but they can still negatively impact your test performance.

Elements of Test Anxiety

As mentioned earlier, test anxiety is considered to be an emotional state, but it has physical and mental components as well. Sometimes you may not even realize that you are suffering from test anxiety until you notice the physical symptoms. These can include trembling hands, rapid heartbeat, sweating, nausea, and tense muscles. Extreme anxiety may lead to fainting or vomiting. Obviously, any of these symptoms can have a negative impact on testing. It is important to recognize them as soon as they begin to occur so that you can address the problem before it damages your performance.

The mental components of test anxiety include trouble focusing and inability to remember learned information. During a test, your mind is on high alert, which can help you recall information and stay focused for an extended period of time. However, anxiety interferes with your mind's natural processes, causing you to blank out, even on the questions you know well. The strain of testing during anxiety makes it difficult to stay focused, especially on a test that may take several hours. Extreme anxiety can take a huge mental toll, making it difficult not only to recall test information but even to understand the test questions or pull your thoughts together.

Effects of Test Anxiety

Test anxiety is like a disease—if left untreated, it will get progressively worse. Anxiety leads to poor performance, and this reinforces the feelings of fear and failure, which in turn lead to poor performances on subsequent tests. It can grow from a mild nervousness to a crippling condition. If allowed to progress, test anxiety can have a big impact on your schooling, and consequently on your future.

Test anxiety can spread to other parts of your life. Anxiety on tests can become anxiety in any stressful situation, and blanking on a test can turn into panicking in a job situation. But fortunately, you don't have to let anxiety rule your testing and determine your grades. There are a number of relatively simple steps you can take to move past anxiety and function normally on a test and in the rest of life.

Physical Steps for Beating Test Anxiety

While test anxiety is a serious problem, the good news is that it can be overcome. It doesn't have to control your ability to think and remember information. While it may take time, you can begin taking steps today to beat anxiety.

Just as your first hint that you may be struggling with anxiety comes from the physical symptoms, the first step to treating it is also physical. Rest is crucial for having a clear, strong mind. If you are tired, it is much easier to give in to anxiety. But if you establish good sleep habits, your body and mind will be ready to perform optimally, without the strain of exhaustion. Additionally, sleeping well helps you to retain information better, so you're more likely to recall the answers when you see the test questions.

Getting good sleep means more than going to bed on time. It's important to allow your brain time to relax. Take study breaks from time to time so it doesn't get overworked, and don't study right before bed. Take time to rest your mind before trying to rest your body, or you may find it difficult to fall asleep.

Along with sleep, other aspects of physical health are important in preparing for a test. Good nutrition is vital for good brain function. Sugary foods and drinks may give a burst of energy but this burst is followed by a crash, both physically and emotionally. Instead, fuel your body with protein and vitamin-rich foods.

Also, drink plenty of water. Dehydration can lead to headaches and exhaustion, especially if your brain is already under stress from the rigors of the test. Particularly if your test is a long one, drink water during the breaks. And if possible, take an energy-boosting snack to eat between sections.

Along with sleep and diet, a third important part of physical health is exercise. Maintaining a steady workout schedule is helpful, but even taking 5-minute study breaks to walk can help get your blood pumping faster and clear your head. Exercise also releases endorphins, which contribute to a positive feeling and can help combat test anxiety.

When you nurture your physical health, you are also contributing to your mental health. If your body is healthy, your mind is much more likely to be healthy as well. So take time to rest, nourish your body with healthy food and water, and get moving as much as possible. Taking these physical steps will make you stronger and more able to take the mental steps necessary to overcome test anxiety.

Mental Steps for Beating Test Anxiety

Working on the mental side of test anxiety can be more challenging, but as with the physical side, there are clear steps you can take to overcome it. As mentioned earlier, test anxiety often stems from lack of preparation, so the obvious solution is to prepare for the test. Effective studying may be the most important weapon you have for beating test anxiety, but you can and should employ several other mental tools to combat fear.

First, boost your confidence by reminding yourself of past success—tests or projects that you aced. If you're putting as much effort into preparing for this test as you did for those, there's no reason you should expect to fail here. Work hard to prepare; then trust your preparation.

Second, surround yourself with encouraging people. It can be helpful to find a study group, but be sure that the people you're around will encourage a positive attitude. If you spend time with others who are anxious or cynical, this will only contribute to your own anxiety. Look for others who are motivated to study hard from a desire to succeed, not from a fear of failure.

Third, reward yourself. A test is physically and mentally tiring, even without anxiety, and it can be helpful to have something to look forward to. Plan an activity following the test, regardless of the outcome, such as going to a movie or getting ice cream.

When you are taking the test, if you find yourself beginning to feel anxious, remind yourself that you know the material. Visualize successfully completing the test. Then take a few deep, relaxing breaths and return to it. Work through the questions carefully but with confidence, knowing that you are capable of succeeding.

Developing a healthy mental approach to test taking will also aid in other areas of life. Test anxiety affects more than just the actual test—it can be damaging to your mental health and even contribute to depression. It's important to beat test anxiety before it becomes a problem for more than testing.

Study Strategy

Being prepared for the test is necessary to combat anxiety, but what does being prepared look like? You may study for hours on end and still not feel prepared. What you need is a strategy for test prep. The next few pages outline our recommended steps to help you plan out and conquer the challenge of preparation.

Step 1: Scope Out the Test

Learn everything you can about the format (multiple choice, essay, etc.) and what will be on the test. Gather any study materials, course outlines, or sample exams that may be available. Not only will this help you to prepare, but knowing what to expect can help to alleviate test anxiety.

Step 2: Map Out the Material

Look through the textbook or study guide and make note of how many chapters or sections it has. Then divide these over the time you have. For example, if a book has 15 chapters and you have five days to study, you need to cover three chapters each day. Even better, if you have the time, leave an extra day at the end for overall review after you have gone through the material in depth.

If time is limited, you may need to prioritize the material. Look through it and make note of which sections you think you already have a good grasp on, and which need review. While you are studying, skim quickly through the familiar sections and take more time on the challenging parts.

Write out your plan so you don't get lost as you go. Having a written plan also helps you feel more in control of the study, so anxiety is less likely to arise from feeling overwhelmed at the amount to cover.

STEP 3: GATHER YOUR TOOLS

Decide what study method works best for you. Do you prefer to highlight in the book as you study and then go back over the highlighted portions? Or do you type out notes of the important information? Or is it helpful to make flashcards that you can carry with you? Assemble the pens, index cards, highlighters, post-it notes, and any other materials you may need so you won't be distracted by getting up to find things while you study.

If you're having a hard time retaining the information or organizing your notes, experiment with different methods. For example, try color-coding by subject with colored pens, highlighters, or post-it notes. If you learn better by hearing, try recording yourself reading your notes so you can listen while in the car, working out, or simply sitting at your desk. Ask a friend to quiz you from your flashcards, or try teaching someone the material to solidify it in your mind.

STEP 4: CREATE YOUR ENVIRONMENT

It's important to avoid distractions while you study. This includes both the obvious distractions like visitors and the subtle distractions like an uncomfortable chair (or a too-comfortable couch that makes you want to fall asleep). Set up the best study environment possible: good lighting and a comfortable work area. If background music helps you focus, you may want to turn it on, but otherwise keep the room quiet. If you are using a computer to take notes, be sure you don't have any other windows open, especially applications like social media, games, or anything else that could distract you. Silence your phone and turn off notifications. Be sure to keep water close by so you stay hydrated while you study (but avoid unhealthy drinks and snacks).

Also, take into account the best time of day to study. Are you freshest first thing in the morning? Try to set aside some time then to work through the material. Is your mind clearer in the afternoon or evening? Schedule your study session then. Another method is to study at the same time of day that you will take the test, so that your brain gets used to working on the material at that time and will be ready to focus at test time.

STEP 5: STUDY!

Once you have done all the study preparation, it's time to settle into the actual studying. Sit down, take a few moments to settle your mind so you can focus, and begin to follow your study plan. Don't give in to distractions or let yourself procrastinate. This is your time to prepare so you'll be ready to fearlessly approach the test. Make the most of the time and stay focused.

Of course, you don't want to burn out. If you study too long you may find that you're not retaining the information very well. Take regular study breaks. For example, taking five minutes out of every hour to walk briskly, breathing deeply and swinging your arms, can help your mind stay fresh.

As you get to the end of each chapter or section, it's a good idea to do a quick review. Remind yourself of what you learned and work on any difficult parts. When you feel that you've mastered the material, move on to the next part. At the end of your study session, briefly skim through your notes again.

But while review is helpful, cramming last minute is NOT. If at all possible, work ahead so that you won't need to fit all your study into the last day. Cramming overloads your brain with more information than it can process and retain, and your tired mind may struggle to recall even previously learned information when it is overwhelmed with last-minute study. Also, the urgent nature of cramming and the stress placed on your brain contribute to anxiety. You'll be more likely to go to the test feeling unprepared and having trouble thinking clearly.

So don't cram, and don't stay up late before the test, even just to review your notes at a leisurely pace. Your brain needs rest more than it needs to go over the information again. In fact, plan to finish your studies by noon or early afternoon the day before the test. Give your brain the rest of the day to relax or focus on other things, and get a good night's sleep. Then you will be fresh for the test and better able to recall what you've studied.

Step 6: Take a Practice Test

Many courses offer sample tests, either online or in the study materials. This is an excellent resource to check whether you have mastered the material, as well as to prepare for the test format and environment.

Check the test format ahead of time: the number of questions, the type (multiple choice, free response, etc.), and the time limit. Then create a plan for working through them. For example, if you have 30 minutes to take a 60-question test, your limit is 30 seconds per question. Spend less time on the questions you know well so that you can take more time on the difficult ones.

If you have time to take several practice tests, take the first one open book, with no time limit. Work through the questions at your own pace and make sure you fully understand them. Gradually work up to taking a test under test conditions: sit at a desk with all study materials put away and set a timer. Pace yourself to make sure you finish the test with time to spare and go back to check your answers if you have time.

After each test, check your answers. On the questions you missed, be sure you understand why you missed them. Did you misread the question (tests can use tricky wording)? Did you forget the information? Or was it something you hadn't learned? Go back and study any shaky areas that the practice tests reveal.

Taking these tests not only helps with your grade, but also aids in combating test anxiety. If you're already used to the test conditions, you're less likely to worry about it, and working through tests until you're scoring well gives you a confidence boost. Go through the practice tests until you feel comfortable, and then you can go into the test knowing that you're ready for it.

Test Tips

On test day, you should be confident, knowing that you've prepared well and are ready to answer the questions. But aside from preparation, there are several test day strategies you can employ to maximize your performance.

First, as stated before, get a good night's sleep the night before the test (and for several nights before that, if possible). Go into the test with a fresh, alert mind rather than staying up late to study.

Try not to change too much about your normal routine on the day of the test. It's important to eat a nutritious breakfast, but if you normally don't eat breakfast at all, consider eating just a protein bar. If you're a coffee drinker, go ahead and have your normal coffee. Just make sure you time it so that the caffeine doesn't wear off right in the middle of your test. Avoid sugary beverages, and drink enough water to stay hydrated but not so much that you need a restroom break 10 minutes into the test. If your test isn't first thing in the morning, consider going for a walk or doing a light workout before the test to get your blood flowing.

Allow yourself enough time to get ready, and leave for the test with plenty of time to spare so you won't have the anxiety of scrambling to arrive in time. Another reason to be early is to select a good seat. It's helpful to sit away from doors and windows, which can be distracting. Find a good seat, get out your supplies, and settle your mind before the test begins.

When the test begins, start by going over the instructions carefully, even if you already know what to expect. Make sure you avoid any careless mistakes by following the directions.

Then begin working through the questions, pacing yourself as you've practiced. If you're not sure on an answer, don't spend too much time on it, and don't let it shake your confidence. Either skip it and come back later, or eliminate as many wrong answers as possible and guess among the remaining ones. Don't dwell on these questions as you continue—put them out of your mind and focus on what lies ahead.

Be sure to read all of the answer choices, even if you're sure the first one is the right answer. Sometimes you'll find a better one if you keep reading. But don't second-guess yourself if you do immediately know the answer. Your gut instinct is usually right. Don't let test anxiety rob you of the information you know.

If you have time at the end of the test (and if the test format allows), go back and review your answers. Be cautious about changing any, since your first instinct tends to be correct, but make sure you didn't misread any of the questions or accidentally mark the wrong answer choice. Look over any you skipped and make an educated guess.

At the end, leave the test feeling confident. You've done your best, so don't waste time worrying about your performance or wishing you could change anything. Instead, celebrate the successful completion of this test. And finally, use this test to learn how to deal with anxiety even better next time.

Review Video: Test Anxiety
Visit mometrix.com/academy and enter code: 100340

Important Qualification

Not all anxiety is created equal. If your test anxiety is causing major issues in your life beyond the classroom or testing center, or if you are experiencing troubling physical symptoms related to your anxiety, it may be a sign of a serious physiological or psychological condition. If this sounds like your situation, we strongly encourage you to seek professional help.

Online Resources

Due to our efforts to try to keep this book to a manageable length, we've created a link that will give you access to all of your online resources:

mometrix.com/resources719/terranextg6rl

It's Your Moment, Let's Celebrate It!

Share your story @mometrixtestpreparation